JESUS THE STORYTELLER

JESUS THE STORYTELLER

STEPHEN I. WRIGHT

WESTMINSTER
JOHN KNOX PRESS
LOUISVILLE · KENTUCKY

First published in Great Britain in 2014
by Society for Promoting Christian Knowledge

Published in the United States of America in 2015 by
Westminster John Knox Press
100 Witherspoon Street
Louisville, KY 40202

15 16 17 18 19 20 21 22 23 24—10 9 8 7 6 5 4 3 2 1

Cover design by Barbara LeVan Fisher / levanfisherstudio.com

Library of Congress Cataloging-in-Publication Data

Wright, Stephen I.
  Jesus the storyteller / Stephen I. Wright.
      pages cm
  Originally published: London : SPCK, 2014.
  Includes bibliographical references and index.
  ISBN 978-0-664-26044-6 (alk. paper)
  1. Jesus Christ--Parables. 2. Storytelling--Religious aspects--Christianity. I. Title.
  BT375.3.W75 2015
  226.8'06--dc23

                                                              2015019366

♾ The paper used in this publication meets the minimum requirements
of the American National Standard for Information Sciences—Permanence
of Paper for Printed Library Materials, ANSI Z39.48-1992.

Most Westminster John Knox Press books are available at special quantity
discounts when purchased in bulk by corporations, organizations, and special-interest
groups. For more information, please e-mail SpecialSales@wjkbooks.com.

Contents

Preface and acknowledgements

This book is a development of work which I have done on the parables of Jesus since starting my doctoral studies in Durham in 1994. It builds on, expands and attempts to balance out my published thesis *The Voice of Jesus*, which appeared in 2000. But it also seeks to incorporate fresh insights from different angles and sources, and to do so in a way which, I trust, will be accessible beyond the confines of academic biblical studies.

Those who are not so interested in the history of the last couple of centuries of parable scholarship, and want to dive straight into the stories themselves, can skip Part 1. In fact, having done so, they could even choose between Parts 2 and 3, depending on whether they would like a fairly quick overview of how Jesus' stories fit into the Synoptic Gospels (Part 2) or a more detailed study of how they fit into his life and work (Part 3). My popular-level work *Tales Jesus Told* is now out of print, and I have attempted to make Parts 2 and 3, especially, accessible to a wide audience while remaining, I hope, of interest to the academics. Of course, I would be gratified if many read the whole book!

My thanks are due to Philip Law of SPCK for his encouragement of this project from the start. I have benefited greatly from the positive and supportive atmosphere of Spurgeon's College, London, where I work with marvellous colleagues and students. I am grateful to its Academic Board for granting me study leave in the autumn term of 2011 when I was able to catch up (a little) with some of the mass of scholarship, recent and older, on Jesus as a historical figure. I am grateful to have been invited to give a paper at the Ehrhardt Seminar in the University of Manchester in May 2013 where I floated something of the basic shape of the project, and to the encouraging audience on that occasion. I was glad also of the opportunity to give a paper on the theme at the Jesus Seminar of the British New Testament Conference in St Andrews in August 2013. I am especially grateful for comments and questions received from Todd Brewer, David Bryan, Alison Jack, and Professors Larry Hurtado and Francis Watson. They have encouraged me to sharpen my argument in certain places. Naturally, I remain solely responsible for the outcome and for any errors and lacunae that remain.

My wife and family have given me the priceless support of a loving and understanding home, without which the will to persevere with a project like this might well elude me, and to them I owe a very special debt of thanks.

Stephen I. Wright

Introduction

It is widely acknowledged that Jesus of Nazareth told stories. Much less agreement exists on why he did so or how these stories contributed to his wider activity and brief career. This book approaches this topic afresh in an attempt to gather some of the wisdom of scholarship past and present into a new synthesis.

There are three reasons why I believe this enquiry is important. First, although the 'parables of Jesus' have been examined from every conceivable angle over the last century and a half, their character as stories, and its implications, has been surprisingly neglected. This is because the stories have been placed in the category of 'parables' along with a range of other, mostly shorter sayings which are quite distinct rhetorically from stories. Attention to the genre and strategy of 'parable' has tended to exclude a steady concentration on the dynamics of narrative.

There is good reason for this: above all, the use of the term 'parables' by the Evangelists as a summary characterization of the way in which Jesus 'spoke the word' to people (Mark 4.33–34), and the obviously narrative element of many of these sayings. By focusing on the category of 'story' or 'narrative', I do not propose that we dispense with that of 'parable'. Indeed, narrative may rightly be seen as the 'classic' parable form (Hedrick, 2004, p. 10). But it has long been recognized that the use of the word 'parable' to describe a wide range of recorded sayings of Jesus may not take us very far in understanding their meaning or force. Even what counts as a 'parable' in the Gospels is disputed: not surprisingly, since the Evangelists' use of the word to designate particular sayings is relatively loose.[1] Not all utterances that are normally grouped as 'parables' by scholars are labelled as such by the Evangelists, while they include a few utterances as 'parables' which scholars would be more inclined to label a riddle, a proverb, a simple analogy, or an instruction – a range of forms all covered, along with others, by the Hebrew *māshāl*.[2]

When scholars come up with a list of 'parables', according to their preferred definition, it always seems necessary to create sub-categories. The division may be according to perceived rhetorical form, as in Adolf Jülicher's seminal work (1910 (1886, 1898, 1899)). He divided parables into three categories: the short similitude (*Gleichnis*), the story parable (*Parabel*) and the example story (*Beispielerzählung*) (1910, I, pp. 80, 98, 114). The difference between the latter two categories, for Jülicher, is that the story parable is intended to point beyond the situation pictured to a general truth which it somehow resembles (for instance, God's love for humanity is 'like' the love of the father for his son in The Prodigal Son: 1910, II, p. 362), while the example story presents the general truth in the clothing of a specific instance (thus, The Good Samaritan embodies the truth that 'the gladly-offered exercise of love earns the highest worth in the eyes of God and humans': 1910, II, p. 596). Jülicher distinguishes all three categories sharply from allegory, in which a whole series of terms is exchanged for another series (1910, I, p. 80). But his insistence on the story parables, of either kind, expressing a general truth obscured their contours as stories.

The problematic nature of such sub-categories has been discussed by Ruben Zimmermann (2009). In this article Zimmermann explains that his solution, in the major volume he edited (2007), was to do away with them (and the sometimes misleading directions in which they took interpretation of the texts themselves) by producing a supposedly all-encompassing, six-point character-ization of the genre parable (2009, p. 170). First among these points was that a parable is always narrative. The danger Zimmermann courts is the old one he tries to combat, however, that of subsuming parables within a predetermined definition of their characteristics. Thus, while accepting the depth of 'narrative' structure in many short proverbial sayings, one might reasonably argue that to treat such a saying within essentially the same analytical matrix as a full-length 'story' is to invite the blurring of important rhetorical distinctions.

To appreciate Jesus' stories in their force and distinctiveness, scholars have often turned to comparative studies of ancient literature and rhetoric. Such studies may give us helpful material with which to illuminate what Jesus was saying and doing. The Old Testament (OT), the parables of the Jewish Rabbis, the rhetorical handbooks of Aristotle or Quintilian and the fables of Aesop have all been used to seek such illumination.

We must be cautious, however, about making such comparisons bear more weight than they can reasonably carry, and the net effect of them has often been, again, to downplay the clearly narrative character of Jesus' most memorable 'parables'. It does not follow, for instance, from the fact that the Rabbis told parables with a standard structure involving the comparison of two entities or situations (see McArthur and Johnston, 1990), that Jesus' parables functioned in the same manner (despite the implications of some, such as Young, 1998). A recurring theme of my study is that to jump to a supposed 'comparative' force in a story is to fail to apprehend its narrative rhetoric.

When they have drawn on Aristotle to illuminate Jesus' parables, scholars have tended to look to his *Rhetoric* (a handbook for those who fulfilled specific public roles within Greek society) rather than his *Poetics*, which includes his seminal account of narrative and its workings within popular drama.[3] The dominant model for understanding the parables has thus been rhetorical persuasion rather than the experience of entering a narrative. This study seeks to redress this balance by drawing particularly on contemporary 'narrative criticism' which finds its roots in Aristotle's *Poetics*. This entails no claim that Jesus was influenced by this work, just the recognition that insights deriving from it have universal application to the workings of story. Moreover, we will focus on the dynamics of the stories as the Gospel texts have mediated them to us. A comparative study setting Jesus' stories in the wider field of storytelling in the ancient world, Jewish and non-Jewish, is for another time.

The second reason why I believe this study is worthwhile is this. A further feature of most modern scholarship on Jesus' parables is that, when they have been treated as a corpus, they have usually not been integrated into an overarching portrait of the work of Jesus but treated either as individual units, relating to historical background generally but not to a specific hypothesis about his strategy (e.g. Hultgren, 2000; Snodgrass, 2008; Blomberg, 2012 (1990)), or as part of the tapestry of the Evangelists' presentation of Jesus (e.g. Drury, 1985; Donahue, 1988). Partial exceptions are the classic works of Jülicher (1910 (1886, 1888, 1898)), Dodd (1936 (1935)) and Jeremias (1963 (1947)).[4] Jülicher's reading of the parables was clearly intertwined with the typically nineteenth-century hypothesis that Jesus was an ideal moral teacher. Dodd's book was key to advancing his argument that Jesus believed the 'kingdom of God' had actually dawned with his coming. Jeremias emphasized the role of the parables in Jesus' defence of his ministry against his critics. Though these works made strides in their different ways in careful historical appraisal of the parables as parables of Jesus, however, their concentrated focus on the parables did not allow much engagement with other Gospel material that might corroborate, challenge or nuance the picture of Jesus which emerged.

The reluctance to integrate the parables into an overarching reconstruction of Jesus' ministry has no doubt been a symptom of the general reluctance through much of the twentieth century, in the wake of both Albert Schweitzer's critique of the nineteenth-century 'questers' and Rudolf Bultmann's historical scepticism, to claim that it is now possible to draw a genuinely historical portrait of Jesus. The reluctance is often conditioned by commendable scholarly caution. Biblical commentators, for instance, are more likely to offer detailed material on the background of an individual parable, and/or the way it fits as a literary unit into the Gospel where it is now found, than to hazard opinions as to how it fits into the ministry of the historical Jesus – even that ministry as the particular Evangelist has reconstructed it. There is also understandable caution about 'psychologizing' Jesus. While those concerned with the continuing reception and usefulness of Jesus' stories have been happy to import psychological categories into their interpretations (e.g. Tolbert, 1979; Ford, 1997), historians have tended to shun them as, almost inevitably, going beyond the evidence. As James Breech perceptively showed, however, although the parables themselves give us remarkably few overt clues about Jesus' personality, self-understanding or aims, we might find his very silence on these things deeply instructive (1983, esp. pp. 213–22).

Conversely, when the focus of scholars has been on the career of Jesus as a whole, there has been an understandable compression in their treatment of the parables, which inevitably tends to flatten their diversity and allow only limited attention to individual stories in their peculiarity. N. T. Wright has some highly suggestive comments about the parables in relationship to Jewish prophetic and apocalyptic tradition within his major construal of Jesus' ministry (1996, pp. 125–31, 174–82) and some play a key role in the argument: note especially the reading of The Pounds and The Talents as speaking of YHWH's return to Zion (1996, pp. 632–9). Oddly, however, John Dominic Crossan, author of two creative books on the parables, deals only very briefly with them in his major work on Jesus (1991).[5] The phenomenon I am describing has been well summed up by Snodgrass (2013, pp. 45–6, n. 2): 'Most works on the historical Jesus ... give minimal attention to the parables, and books on parables often give inadequate attention to the historical Jesus.'

Not only, then, is there a gap in the scholarly study of certain parables of Jesus as stories, there is a gap in the study of them as stories told by Jesus. Fuller justification for these statements will emerge in Chapters 1 and 2. The upshot is that there remains a surprising divergence of views on the nature and purpose of Jesus' storytelling. This divergence is easily masked by frequent reference to Jesus as a storyteller, without corresponding frequency of enquiry about what sort of stories they really were and what they might imply about their teller. And though some of the stories get the regular epithet 'well-loved' – not least The Good Samaritan and The Prodigal Son – there are probably more which continue to puzzle, challenge and even offend. As they continue to be discussed and meditated upon, especially in church settings, blank looks greet Jesus' apparent commendation of a steward's dishonesty (Luke 16.1–8); people wonder what exactly we are to learn from a king who sends an unforgiving debtor to the torturers (Matt. 18.23–35); and preachers take evasive action when it comes to the king who first burns a city in response to the refusal of a wedding invitation, then imprisons one who has accepted it because he is not wearing the right clothes (Matt. 22.1–14). The gap in scholarship is surprising given the extraordinary scholarly interest in narrative as a category that has emerged in many disciplines in the last half-century or so,[6] though much important headway has been made on particular stories and particular aspects of Jesus' ministry, and I draw gratefully from a number of relevant works.

The third reason for my focus is that Jesus is often claimed as a champion for storytelling as a powerful and central medium for communication (particularly Christian communication). There is a danger of superficiality in this, if the range of possible purposes of Jesus' own storytelling is overlooked. Like any rhetorical form, story is not a mere innocent dress in which one can present any message one likes. Message and medium are bound up together. Nor is it merely a vehicle for conveying meaning. It does something as well as saying something, and through saying something.

Jesus' activity as a narrator of tales plays a wider role too in Christian theology and praxis. For example, it may enhance an image of him as a wandering charismatic holy man, which some will find more credible and perhaps comfortable than the apocalyptic or *Christus Victor* images of Christian tradition (see for example the various works of Marcus Borg, e.g. 2011). Alternatively, the tales themselves may be interpreted in an apocalyptic light, thus yielding a Jesus who conforms somewhat more to the traditional Christian picture (N. T. Wright, 1996). In the arguments for a 'narrative theology', the central impetus of Jesus as a storyteller is acknowledged (McFague, 1975). But in what sense, if any, did Jesus' stories constitute 'theology'? That is far from being agreed, though writers continue to offer suggestive explorations of the theme (e.g. Blomberg, 2012 (1990), pp. 408–46). I hope to shed further light on this question.

Two further introductory observations before I describe how the book unfolds. First, since the stories Jesus told are, on the whole, the longer utterances among those that are loosely called 'parables', they inevitably offer more scope for variety in understanding than the rest. The present study does not seek to eliminate plurality of readings; like Zimmermann (2009, pp. 175–6), I regard such plurality as inherent to the dynamics of telling and hearing parables, and I would include stories especially in this. As we shall see, however, recent scholars have given markedly different interpretations to Jesus' stories, which cannot really coexist compatibly within a single coherent account of his aims and teaching. Without imposing artificial rules of 'legitimacy' on contemporary readings, improbable limitations on the spectrum of what Jesus' first hearers may have gleaned from his stories, or a narrow presumption that they must all 'work' alike, I think it is reasonable and profitable to do some sifting among the diverse 'hearings' of the stories in order to see what hints they may offer about the stance and strategy of Jesus.

Second, I do not propose to engage in the wider debate about the justification for 'the quest of the historical Jesus' in the various forms that the quest has taken and continues to take. It will be clear, however, that I believe that working towards an accurate historical portrayal of Jesus is no less important than working towards such a portrayal of any other influential historical figure, and arguably a good deal more. The often angst-ridden dealings between people of Christian faith (of various hues), other faiths and no faith are ill-served by substituting tendentious assumptions (from any quarter) for serious discussion. I will outline the rationale for my own approach more fully in Chapter 3. Here I will just say that, though all scholars bring certain assumptions to their work, I am not among those who despair of attaining a level of cool rationality as a medium of shared debate and apprehension of historical reality. As a Christian I do not hide my practical concerns about the relevance of this discussion (as just outlined). Nor can I claim to be free from bias, but I will be glad to hear from any student of Jesus, Christian or not, who thinks that bias has unduly coloured the picture I paint here, and seek to correct it.

My study will proceed as follows. In Part 1, Chapters 1 and 2 survey the real though partial insights into Jesus as a storyteller which do indeed emerge from modern scholarship on the historical Jesus and on the parables, despite the lack of clear focus on 'story' as such. I recount this selective 'history of scholarship' as a tale of the eclipse of Jesus' stories through the nineteenth century (Chapter 1) and the gradual but partial recovery of them through the twentieth

(Chapter 2). As I argued in an earlier work (S. I. Wright, 2000b), important insights emerge also from 'pre-modern' scholarship on the parables; but that is beyond my scope here. After these chapters, we will then be in a position to delineate more precisely the investigation which needs to be carried out, and Chapter 3 lays the methodological groundwork for that investigation. Here I introduce key categories in the recent and contemporary study of Jesus and the Gospels which now seem to invite application in a more concerted way to his stories: orality, testimony, memory, performance, reception history and above all narrative. I offer a justification for the way in which I seek a fresh appraisal of the nature, purpose and import of Jesus' storytelling through these lenses, especially the last, and for the way in which I attempt to relate the Gospel renderings of the stories to suppositions about the historical Jesus.

In Part 2, we will seek to imagine how the stories would have resonated with hearers as part of an early oral performance of the Gospels, taking each of the Synoptic Gospels in turn in Chapters 4—6. In Part 3 we will try to enter the dynamics of the original oral exchange between Jesus and his hearers, dividing the stories up for convenience in Chapters 7—10 according to the spatial and temporal location given them by the Evangelists. Finally, Part 4 (Chapter 11) 'gathers the echoes' in an attempt to sketch the outlines of the purpose(s) of the stories as they relate to Jesus' activity, and of the storyteller himself insofar as they reveal him.

Part 1
LAYING THE FOUNDATIONS

1

Eclipsing the stories of Jesus: from Reimarus to Jülicher

The stories Jesus told, and Jesus' activity as a storyteller, have been strange and usually unintended casualties of the modern quest for the historical Jesus. Repeatedly, this element of his life has been marginalized, and the stories themselves have been, in effect, transposed into other rhetorical forms, sometimes in the effort to establish criteria for distinguishing the Evangelists' implied interpretation of the stories within the Gospels from the force they would have carried for Jesus and his hearers.

It had not always been so. A noteworthy feature of the 'pre-critical' phase of interpreting Jesus' parables, which lasted from the first century well into the nineteenth, was that their narrative richness was often preserved. Although modern scholars have surely been right to regard the allegorical readings developed by the early and mediaeval Church as mostly implausible construals of the parables' original force for their speaker or hearers, these readings did often have the merit of mirroring the pattern of the story. To take the most famous example, the interpretation of The Good Samaritan well known from Augustine (but present in earlier interpreters including Origen and Ambrose), which reads the story as an allegory of the events of salvation in which the Samaritan stands for Christ, may be fanciful in its details but reflects the sweep of narrative time and the plot-dynamics of disaster and rescue in the biblical text.[1]

The early students of Jesus from a modern historical perspective, however, had concerns understandably different from Jesus' storytelling. And the earliest major historical work on the parables, that of Jülicher, with which this chapter ends, determinedly reshaped his stories into similes. To understand something of the background of this move, we must go back to the work of Hermann Samuel Reimarus.

Jesus as political messiah: Hermann Samuel Reimarus

Reimarus's *Fragments* are generally considered the starting point of the modern quest of the historical Jesus. Published by his friend Gotthold Ephraim Lessing after his death in 1768, they contained an incisive attack upon traditional Christian doctrine and upon the veracity of the Gospels themselves. Indeed, the relief into which Reimarus threw the figure of Jesus by setting him within a framework of Jewish thought and language was not to be recapitulated until the late nineteenth century, in the work of Johannes Weiss and then Albert Schweitzer (Schweitzer, 2000 (1913), pp. 22–3). According to Schweitzer, Reimarus's work 'was the first time that a really historical mind, thoroughly conversant with the sources, had undertaken the criticism of the tradition' (Schweitzer, 2000 (1913), p. 16).

Reimarus's basic line of attack was to drive a wedge between the intention and proclamation of Jesus and that of the apostles and Evangelists. Jesus' announcement of God's kingdom, for Reimarus, was entirely conditioned by Jewish expectations of the establishment of an earthly theocracy through the agency of a Messiah, in which Israel would at last throw off the yoke of her enemies. This kingdom was proclaimed by John the Baptist and Jesus as imminent, but when it did not appear, and Jesus was put to death, his followers reconfigured his message radically, introducing the doctrines of a suffering and risen Saviour who would come again in glory, doctrines which shaped the New Testament (NT) writings and all subsequent Christian theology. In this, Reimarus believed, they were drawing on an alternative Jewish Messianic tradition which believed in a supernatural kingdom.[2]

Although Reimarus does not discuss any of Jesus' stories in detail (indeed, much of his discussion treats Jesus' words in quite a generalized fashion), it is important to start our survey with him because he 'takes as his starting-point the question of the content of the preaching of Jesus' (Schweitzer, 2000 (1913), p. 17). Reimarus believes that the Gospels give us access to the substance of what Jesus said, and that this shows Jesus to have been a preacher of repentance from abuses within Judaism (such as those ascribed to the Pharisees) in preparation for the arrival of God's kingdom. Jesus regarded himself, in this view, as the one through whom the kingdom would be established, and thus gathered his followers in Jerusalem for a climactic showdown. This message, says Reimarus, has been overlaid by the retrospective interpretation of the Evangelists, who have depoliticized Jesus and ascribed to him a vocation to suffer and die which he had not in fact possessed (see especially Reimarus, 1970 (1768), pp. 135–50). They were able to carry out this radical reinterpretation because there was in Judaism an alternative conception in which the Messiah came twice, first in misery, then in glory (pp. 212–15).[3]

As a part of his argument, Reimarus refers to the so-called 'parables of the kingdom' found in Matthew 13 and Mark 4 (pp. 74–5, 123–5). He points out that these parables actually tell us very little about the kingdom. Even the story of The Sower, to which is appended an interpretation ascribed to Jesus, seems to tell us little more than that there is hope for the triumph of the kingdom, despite evident resistance to it. This is a key element in Reimarus's argument that Jesus possessed, and assumed in his hearers, a thoroughly traditional Jewish conception of the kingdom. Jesus must have thought that they knew what he was talking about; thus his parables on the subject were not conveying new information so much as expressing encouragement in a vivid way that this kingdom was indeed just around the corner.[4] Jesus' more detailed teaching is read by Reimarus as a reminder of fundamental truths from which his people had strayed, and to which they must return in preparation for God's kingdom. In this connection he refers briefly to The Rich Man and Lazarus as an example of Jesus preaching a 'better righteousness' than that of those who were overconcerned with outward ceremonies (pp. 62–3), by drawing attention to judgement and eternal life.

Despite his lack of discussion of Jesus' stories, Reimarus's understanding of the Gospels is significant for us here in two ways. First, his emphasis that Jesus was not intending to propound new (i.e. what became 'Christian') doctrine or found a new religion was a departure from the thrust of much Christian teaching, and the forerunner of contemporary scholarly emphasis on the Jewishness of Jesus. The stories Jesus told have been, both before and since Reimarus, an important *locus* for the articulation of Jesus' newness in respect to Judaism. Up to the mediaeval period, they were regularly read as encoding the division of Jew and Gentile in salvation history and pointing to the judgement on Judaism expressed in the rise of Christianity (for some examples see S. I. Wright, 2000b, pp. 76–97; Milavec, 1989, pp. 81–4). Since the attempted demolition of allegorical readings by Jülicher, such perceptions have become less tenable, and the emphasis has been on the immediate purpose of Jesus' sayings for his own contemporary context (however that purpose is construed). Yet the attempt to understand Jesus in the light of his Jewish background also impels recognition of the repertoire of images and narratives on which Jesus' stories draw, and this may come close to reintroducing a Jesus who does, indeed – at least indirectly – lay the groundwork for later Christian doctrine, though now in more continuity with Judaism (as in the work of Bailey, 1976, 1980, 2003, 2008; N. T. Wright, 1996).

Second, Reimarus's emphasis on the essential simplicity of Jesus' language also foreshadows Jülicher's work. That which Christians had often seen as intriguingly obscure, admitting of deep and hidden meanings, is 'unmasked'. Hence the stories Jesus told, insofar as Reimarus uses them at all, can be used as simple examples of his 'teaching'. Reimarus, who became a professor of oriental languages (see Talbert's Introduction to Reimarus, 1970 (1768), p. 3), had a clearly (though rudely) articulated perception of Hebraic expression:

> For one can be certain of this much: the Hebraic expressions of the Jews sound swollen and bombastic in the Oriental manner, and one might marvel at what great things seem to be hidden beneath them, but they always mean less than the words seem to imply. So one must learn to divest and strip them of their magnificence; then he will at last understand their speech correctly, and the ideas that prevailed among the Jews will confirm that we have hit upon their meaning.
>
> (Reimarus, 1970 (1768), p. 88)

Reimarus is here discussing Jewish Messianic terminology, but his comments fit the whole thrust of his argument about Jesus' teaching. If only we do a bit of homework about contemporary Judaism, he seems to say, obscurity in

Jesus' words will melt away. In this respect, history seems to have proved Reimarus wrong. But the themes he raised of the distinction between Jesus and the Evangelists, the Jewishness of Jesus and the character of his language have become *leitmotivs* in the study of Jesus' stories.

Parables as problems to be solved: David Friedrich Strauss

Strauss's *Life of Jesus Critically Examined* (1840) took up the historical baton bequeathed by Reimarus. A forerunner of much later Gospel criticism, he subjected the texts to careful scrutiny, exposing (as he saw it) the 'mythological' language in which they are largely written, not least the accounts of miracles, and thus posing fundamental questions about what access we can really gain to the truth of what happened. Although he does not deny a historical basis to the Gospels, the effect of his work was decidedly negative, leaving the impression that very little could be known of the life of Jesus (Schweitzer, 2000 (1913), p. 85).

Strauss discusses the extent to which the Evangelists' arrangement of the parables is true to the circumstances of their original utterance by Jesus (Strauss, 1994 (1840), pp. 345–55). An advance on Reimarus is his sensitivity to Matthew's literary style, as well as to the oral dynamics of this kind of speech, when commenting that, contrary to the impression given by Matthew 13, Jesus would have been unlikely to utter the parables straight after each other:

> The parable, it has been observed, is a kind of problem, to be solved by the reflection of the hearer; hence after every parable a pause is requisite, if it be the object of the teacher to convey real instruction, and not to distract by a multiplicity of ill-understood images.   (p. 345)

Here the assumption that the parables show Jesus as a plain and persuasive teacher rears its head. Strauss comments on the loose way in which parables sometimes seem connected to their contexts, especially in the case of the verses following The Shrewd Manager (Luke 16.9–13) which, Strauss says, will certainly skew our reading of the parable if taken as interpretative of it (pp. 349–50). He rightly shows the difficulty of taking The Rich Man and Lazarus (Luke 16.19–31) as a portrayal of God's moral judgement: 'the guilt of the one appears to lie in his wealth, the merit of the other in his poverty' (p. 351). Recent commentators have taken this insight in a radical direction, seeing the parable as an indictment of society's inequality, rather than a depiction of individuals' destiny (see e.g. Bauckham, 1991). Strauss, however, sees this as a sign of Ebionitism (valorization of poverty) in the Gospel account of Jesus' teaching (and he does not approve).

Especially clear and interesting is Strauss's discussion of the two parables of which Matthew and Luke have different versions: The Wedding Feast and The Talents in Matthew, The Great Banquet and The Pounds in Luke (Strauss, 1994 (1840), pp. 352–5). As noted by most modern commentators, one of each pair (The Wedding Feast in Matthew and The Pounds in Luke) seems to combine two stories. A sub-plot about rebellious subjects and a violent reaction from the overlord appears to have been mixed with another story, about invitations to a banquet, in one case, and the entrusting of money for trade, in the other. (Matthew's conclusion to The Wedding Feast, in which a man is expelled for not having a wedding garment, might, says Strauss, be originally yet another story, 'stitched on' because of its reference to a feast (p. 355).)

Note the hidden literary evaluations at work. Strauss takes these 'composite' parables as necessarily combinations wrought by the tradition rather than the author, because the author as storyteller would surely have achieved a greater consistency (pp. 353–5). Here is an embryonic statement of the popular ideal of simplicity as a lens for reading Jesus' stories, a lens which needs some critical examination,[5] as well as a contrast, familiar in this period, between a Jesus who spoke in a well-honed way and Evangelists who tended to confuse matters by their loose method of associating material. This is a tendentious polarization. Moreover, as we shall see, a grasp of social setting that was not available to Strauss opens up the logic of a number of stories in a way that allows us to read them 'whole'.

Strauss's editor, Peter Hodgson, points out that Strauss says almost nothing about the nature of the parable genre (p. 790). We might add that Strauss says absolutely nothing about the narrative genre as such. In addition, Hodgson draws attention to the fact that Strauss sees The Talents / Pounds and The Great Banquet / Wedding Feast stories, along with The Rebellious Tenants, as referring to the Second Coming. This shows that Strauss is still under the influence of traditional Christological readings (p. 790).

Communicating God-consciousness, founding community: Friedrich D. E. Schleiermacher

Strauss and Schleiermacher stand in a strange relationship. Strauss's massive *Life of Jesus* was first published in 1835 and issued in a fourth edition in 1840. On a visit to Berlin, Strauss had obtained and read a copy of notes from Schleiermacher's lectures on the life of Jesus, which were delivered for the last time in 1832 before Schleiermacher's death in 1834 (Schweitzer, 2000 (1913), p. 67). Schleiermacher's own Life of Jesus, however, was not published till 1864, some 30 years after his death. Schweitzer comments:

> For the questions raised by [Strauss's] *Life of Jesus*, published in 1835, Schleiermacher had no answer, and for the wounds which it made, no healing. When, in 1864, Schleiermacher's work was put on view like an embalmed corpse, Strauss accorded the dead work of the great theologian a dignified and striking funeral oration. (Schweitzer, 2000 (1913), p. 60)

Schleiermacher had approached his task entirely from a theologian's point of view, attempting to show how the Gospel records strike a balance between docetic and Ebionitic pictures of Jesus (i.e. the tendencies to underplay his humanity and divinity respectively) (Schweitzer, 2000 (1913), pp. 59–64). For him, Jesus' vocation is the communication of his God-consciousness. This did, indeed, seem like a backward-gazing direction to take in the wake of the bold historical hypotheses advanced by Reimarus and Strauss, and their negative implications for traditional understandings of Jesus.

Schleiermacher's posthumously published *Life of Jesus* (1997 (1864)) differentiates between Jesus' regular teaching in the synagogues, based on a scriptural text, and the more ad hoc communication of 'his own spiritual existence' when crowds gathered round him (p. 230). Schleiermacher goes on to ask whether the disciples were entrusted by Jesus with an esoteric teaching different from his message to the crowds, and answers in the negative: apparent differences can be explained as 'only a matter of the time at which the message was proclaimed' (p. 231), that is, the disciples were ready for more advanced teaching more quickly because of their more intense relationship with Jesus. This is an implied explanation of the rationale for Jesus' parables, as veiled speech for the 'outsiders', given in Mark 4.10–12. Schleiermacher identifies the 'gnome' or 'aphorism' as the common element between parable and 'consecutive discourse' (1997 (1864), p. 232): the parable is basically a 'pictorial' aphorism and the discourse a 'didactic' one. Note, again, the absence of the category of narrative.

The theological convictions driving Schleiermacher's work are seen in statements such as this: '[W]e see that [Christ's teaching] must have been at the same time a teaching concerning himself and not just concerning general human affairs' (1997 (1864), p. 234). All Christ's teaching is aimed at laying a basis 'for a specific human community': 'The teaching of the kingdom of God could only have been an invitation to belong to it and an encouragement to do what it demands' (p. 234). Schleiermacher explicitly brings the parables under this umbrella: 'Most of them are concerned with the kingdom of God, and likewise refer to it by way of Christ's founding of a community' (p. 234). This determination to see all Jesus' teaching as centred in the announcement of God's kingdom is important, not least in Schleiermacher's observation that we cannot divide the theoretical idea of the kingdom from its practical outworking (p. 235). In parable studies, there has indeed been division along these lines: some parables (such as The Good Samaritan) have often been seen as fundamentally practical, indeed moralistic, while others (such as The Prodigal Son) have often been seen as fundamentally theoretical, teaching doctrine about God. I have attempted to show the invalidity of this distinction elsewhere (S. I. Wright, 2000b, esp. p. 202), as has Jeffrey Tucker at greater length (1998). It is the category of narrative which enables us to see that more clearly.

Schleiermacher stresses that we must distinguish between that which was original to Jesus and that which he took from the Scriptures or later developments in Jewish thinking. He illustrates this from the 'parable'[6] of The Sheep and the Goats: the saying about what is done to the least of his brethren being done to Christ is the key, original message, and 'the idea of the last judgment is just the form it takes' (1997 (1864)), p. 238). Whether or not he is right about that passage, there is a literary and historical sensibility at work here, though not applied to a story. In a similar way, most recent scholars stress that the story of The Rich Man and Lazarus does not set out to teach a particular conception of the afterlife, but uses a standard conception current at the time to develop its plot.

Schleiermacher argues that this distinction between an original message and its dressing in current language is most difficult to make when Jesus is speaking in an 'apologetic and polemical' context, because there it will be natural to use, to some extent, the thought-forms of the opponent (1997 (1864), p. 242). Schleiermacher's editor, Jack Verheyden, points to the parallel here with Joachim Jeremias's influential work on the parables (Jeremias, 1963 (1947)): Jeremias identified the parables as largely polemical. But Verheyden points also to the key difference, that Jeremias thought that this polemic opened a window on what was most distinctive about Jesus, whereas for Schleiermacher the polemic obscured it; for him, the characteristic Jesus was most clearly revealed in the (serenely self-disclosing) discourses of the Fourth Gospel (p. 242). Without fully adopting Jeremias's construal, recent scholarship moves inexorably towards identifying the deeply conflicted nature of Jesus' world and therefore of the environment in which his stories were heard.

Schleiermacher's, in fact, was the last major Life of Jesus to take the Gospel of John as the 'controlling' Gospel. This also happens to be the Gospel in which Jesus tells no stories, but utters a range of highly self-referential discourses. It is thus natural that Schleiermacher should generalize about Jesus' speech as the communication of 'his own spiritual existence in the form of thought' (1997 (1864), p. 230). Such a rubric does little to hint at the earthy nature of Jesus' stories as recorded in the Synoptics, though Schleiermacher is confident in asserting that Jesus' teaching about himself, his mission and the kingdom is all of a piece (p. 243).

Schleiermacher's interpretation of Jesus' preaching of the kingdom as his 'communication of his God-consciousness' (p. 280 n.), incorporating also his 'self-consciousness' which was also 'the consciousness of the complete development of the human spirit and the human race that took place from this point on' (p. 337), is bound to have a significant effect on our understanding of Jesus' stories, inclining us towards a self-revealing interpretation. Associated with this is Schleiermacher's opposition to any idea that Christ 'had a *plan*':

> Once we admit the existence of that direction of life that led Christ to preach himself, redemption through him, and the kingdom of God, we have to agree that in all individual cases Christ and the apostles let themselves be governed by the circumstances, without formulating a specific design or determining by human reflection that something should be done here or there that would most effectively spread the gospel. (p. 328)

For such a view, it is natural that the stories Jesus told should not be thought to relate at all to the strategy of Jesus' mission, for there was no such strategy. While Schleiermacher was surely right to stress the contingency of Jesus' utterances on circumstances, he underplays the sharpness with which they reflect and relate to the world around them, because he wants us to see the eternal truth beneath that response to circumstances. He minimizes the moral force of Jesus' speech, seeing its moral content as 'predominantly only the polemic against those who oppose the kingdom' (p. 337). The reality of his consciousness of God is, for Schleiermacher, the sum of what Jesus desired to communicate, and thus we must hear through all the contingent detail in which his teaching is couched the message of faith working through love (p. 338).

Images from nature: Ernest Renan

Little fresh insight emerges into Jesus' stories from the sentimental portrait of Jesus painted by Ernest Renan in his *La Vie de Jésus* (1863). But he does perceive the link revealed in those stories between Jesus' teaching and his natural environment:

> His preaching was gentle and pleasing, breathing nature and the perfume of the fields. He loved the flowers, and took from them his most charming lessons. The birds of heaven, the sea, the mountains, and the games of children furnished in turn the subject of his instructions. His style had nothing of the Grecian in it, but approached much more to that of the Hebrew parabolists, and especially of sentences from the Jewish doctors, his contemporaries, such as we read them in the 'Pirke Aboth'.   (Renan, 1935 (1863), ch. X)

For Renan, however, it was strictly his *natural*, not his political environment which influenced Jesus: 'The charming impossibilities with which his parables abound, when he brings kings and the mighty ones on the stage, prove that he never conceived of aristocratic society but as a young villager who sees the world through the prism of his simplicity' (Renan, 1935 (1863), ch. III). Later scholarship overturns this picture of the naïve country boy with little notion of the powers in the land. The influence of Roman rule and overbearing aristocracy was all too evident amidst the beauties of the rural scene.

There may at first sight be an element of contradiction between the picture of the imagery Jesus so readily drew from nature and Renan's summary of the 'parables of the kingdom': 'A series of parables, often obscure, was designed to express the suddenness of this advent, its apparent injustice, and its inevitable and final character' (Renan, 1935 (1863), ch. VII). If these parables are drawn from nature, in what sense does Renan think they are 'obscure'? In fact Renan here seems to express an abiding intuition about the parables, namely, that they both reveal and conceal. There is something deceptive about the naturalness of their language, because they hauntingly evoke that which is beyond nature: and it may be narrative form itself which brings this to the fore most sharply.

Renan contrasts the strategy of Jesus during most of his ministry, which was to explain to the disciples the full but secret truth about himself that he could not communicate to the crowds (ch. XVIII), and Jesus' approach as the final conflict looms: 'The title "Son of God," which he openly assumed in striking parables, wherein his enemies appeared as murderers of the heavenly messengers, was as an open defiance to the Judaism of the Law' (ch. XXI). This exaggerates the difference, however. Renan seems to be referring to The Rebellious Tenants and The Wedding Feast, both set in Jesus' last week, but neither of these can be regarded as an 'open' assumption of the title 'Son of God' by Jesus. Couched as they are in the third person, the stories are not directly self-referential, and any such self-reference by Jesus can only be derived by hearers/readers through an interpretation of the vineyard owner and king as God, and a further interpretation of the son in both stories as Jesus.

Jesus the teacher of universal truth: Adolf Jülicher

After over a century of 'historical Jesus' study, it was not until Jülicher's major work (Jülicher, 1910 (1886, 1898, 1899)) that the parables of Jesus were given thoroughgoing and sustained attention in a way that would influence subsequent debate. I have discussed Jülicher's approach in detail elsewhere (S. I. Wright, 2000b, pp. 113–50), and will focus here on the absence of 'story' as a category in his interpretation.

Jülicher's study of the parables allowed him to present a Jesus who is an original genius in the Romantic mould (S. I. Wright, 2000b, pp. 137–8). The recognition, in this phase of historical criticism, that with the parables we are in touch with some of the most reliable tradition of Jesus' sayings meant that the parables in effect took centre stage in defining Jesus' character and purpose. However, since Jülicher did not to any great extent set his study in the context of Jesus' other sayings and actions, his construal of the parables was overdetermined by standard views of Jesus inherited from nineteenth-century theology. Jesus was the supreme God-conscious moralist. Although Weiss's work arguing that Jesus' sayings must be understood in an eschatological light had appeared in 1892, it did not much affect Jülicher's second volume in 1898, or the second edition of the first volume in 1899. It would not be until the work of Dodd in the 1930s and especially that of Jeremias in the 1940s that the insights into Jesus' eschatology from Weiss and Schweitzer made themselves felt in a serious way in parable scholarship.

Thus Jülicher appropriately comes at the end of this chapter, because, despite his pioneering work in parable scholarship, the picture of Jesus as the ideal moral teacher which both presupposed and was bolstered by it was a typically nineteenth-century one. This was the age in which Christianity was seeking a recovered acceptability in Western culture, partly by presenting its core teachings (not least those of its founder) as expressions of universally recognized truth. In fact Jülicher's Jesus is much more similar to

Schleiermacher's (notwithstanding the different theological assumptions at work) even than the Jewish Jesus of Reimarus, and certainly than the Jesus of Jülicher's own contemporaries Weiss and Schweitzer.

In order to understand Jülicher's approach it is vital to see what he was reacting against (S. I. Wright, 2000b, pp. 127–50). The handling of the parables by the Fathers and mediaeval commentators had often been richly imaginative. All kinds of deeper meanings and links with other parts of Scripture had been 'discerned' and this, thought Jülicher, militated perniciously against grasping Jesus' true meaning. Jülicher overreacted to this approach. In seeking to 'save' the parables from what he saw as the wantonly allegorizing treatment they had received for much of Church history, he overstated the case that they were basically clear in their message. In particular, he asserted that they shared a common underlying structure of simile: 'this is like that'. In so doing, he obscured the rhetorical character of story which many of the parables possess.

This is clearly illustrated in Jülicher's treatment of The Prodigal Son. His summary of this story is a general statement of comparison: 'As a father of two sons ... greets [his son] as soon as he returns in contrition, with warmth ... so the way to the father-heart of God stands always open, even to the most rotten sinner' (Jülicher, 1910, II, p. 362). The interpretation elides the narrative dynamics completely in favour of the statement of a universal truth (S. I. Wright, 2000b, pp. 119–22). Not surprisingly, Jülicher's attempt to read all the parables as comparisons runs into particular difficulties with those he named *Beispielerzählungen*, 'example stories', those that clearly picture scenes from real life in which characters appear as models, either positive or negative. He himself notes, for instance, that it does not make sense to read in Luke 18.9–14 an implied *comparison* between the Pharisee and 'all the haughty': 'can one seriously *compare* all the haughty with one haughty person, and thus the category with the individual belonging to it?' (Jülicher, 1910, I, p. 112; S. I. Wright, 2000b, pp. 136–7). Of course not, indeed: the structure of story is not that of rhetorical comparison ('this is like that') but rather an implied invitation to imagine a set of events ('consider this'). Not only with the so-called 'example stories', but with the other narrative parables too, the overlooking of the simple fact of their narrative character has been detrimental to our understanding of what Jesus was about.

Certainly, the earlier Christian interpreters were sometimes no more attentive to the narrative quality and structure of Jesus' parables than Jülicher was (the other side of the picture I presented at the start of this chapter). They had this in their support, however, that they were seeking connections between these mini-stories and the grand, overarching story of redemption in which they believed. The integrity of the individual stories may have been sacrificed in the process, but for them that was less important than the placement of the parables in a universal web of divine meaning (S. I. Wright, 2000b, pp. 62–112). For his framework, Jülicher has only the nineteenth-century delineation of Jesus as the ideal teacher. Perhaps the 'eclipse of biblical narrative' which Hans Frei (1974) traced from the seventeenth through to the nineteenth century here reached its nadir, with the eclipse of the narrative structure of the stories Jesus himself told.

2

Recovering the stories of Jesus: from Wrede to the present

As we enter the twentieth century, a fresh appreciation for Jesus' specifically Jewish context starts to take hold of Jesus-studies, and in due course makes its impact on studies of his parables. As we shall observe, this appreciation does not automatically lead to careful appraisal of his stories as stories (notwith-standing the large number of stories in Judaism's sacred texts). Nevertheless, the 'eclipse' we traced in the earlier period starts to recede, as important insights on narrative start to be applied.

The eschatological secret: William Wrede and Albert Schweitzer

In two important works first published in the first decade of the twentieth century, the issue of the obscurity or clarity of the parables contributed significantly to the arguments about Jesus. This has a close bearing on the issue of story, since even short stories are capable of bearing a range of meanings, and are not reducible to one 'obvious' one. William Wrede's *The Messianic Secret* (1901) saw the Gospels' account of Jesus' private explanations of parables to his disciples (e.g. Mark 4.10–20) as an editorial insertion by the Evangelists. This insertion, he argued, was designed to cover up the fact that Jesus had never claimed to be Messiah, by asserting that this knowledge had been given by secret revelations to the select few.[1] This is Wrede's sophisticated rationale for saying, as Jülicher had already asserted, that since Jesus must have spoken in parables which were clear and straightforward, any more hidden meanings in them must be attributed to early, or later, Christian interpretation. Thus in Wrede the story-character of many of Jesus' parables continues to be eclipsed by overreaction to pre-critical allegorization, as well as by an assumed contrast between the plain speech of Jesus and its dressing-up by the Evangelists.

Albert Schweitzer's *The Quest of the Historical Jesus*, first appearing in 1906, made the case forcefully that Jesus' words and activity were entirely conditioned by eschatological hope (Schweitzer, 2000 (1913), pp. 303–54). It was consistent with this that, *pace* Wrede, Jesus should indeed have intended his parabolic teaching as secretive. Though harking back to Reimarus in some respects, Schweitzer's position is distinguished from that of Reimarus in three ways above all: his belief that this hope was for a supernatural, not an earthly kingdom; his belief that Jesus' eschatological expectation was 'thoroughgoing' (*konsequente*), that is, that it drove all his actions, including his decision to go to Jerusalem to die; and Schweitzer's own passionate faith that this Jesus could still be followed, notwithstanding the strangeness of his eschatological world-view for the modern world (on this see especially his famous Conclusion, pp. 478–87). For Schweitzer, Jesus expected an imminent, supernaturally wrought kingdom of God, and within it the revelation of himself as Messiah. When this did not happen as soon as he expected, Schweitzer's Jesus believed he was being called to usher it in through himself bearing its birth pangs through suffering and death. This, for Schweitzer, is the background framework of thought which makes sense of the mysterious history recounted in the Gospels of Mark and Matthew. Insofar as he discusses the stories told by Jesus, this, therefore, is the framework within which he interprets them.

In contrast to the nineteenth-century 'liberal' Jesus, delineated for instance by Jülicher, a Jesus whose words are all honed towards the clear communication of a universal moral message, Schweitzer's Jesus is torn between 'the urge to teach and the duty he felt to preserve the secret of his person … He teaches, but like one who knows that he should not do so too clearly or too convincingly' (Schweitzer, 2000 (1913), p. 322). Rather than attributing the words about the parables' 'veiling' purpose (Mark 4.10–12) to the early Church, as Jülicher and Wrede had done, Schweitzer sees them as representing the intention of Jesus: not, to be sure, in everything he said, but particularly in the parables in Mark 4. Schweitzer regards a strong view of predestination as integral to Jesus' eschatological outlook. Beyond the basic message to repent in view of the kingdom's nearness (Mark 1.15), anything Jesus proclaims in public must be in parables, 'in order that only those who are shown to possess predestination by having the initial knowledge which enables them to understand the parables may receive a more advanced knowledge' (Schweitzer, 2000 (1913), p. 323). The story of the wedding feast from which someone is excluded for not wearing the right garment (Matt. 22.1–14) is interpreted by Schweitzer as the ultimate demonstration of this predestinarian outlook. The king's invitation has been publicly issued, but the man's appearance demonstrates that he is not 'chosen' (see especially v. 14; Schweitzer, 2000 (1913), p. 323). The assumption that Jesus was completely controlled by his eschatological beliefs might indeed help to explain this and other puzzling parables. That which makes them morally perturbing to us may be precisely that which makes them comprehensible in an eschatological framework which, as Schweitzer recognized, seems so alien to a modern outlook. But, as we shall see, this may not be the complete, or only possible, explanation for them.

Narrative starts to make an exciting (re-)appearance with Schweitzer's reading of the parables of Mark 4 – The Sower, The Seed Growing Secretly, and The Mustard Seed. Here he emphasizes not the idea of gradual development (as in the interpretation of C. H. Dodd), but rather that of immediacy. Something comes about in the natural world, following an apparently insignificant human act, through the mysterious power of God (Schweitzer, 2000 (1913), p. 324). The 'initial fact' that they reflect is understood by Schweitzer as 'the movement of repentance evoked by the Baptist and now intensified by [Jesus'] own preaching', which 'compels the bringing in of the kingdom by the power of God, as man's sowing necessitates the giving of the harvest by the same infinite Power'. Schweitzer continues:

> Anyone who knows this sees with different eyes the corn growing in the fields and the harvest ripening, for he sees the one fact in the other, and awaits along with the earthly harvest the heavenly harvest, the revelation of the kingdom of God.
>
> If we look into the thought more closely, we see that the coming of the kingdom of God is connected with the harvest not only symbolically or analogically, but also really and temporally. The harvest ripening upon earth is the last! With it comes the kingdom of God which brings in the new age. When the reapers are sent into the fields, the Lord in heaven will cause his harvest to be reaped by the holy angels.   (Schweitzer, 2000 (1913), p. 325)

The particular historical reference given to this parable here (that it points to the imminent, literal harvest as the one Jesus predicted to be the last ever) is striking. Schweitzer's belief that Jesus expected the overwhelming appearance of God's kingdom as imminently as this is not widely held today. But he shows important insight into the way the parable 'works'. It is not a mere analogy; in fact, in grammatical structure it is not an analogy at all; there is no 'just as ... so' (an analogical expansion only enters with the subsequent explanation to the disciples). It is a *story*, and, though Schweitzer does not say so explicitly, he sees that in its form it invites hearers to consider a past fact as present, 'as certainly present as the time of the sowing is past at the moment when Jesus speaks' (Schweitzer, 2000 (1913), p. 325).[2] Because of the 'naturalness' or 'normality' of the progression from seedtime to harvest (though, of course, it is a divine progression), the hearers are invited to consider the ultimate yield – notwithstanding resistant factors – as something already certain.

Thus, though we may not agree that Jesus thought that the coming harvest was literally the last before the dawn of the new age, Schweitzer helps us to see how the parable in its narrative logic calls its hearers to see 'the one fact in the other', the certainty of the kingdom's coming in the certainty of the seed's growth. Observation of the 'natural' process should lead to conviction about the certainty of the 'spiritual' process. And the latter is no vague generality, but is rooted in the narrative of historical events that are unfolding as Jesus speaks. Schweitzer's identification of the 'sowing' with the initial preaching of John and Jesus implies a Jesus who tells this short story with the intent that hearers will place themselves in the time shortly before the harvest. Indeed, the 'mystery of the kingdom of God' (Mark 4.10), on this reading, is precisely the kingdom's imminence at this historical moment (Schweitzer, 2000 (1913), p. 326). This understanding is supported by Schweitzer with reference to

Matthew 9.37–38, in which Jesus tells his disciples, immediately before sending them out on their mission, to pray God 'to send out labourers into his harvest'.[3]

Schweitzer does not discuss the interpretation given to the parable by the Evangelists, but one merit of his reading is that it invites us to listen for the parable's original (uninterpreted) force, rather than hearing it only through the filter of the interpretation. At the same time, it enables us to see more clearly the logic of the interpretation. In its present-tense form, the interpretation reads like a re-presentation of the parable's message for a Christian age in which the kingdom had not yet dawned, indeed still faced resistance, but remained the object of hope, hope realized already in part through the people in whom the good seed is bearing fruit. But this does not mean that the interpretation could have had no logic for Jesus himself. On Schweitzer's reading, accepting Mark at face value, the interpretation is given to the disciples precisely as the elect, those to whom 'has been given the secret of the kingdom of God'. Their request for more clarity (Mark 4.10) may draw a mild rebuke from Jesus (v. 13), but the fact that he goes on to spell out in more detail the truth concerning the spiritual significance of the time shows that he believes them to have enough understanding to be worthy of further enlightenment. The predestinarian overtones of the interpretation fit Schweitzer's construal of the parable exactly: there is a mystery to human response to the proclamation of repentance which cannot be explained in purely human terms but is very appropriate to the image of different kinds of soil. The present tense gives a more general, timeless air to the interpretation than the definite urgency evoked by the past tense of the story itself, but it is not difficult to hear even in the story's interpretation the tones of a highly expectant Jesus commenting on the actual realities of human response, and lack of it, which he observes all around him at this crucial moment in history. Schweitzer's reading is perhaps one of the first from a modern scholar to capture the narrative force of The Sower.

What kind of eschatology? Rudolf Bultmann, C. H. Dodd and Joachim Jeremias

Three contributions from the 1920s, 1930s and 1940s respectively merit our attention here. Rudolf Bultmann, C. H. Dodd and Joachim Jeremias all built on Schweitzer's eschatological understanding of Jesus' activity. Bultmann stressed the existential implications of Jesus' announcement of a future kingdom; Dodd believed that Jesus announced the kingdom as present, but that his followers sometimes misunderstood his words as applying to the future; Jeremias said that Jesus' proclamation 'inaugurated' the kingdom of God (rather than 'realizing' it, as Dodd believed).

All followed Jülicher in insisting that a parable normally just has one 'point'. Bultmann (1963 (1921), pp. 187–92) has left us with a very useful summary of standard narrative techniques as they may be found in Jesus' stories, but the net effect of his study of narrative technique is to diminish the significance of specific elements in parables as being simply elements of the storyteller's art, to be discarded in the quest for the existential kernel. Dodd (1936 (1935)) used the parables as the basis for his argument that Jesus believed the eschaton had dawned in his own ministry, but at the cost of diminishing their narrative quality. Jeremias (1963 (1947)) identified the parables as weapons in Jesus' controversy with his opponents, and thus tended to 'filter' narrative through the lens of argument. We will consider each of these scholars in more detail.[4]

Bultmann's *History of the Synoptic Tradition* (1963 (1921)) gave the detailed fruits of his study of the Synoptic Gospels using the newly developed approach of 'form criticism'. He analysed the material according to its various literary forms and used this analysis to make judgements about how the process of tradition had affected the texts in the form they now possess in the Gospels. He has a section on 'similitudes and similar forms' (pp. 166–205), within which he treats those parables which have obvious narrative features (esp. pp. 174–9). He thus continued Jülicher's approach of subsuming 'narrative' within 'similitude', understood as a straightforward comparison, while turning his back on Schweitzer's belief that Jesus taught in an esoteric manner; Bultmann regarded Mark 4.10–12, 'where the similitudes are treated as quite esoteric utterances', as 'quite secondary' (i.e. expressing the view of the tradition or Evangelist, not that of Jesus) (1963 (1921), p. 199).

Bultmann's short book on Jesus shows that he has a quite standard understanding of parables, including story parables, as simile or metaphor, the straightforward identification of a material scene with a spiritual reality. He comments on The Master and His Slave and The Labourers in the Vineyard: 'Both parables express as strongly as possible the conviction that man can have no claim on God' (1935 (1926), p. 74).[5] This is Jülicher's generalized style of reading transposed into Bultmann's particular eschatological–existentialist key.[6] There is no thorough integration of those stories into Jesus' wider ministry, and this tallies with Sanders's comment that Bultmann's treatment of Jesus gives no explanation of Jesus' teaching, the movement he began, or his death (Sanders, 1985, p. 27).

Bultmann's work has left both a negative and a positive legacy with respect to our present subject. Negatively, it appeared to show how difficult it was to reach any confident knowledge about the profile of Jesus, so many were the possible adaptations of oral tradition, redactions of the Evangelists and so on. Indeed, Bultmann himself is over-confident on the basis of the evidence he produces, not least when we note his anti-Jewish prejudice. Here is an early statement of what would become well known as the 'criterion of dissimilarity':

> We can only count on possessing a genuine similitude of Jesus where, on the one hand, expression is given to the contrast between Jewish morality and piety and the distinctive eschatological temper which characterized the preaching of Jesus; and where on the other hand we find no specifically Christian features.
>
> (Bultmann, 1963 (1921), p. 205)

The general problems with the use of such a criterion have been widely discussed recently.[7] Bultmann's whole approach to examining the sayings of Jesus, which became influential for a generation, is now called into question: the oddly atomistic procedure whereby scholars construct a picture of Jesus by extracting individual *logia* from the Gospels and setting them in the scholars' own framework of meaning – whether it be that of an 'existential–eschatological' Jesus, an 'apocalyptic' Jesus, a 'sapiential' Jesus or anything else (see Horsley, 2012, pp. 3–4, 68–71).

In particular, Bultmann's sometimes unsavoury application of the criterion of dissimilarity is exemplified in his judgement about The Rich Man and Lazarus: the first part of the story, he says (Luke 16.19–26), 'can hardly have come from Jesus or the Church, for it breathes the rancorousness of Judaism as it pervades the last chapter of Eth. Enoch, and treats sinners and rich men, the pious and the poor alike' (Bultmann, 1963 (1921), p. 203). Indeed, although Bultmann has often been cited as the one who made study of the historical Jesus (deliberately?) problematic and full of uncertainties by exposing the changes that accounts and sayings of Jesus have undergone, the greater problem of his legacy is perhaps the prejudiced dogmatism with which he did decree what Jesus himself could or could not have said.

Positively, however, a real advance in scholarship is signalled by Bultmann's section highlighting characteristic features of narrative as they are seen in Jesus' stories (1963 (1921), pp. 187–92). Although based quite narrowly on studies of folklore available to him at the time, this list draws attention to features which are still widely recognized as key to the way many stories work. It forms a useful reference point for the exploration of the stories in Part 3 of this book. He mentions the conciseness of the narratives, with only the necessary persons appearing (usually one, two or three, with groups often treated as individuals) (p. 188). He notes the laws of 'stage duality', whereby only two persons speak or act in the same scene of the story, and of the 'single perspective', whereby 'one is not asked to watch two different series of events happening at the same time' (p. 188). He comments that people in the stories are mostly characterized by their words or actions, rather than the narrator's judgements; that feelings and motives are largely left unexpressed (p. 189). Unnecessary elements are omitted from plots, including conclusions not germane to the storyteller's thrust (p. 190). The use of direct speech and repetition, and the law of 'end-stress', putting the most important element of the story at the end, are all evident (pp. 190–1). Finally, the narrator has various ways of inviting hearers to make a judgement on characters and events (pp. 191–2). All this is part of the 'wise economy of popular story telling' (p. 189). As we shall see, a detailed study of Jesus' stories with attention to such techniques yields great dividends, though also far more ambiguity than Bultmann allows for; the identification of narrative techniques need not and should not merely serve the purpose of penetrating beneath the artistic 'surface' to the 'one point' beneath.

In C. H. Dodd's view (1936 (1935)), Jesus announced a kingdom which was fully present, thus not only proclaiming the fulfilment of Jewish hopes but also redefining them radically. The key difference from Schweitzer's understanding is seen in Dodd's interpretation of The Seed Growing Secretly. Where Schweitzer had identified the moment of sowing with John the Baptist's preaching, and the harvest as something imminent but yet to come, Dodd identifies the harvest as the present moment of crisis. He supports this with reference to the 'harvest' saying of Matthew 9.37–38 / Luke 10.2. The stages of growth are seen not as the months and years of preparation now shortly to reach their apogee, but as the long preparation of God through the prophets for a moment actually reached (1936 (1935), pp. 178–80). Jesus is 'standing in the presence of the ripe crop, and taking active steps to "put in the sickle"' (p. 179). Thus, like Schweitzer, Dodd took seriously the narrative dimension of the seed parables. As mini-stories, their temporal unfolding was seen as mapping on to the events of history, whether on a brief timeline still to be completed (Schweitzer) or a long one that has reached its end (Dodd).

For Dodd, however, unlike Schweitzer, there is no secrecy; he hears Jesus as announcing the kingdom openly as present and the parables illustrating that announcement. In this respect his approach bears much more affinity with Jülicher's. Dodd's emphasis on the homeliness of the parables tends towards emphasizing their clarity, although his famous definition of a parable does allow for an element of ambiguity in them:

> At its simplest the parable is a metaphor or simile drawn from nature or common life, arresting the hearer by its vividness and strangeness, and leaving the mind in sufficient doubt about its precise application to tease it into active thought.
>
> (1936 (1935), p. 16)

The introduction of the label 'metaphor', which entails an implied rather than an explicit identification or comparison between two entities, allows for more mystery or 'strangeness' than does Jülicher's analysis of all the parables as 'similes'.[8] But rhetorically it does not take Dodd much further. Acknowledging that 'simple' metaphors may be elaborated into more detailed pictures, or short stories, or longer ones (1936 (1935), pp. 16–18), he writes that in all these types

> it is clear that . . . we have nothing but the elaboration of a single comparison, all the details being designed to set the situation or series of events in the clearest possible light, so as to catch the imagination.   (1936 (1935), pp. 18–19)

He goes on:

> This leads us at once to the most important principle of interpretation. The typical parable, whether it be a single metaphor, or a more elaborate similitude, or a full-length story, presents one single point of comparison. The details are not intended to have independent significance.   (1936 (1935), p. 19)

What Dodd overlooks here is that even if a single metaphor is the germ of a narrative, its expression as narrative makes it far more complex and ambiguous, often evoking an entire metaphorical field whose associations for hearers are impossible to control.[9] For example, it is not clear from the surface of the short image (or implied narrative) of The Seed Growing Secretly, or the story of The Sower, whether Schweitzer or Dodd is more on target in identifying the time of the harvest in Jesus' mind. The narratives themselves are suggestive rather than definitive. And Dodd's account of how a story that originally had a simple point for Jesus' Jewish hearers was later developed in Christian tradition for paraenetic and then eschatological purposes is oversimplistic (see his discussion of The Talents / The Pounds on pp. 146–53, taking it as originally a challenge to the 'selfish exclusiveness' of Pharisaim, p. 151; Jeremias would offer a more elaborate account of the process, which, however, remained over-schematic). At all stages of transmission, the semantic and emotive associations opened up even by a 'simple' story of Jesus are too numerous and complex to admit of straightforward tracing of a tradition of interpretation.[10]

Jeremias treated the parables of Jesus in a separate volume from his treatment of his wider teaching and career (1963 (1947); 1971). He certainly took narrative features of the parables seriously. For example, he recognizes that one cannot take the father in The Prodigal Son as God *tout court* without upsetting the realism and verisimilitude of the narrative:

> The parable is not an allegory, but a story drawn from life, as is shown by vv. 18, 21, where, in a paraphrastic way, God is named: 'Father, I have sinned against heaven (i.e. God) and against thee.' Thus the father is not God, but an earthly father ... (1963 (1947), p. 128)

Yet Jeremias immediately turns away from drawing out further implications of this being a realistic narrative to assert that 'some of the expressions used are meant to reveal that in his love he is an image of God' (1963 (1947), p. 128): he mentions the Greek expressions for 'before you' in verses 18, 21, 'had compassion' in verse 20 and 'command' in verse 29. Certainly, Jesus and his hearers, Luke and his readers, and subsequent interpreters of the parable may have experienced these resonances. But Jeremias, similarly to Jülicher, turns subtle, ambiguous resonance into open simile, proclamation and argument, and erases narrativity in the process: 'The parable describes with touching simplicity what God is like, his goodness, his grace, his boundless mercy, his abounding love.' It specifically addresses those 'offended at the Gospel', saying,

> Behold the greatness of God's love for his lost children, and contrast it with your own joyless, loveless, thankless and self-righteous lives. Cease then from your loveless ways, and be merciful. The spiritually dead are rising to new life, the lost are returning home, rejoice with them. (1963 (1947), p. 131)

If Jeremias had used the word 'evokes' rather than 'describes' in the first of these quotations, and if the second had given more sense that the parable is neither a direct unveiling of God's love nor a direct exhortation, he would have been nearer capturing its narrative quality.

Furthermore, shoeing the parables into the over-narrow rhetorical space of Jesus' controversy with his opponents not only made 'argument' a more important category than 'narrative' in Jeremias's treatment – the parables 'correct, reprove, attack' (1963 (1947), p. 21). It also played naturally into his tendency to overemphasize, in the Reformation tradition, the differences between Jesus and Judaism rather than their commonality (on this see Sanders, 1985, pp. 277–8 and 403, nn. 38–40). His highly suggestive principles of 'transformation' whereby we can supposedly identify various ways in which the early Church altered the meaning of parables from that which they possessed in Jesus' time is in general vulnerable to the arbitrariness of such overarching constructions of the relationships between Judaism, Jesus and the early Church.

Parables as performative speech

Bultmann left in his wake scepticism with regard to the possibility of reconstructing the historical Jesus in any detail, as well as doubt about its theological desirability. For him, the historical contingencies of Jesus' life were irrelevant to the existential challenge represented by the great fact of his life, death and resurrection.[11] It was an important shift, then, when in a lecture in 1953 Ernst Käsemann reaffirmed the necessity, for theological purposes, of making some link between the historical proclamation and activity of Jesus and the *kerygma* proclaimed about him after his death (1964 (1960), pp. 15–47; see N. T. Wright, 1996, p. 23). In this 'New Quest', the parables of Jesus played a vital role, for they were seen precisely as that characteristic mode of speech by which Jesus proclaimed the faith which was later, in expanded form, to be proclaimed by the Church. They formed the crucial link between the pre-Easter Jesus and Paul's gospel. In this respect they were far more important than, for example, titles ascribed to Jesus in the Gospels, which continued to be seen as largely retrojected by the early Church. As Eberhard Jüngel put it: 'The parables of Jesus lead us ... not only into the centre of Jesus' preaching, but refer at the same time to the person of the preacher, to the secret of Jesus himself' (1962, p. 87, my translation). The 'New Quest' laid a wager that the parables could somehow provide the missing link, both historical and theological, between the life of the earthly Jesus and the proclamation of the Church. They were foreshadowings of the *kerygma*, before the *kerygma* proper that was the 'word of the cross' (1 Cor. 1.18).

It was not, however, the words of the parables alone which fulfilled this connecting function. It was the fact that (according to Ernst Fuchs) they reflected and expressed the activity of Jesus. '*Jesus' conduct* was itself the framework of his proclamation' (1964, p. 21, italics original). For example, Fuchs reads The Labourers in the Vineyard as a proclamation of God's act of kindness in Jesus (pp. 32–8):

> The parable by no means simply contains the pallid requirement that sinful man
> should believe in God's kindness. Instead it contains, in a concrete way, first

Jesus' *pledge*, which says that there will be no disappointment for those who, in face of a cry of 'guilty', nevertheless found their hope on an act of God's kindness; and, secondly, Jesus' *determination* to give up everything else for this faith.

(Fuchs, 1964, p. 37, italics original)

Thus Fuchs turns his back decisively on Jülicher's dictum that the parables teach a truth of the widest possible generality. They are not only parables *of* Jesus, but, in an important way, parables *about* Jesus and what he is doing. Their stories are in some way reflective of his own story. Moreover, they are themselves acts as well as words.

Fuchs has an interesting comment about the parables as narratives:

> We should not be misled by the completeness of the parables. In them the result is only parabolically presupposed or anticipated, as in the parable of the prodigal sons (and) ... Matt. 20.1–16 and ... Mark 4.3–9 par. The end is only seen by the one who comes last; the first-comers do not see it.   (pp. 25–6)

The fact that these stories have a dénouement, in other words, should not distract us from the fact that Jesus is still living them out. Only with the end of his story will the end of their story come about and be seen to be true. Fuchs sees the parable-stories as a window into Jesus' own suffering; as he tells them, his own end is not yet. Through them, he 'inspires confidence in God's action' (p. 73). Various parables are even seen as proof that 'Jesus prayed *for* his own' (p. 62, italics original).

In parallel with the 'New Quest' went a New Hermeneutic which, desiring to give a more positive place to the life of the historical Jesus in theology, argued that the power of his words continued to be transformative down the centuries. Critical scholarship on Jesus, especially that which had produced such negative 'results' as Bultmann's, did not, it was argued, have the last word in the Church's task of interpreting Jesus for today, for Jesus' words interpreted us, and the overriding present task for the theologian and preacher was not historical reconstruction but receptive attention to the world-redefining words that Jesus had spoken.

The fact that the parables were regarded, in any case, as the most recognizably authentic of Jesus' sayings played into the hands of these 'New Hermeneutic' scholars such as Fuchs, Gerhard Ebeling, Eberhard Jüngel, Eta Linnemann and Robert Funk. (Linnemann and Funk were the only ones of these to write at length on the parables specifically.) But there was unwitting sleight-of-hand in this argument. The striking presence and quality of the parables in the Gospel narratives could not prove their authenticity, however theologically attractive they might be. Nor did it prove that they were the key to unlocking the continuity between the pre-Calvary and post-Easter Jesus. It was theologically convenient to see them thus, but this linking had the inevitable result of bringing the message that Jesus spoke and the message that his followers later spoke about him too close. Once the parables became a necessary link in a chronological and kerygmatic chain, it was hard to hear them saying anything strange or uniquely applicable to the time of Jesus' ministry or different from the post-Easter *kerygma*. And once more, now under the influence of the existentialist thinking that shaped the theology of the time, appreciation of their narrative character suffered under the need to hear them as proto-kerygmatic utterances. Thus Linnemann could say that 'A direct line leads from the parables of Jesus to his crucifixion' (1966 (1961), p. 41), and Eduard Schweizer could speak of Jesus dying for the truth of his parables (1971 (1968), p. 29; see critique by Sanders (1985), p. 39).

Linnemann (1966 (1961), pp. 12–16) quotes in abbreviated form the 'laws of popular narrative' as outlined by Bultmann (1963 (1921), pp. 187–92), and discussed above. But she moves on quickly from this focus on narrative to write of the variety of ways in which a parable can be used:

> A parable is an urgent endeavour on the part of the speaker towards the listener ... It is of the essence of a parable that there is achieved in it a *dialegesthai*, a conversation, a dialogue *between* the narrator and the listener ... A parable can be used for *instruction* ... for *exhortation*.   (p. 19, her italics)

She goes on to present the parable as a form of argument, drawing from Rabbinic and classical examples (pp. 20–3), using the standard distinction between 'picture part' and 'reality part', joined by a *tertium comparationis* or point of comparison, standard since Jülicher. The climax of her introductory material on basic principles of parable interpretation is the assertion that the parables of Jesus are 'language-events' with the power to create a new existence:

> A successful parable is an event that decisively alters the situation. It creates a new possibility that did not exist before, the possibility that the man addressed can come to an understanding with the man addressing him across the opposition that exists between them.   (p. 30)

> Jesus, by compelling his listeners to a decision through telling a parable, gives them the possibility of making a change of existence, of understanding themselves anew from the depths up, of achieving a 'new life'.   (p. 31)

This insight of the New Hermeneutic that the parables were performative acts, events of language, not simply repositories of abstract 'meaning', has been a very important and enduring contribution to parable scholarship, which links it vitally with study of the historical Jesus. But the way in which the scholars of this period spoke of the parables' 'compulsion' of their hearers to existential decision owed more to the philosophical mood of the period's theology than to actual analysis of their rhetoric, and particularly the rhetoric of story. It also inevitably tended towards focusing on a general (if profound) challenge, rather than the specific resonance of a story with the circumstances of Jesus' hearers.

The emphasis on the parables as language-events merges creatively in this period with increasing attention to their literary qualities. Geraint Vaughan Jones (1964) linked the parables' 'truth' to their 'art'. Dan Otto Via's analysis of the parables in the categories of tragedy and comedy (1967) is very suggestive, and his intuition that historical criticism alone could not enable us to appreciate them was prophetic. John Dominic Crossan (1973) drew on structuralist literary theory to divide the parables into three categories of 'advent', 'reversal' and 'action'. (On a structuralist approach to Jesus' narratives, see Theissen and Merz, 1998 (1996), pp. 331–4.) All this constituted welcome recognition that there was far more to the parables than single points, and that they were not necessarily to be pressed into immediate theological service. Yet this deeper attention to narrative art does not, on its own, enable us to 'place' Jesus' stories as elements of his historical activity. Further steps are needed, which will be outlined in Chapter 3. And it is telling that all these scholars described the impact of the parables in terms of existential challenge, a natural philosophical counterpart to the perception of art as timeless. In this we may see the desire for contemporary impact, entirely understandable from a theological perspective, interfering with sensitivity to historical contingency. For instance, Via in his final chapter (1967, pp. 177–205) enquires how his reading of the parables as 'aesthetic objects' relates to study of the historical Jesus. Rather than aligning it with either the 'thoroughgoing' eschatology of Schweitzer or the 'realized' eschatology of Dodd, he essentially follows Bultmann by calling the parables (awkwardly) an 'aesthetic expression of the existential intention of the eschatology' (p. 188).

Within this section we will mention the unique work of Kenneth Bailey (1976, 1980, 2003, 2008) who, by contrast to the authors of the 'New Quest' and New Hermeneutic movement, has dealt at length with the cultural context of the parables, drawing from long immersion in the Middle East. Although he has been criticized for assuming too readily that the present culture of this area is sufficiently similar to that of Jesus' time for us to draw interpretative conclusions from it (see e.g. Hedrick, 1994, pp. 44–6), Bailey has at least compelled many Western readers to remove their own cultural spectacles and imagine the meanings of Jesus' stories and sayings in their original setting. In addition to this, he brought to his task a formidable knowledge of Arabic and other New Testament versions.

It is surprising, then, that the picture which emerges of Jesus is a remarkably traditional one. Where Bultmann and the New Hermeneutic 'heard' theological challenges couched in existential terms, Bailey heard, essentially, lessons in Christian doctrine, outlined in the 'theological clusters' with which he summarizes his expositions (1976, 1980; 2003, pp. 205–11). The Prodigal Son 'provides a clear picture of Jesus of Nazareth, the theologian' (2003, p. 208). The readings of the parables in his 2008 work follow a similar pattern. Bailey's brilliantly fresh insights into the cultural overtones of the stories – famously, for instance, the cultural shamefulness and costliness of a Near-Eastern patriarch running the gauntlet of the local village to greet his wayward son (1976, pp. 181–2) – are not matched by a sufficiently down-to-earth imagination of the overall rhetorical force of the story for the immediate hearers. Deborah Storie points to one aspect of this weakness: Bailey's tendency to 'overlook dynamics of power and vulnerability and their effects on social relationships' (2009, pp. 100–1).[12] We might add that his careful analysis of the parables' (possible) poetic structure tends to draw attention to them as literary products rather than oral events. In the end, these vivid tales are read, as by so many others, as pointers away from themselves to some abiding spiritual truth.

Approaching Jesus' aims afresh: Ben Meyer, E. P. Sanders

A decisive shift in the study of Jesus was marked by Ben F. Meyer's *The Aims of Jesus* (1979). Meyer's verdict on the New Quest, discussed above, is that it 'was an effort by a school of theologians to meet problems in some measure peculiar to the school and to do so partly in accord with, partly in violation of, the school's inherited canons of theological legitimacy' (p. 20).

Meyer, in contrast, aims 'to understand the Jesus of ancient Palestine' in a much more full-blooded way than those, such as Strauss, Wrede and Bultmann, whose historical work has been strangely constrained by their religious interests (p. 19). History, for Meyer, is 'reconstruction through hypothesis and verification':

> Its topic is 'aims and consequences', for history involves, first of all, the grasp of aims in relation to the dynamics of the time, i.e., the springs of actually advancing movements. They say where the action is and supply the terms of its explanation.
>
> (Meyer, 1979, p. 19)

Meyer, like many of those engaged in what has come to be called the 'Third Quest' for the historical Jesus, is concerned to let historical study breathe without, as it were, having theology peering over its shoulder all the time asking the 'so what for now?' questions. He is also concerned not with the often atomistic business of deciding on the 'authenticity' or 'historicity' of particular sayings or narrated events in the Gospels but rather with the genuinely constructive business of understanding and delineating 'the goal informing Jesus' career' (1979, p. 2). Such an approach is not driven by any theological need to find (e.g. as in the 'New Quest') that the parables form a key link between the proclamation of Jesus and that of the Church.

Meyer separates Jesus' public acts and proclamation from his 'esoteric teaching'. The parables fall into the former sphere as essentially defences in public debate about his proclamation (1979, pp. 163–4) and warnings and appeals to follow it up (p. 165). While acknowledging that explanations of parables form part of the 'esoteric teaching', he asserts that these do not constitute the core of that teaching, which is reserved for the sequel to Simon's confession at Caesarea Philippi (p. 175). Meyer's general claim that '(i)n Jesus proclaimer and teacher were one and that proclamation determined teaching at every point and accounted for all its traits' (p. 137) is, however, an important benchmark for understanding the parables, emphasizing as it does that, like his other public sayings, they have a performative and proclamatory quality. For Meyer, Jesus' public actions and proclamation were his 'performance', and his private explanation of them, his 'theme'; they related to each other as 'riddle' to 'solution' (1979, p. 174).

Meyer's colleague E. P. Sanders (1985) probes in more detail the chains of cause and effect between the ministry of Jesus, his death and the emergence of the Church – all within the context of first-century Palestinian Judaism. With regard to our topic, especially pertinent is Sanders's critique of Eduard Schweizer's view, noted above, that 'Jesus identifies himself so with the cause of God that he dies for the truth of his parables' (Schweizer, 1971 (1968), p. 29, cited in Sanders, 1985, p. 39).

> Where [Sanders asks] is the evidence that there is a connection between Jesus' parabolic teaching, the accusation of blasphemy, and the crucifixion? ... Were the Romans offended by the 'blasphemy' of the offer of grace to sinners? There is here an apparent loss of touch with historical reality.
>
> (p. 40, and see his further comments on pp. 202, 279)

There is an implicit warning here against drawing too direct a link between two of the distinctive and widely accepted facts about Jesus: his parabolic teaching and his death by crucifixion at Roman hands. Yet, perhaps crucially, both Schweizer and Sanders seem to miss the fact that though the parables may not indeed have provoked opposition by their content, the persona and pointedness of Jesus as a parabolist or storyteller might have been sharply troubling. (B. B. Scott, discussing the 'disappearance' of parables in historical-Jesus study, commented that Sanders preferred to focus on the deeds of Jesus rather than his words, because of the uncertainty of interpreting words (2007b, p. 96): but, as we have seen, words – and especially combinations such as parables or stories – are also deeds.)

Sanders is also critical of implicit anti-Judaism in Jeremias's understanding of the parables as Jesus' defence against his Jewish opponents.[13] For Sanders, Jeremias buys in too naïvely to the setting in which Luke places the parables of 'lostness' in chapter 15 (1985, p. 278), that of Jesus' response to those who criticize his table fellowship with 'sinners'. These parables, in Sanders's view – like Jesus' teaching generally – concern the action of God rather than the (negatively viewed) self-righteous posture of human beings (p. 281) or the call to repentance (p. 109). In addition, Sanders argues that 'repentance' has to be read into, rather than out of, other parables sometimes adduced as evidence that it was central to Jesus' message: The Sheep and the Goats, The Sower, The Shrewd Manager, The Wedding Feast, The Wheat and the Weeds, and The Net (p. 111). In Sanders's view, the Evangelists' explicit emphasis on repentance is redactional, not authentic to Jesus (p. 113). This 'either/or' approach to the parables – that, if they concern God's action, therefore they *do not* imply human response – may be challenged on the basis of the structure of narrative and its potentially wide resonances.

Cynic, sage, mystic, poet: the Jesus Seminar

One strand of scholarship on Jesus that emerged from the developments of the 1960s was the continuation, to a radical extent, of Bultmann's intense focus on the sayings of Jesus and his exposure of their uncertain tradition-history. The American 'Jesus Seminar', famous for its edition of the Gospels colour-coding Jesus' sayings according to the level of likelihood that they are 'authentic' (Funk, Hoover and The Jesus Seminar (1997)), has produced creative and important work on the parables of Jesus in particular, work yielding important insights despite the criticisms that have been, and can be, levelled against both its methods and its conclusions. A significant influence on the Seminar was the work of Norman Perrin (1976), especially in his argument that scholars such as Jeremias had been too confident in locating the parables as specific rhetorical tools in a strategy of Jesus. If we take such sayings seriously, Perrin argued, we will recognize their 'occasional' nature, respecting their autonomy rather than trying to squeeze them tightly into any reconstruction of Jesus' ministry (see Hedrick's acknowledgement of his debt to Perrin in 2004, pp. 37–9). Here we will consider a couple of works on Jesus and a couple of works on the parables by some of the Seminar's leading members.

In his *magnum opus* on Jesus (1991), Crossan characterizes Jesus as a 'peasant Jewish cynic' (p. 421). Key to this construal of Jesus is the sense that it was the praxis of Jesus as much as, or more than, his 'teaching' to which we must look for his historical distinctiveness. The parables as a particular form of speech constitute part of this praxis:

> Miracle and parable, healing and eating were calculated to force individuals into unmediated physical and spiritual contact with God and unmediated physical and spiritual contact with one another. He announced, in other words, the brokerless kingdom of God.　　　　　　　　　　　　　　　　　　　　　　(1991, p. 422)

This emphasis on praxis may help to explain a curious feature of this major work of Crossan: that although a good number of Jesus' narrative parabolic sayings appear in his 'reconstructed inventory' of Gospel sayings that go back to Jesus himself (pp. xiii–xxvi), there are few discussions in the body of his book of these sayings or their significance. He has a short section on the brief kingdom-parables of Matthew 13 (pp. 276–82), but no substantive treatment of any major narrative parable. He comments briefly on The Sower as a 'platitudinous image' communicating 'serenity and security' from 'watching nature's rhythms here and now' (p. 295). There is no hint as to what its narrative form might betoken.

It seems that the fact that Jesus used a parabolic mode of speech is as important to Crossan as whatever its content might be thought to signify. This would chime with the tenor of his 1980 work *Cliffs of Fall*, in which the parables are construed, Derrida-like, as having endlessly deferrable 'meaning': The Sower, above all, may be forever deconstructed. It is therefore the act, rather than the meaning of the parables which becomes crucial to our sense of their place in the pattern of Jesus' life. Indeed, 'performance' is a category introduced in the first sentence of Crossan's book: '*In the beginning* was the performance; not the word alone, not the deed alone, but both, each indelibly marked with the other forever' (1991, p. xi, his italics). Crossan's emphasis on the performative nature of Jesus' use of parables is important, picking up the emphasis of the New Hermeneutic, though it is overplayed to the extent that he undervalues the content of what Jesus said in those parables. In this he is like Sanders (above) and Allison (below), who are likewise reluctant to allow the parables' content to play a significant role in reconstructions of the historical Jesus. In their case, it is on account of the parables' figurativeness and ambiguity. In Crossan's, as noted by Scott (2007b, p. 96), it is because he has selected for his account of Jesus only material from 'the earliest stages of the Jesus tradition'. Since one of his key criteria for identifying this material is 'multiple attestation', and few of Jesus' parables occur in more than two of our sources (many of the full narratives occur only in Matthew or Luke), most of them are excluded.

One narrative parable in three variations to which Crossan does pay brief attention is The Great Banquet / The Wedding Feast. It is significant that he sees this tale in its supposedly original form as pointing to the concrete activity of Jesus in eating with all kinds of people: 'The social challenge of such egalitarian commensality is the radical threat of the parable's vision' (Crossan, 1991, p. 262). This is the kind of perceived mirroring of praxis in parable which will be developed much more fully in the work of Herzog and Schottroff.

In his 2011 book, Marcus Borg draws together threads from earlier work to give an account of a Jesus who is (characteristically for the Jesus Seminar) 'non-apocalyptic'. For Borg, Jesus is a 'mystic' (pp. 131–5) for whom 'the world has a positive value . . . it is filled with the glory of God. It is where we live – but it needs to be changed' (p. 134). The importance for Jesus of his mundane environment is a key insight for appreciating his stories, which have a much more significant place in Borg's book than in Crossan's. This is Borg's summary of Jesus' parabolic mode of teaching (pp. 151–5):

> Parables work by being good stories. They draw the audience into the narrative. They need to be good stories not only to avoid being tedious, but because fanciful or unrealistic details would get in the way of the audience's entering the story. They may describe surprising behavior, and often do, but not behavior that leaves the realm of the credible . . . Parables invite the audience to make a judgment [p. 152] . . . Parables are an interactive form of teaching [p. 153] . . . they do not depend on Scripture to make their point [p. 154] . . . the parables are invitational rather than imperatival. [p. 155[

Such features of parables may be discerned particularly in the narrative form, as we will be exploring later in this book.

Borg's treatment of specific parables uses a multifaceted approach which builds on the strengths of much previous scholarship and suggests their polyvalence. This is helpful, though it leaves open the issue of whether, and how, we might attain greater precision in descrying how Jesus' hearers might have received them. Thus, for instance, The Prodigal Son illustrates Jesus' teaching about the character of God (pp. 169–73, reprising the understanding of the Church since early times). The son's departure to a foreign land is heard as evoking the exit of Adam and Eve from Eden and the exile of the Jewish people (p. 170; compare the reading of N. T. Wright, 1996, pp. 125–31), and thus inviting the question 'Is this a story about a particularly foolish son? Or is it a story about all of us?' (Borg, 2011, p. 171). The scene of his return prompts questions about God: 'Are we supposed to think God is like this? Do you think God is like this?' (p. 172). Finally, the older brother's resentment also provokes enquiry: 'Should life be the way he thinks it should be?' (p. 173). Borg's suggestions about the questions the parable provokes point in the right direction for an appreciation of narrative's dynamics.

Borg proposes that the picture of a compassionate God found in The Prodigal Son comes from Jesus' own experience (p. 173), an interesting return to Schleiermacher's conception of the 'God-consciousness' of Jesus informing all his words and actions, as well as a hint as to what narrative criticism might be able to say about their 'implied author'.

Bernard Brandon Scott's major work on the parables (1989) reflects the Jesus Seminar's focus on the words of Jesus and their reluctance to be too confident about the particular setting of those words in Jesus' life. It was also the first significant contribution to parable study to make use of some of the key categories of narrative criticism, such as 'the implied hearer'. I have discussed Scott's work in detail elsewhere (S. I. Wright, 2000b, pp. 155–85). For our purposes here, there are two key features to note.

First, Scott defines parable in this way: 'A parable is a *mashal* that uses a short narrative fiction to reference a transcendent symbol' (1989, p. 8). The 'symbol', for Scott, is the kingdom of God, which he regards as 'plastic' in its first-century Palestinian meaning (p. 62). This is a subtle definition of parable which takes the narrative quality of parables seriously. Scott also deploys contemporary understanding of metaphor skilfully, pointing out that hearers are invited to allow the parables to inform their conception of the kingdom, not merely illustrate an existing understanding, for metaphor has cognitive not just ornamental value (pp. 42–51). The corollary of this is that the narrative itself must be taken with full seriousness, not 'left behind' in the interests of its 'meaning'. Yet we may ask whether even this goes far enough in allowing the narratives their force, since their labelling as metaphor, and even (often) as parable, is imposed on the texts rather than found within them.

Second, the Jesus Seminar's reluctance to earth Jesus' sayings too precisely in elements of his career leads Scott, perhaps inevitably, to conclusions about his message which tend to the general rather than the specific. Although Scott focuses on the 'hearing' rather than the 'intention' of the parables, the outlines of an intention nevertheless emerge (see S. I. Wright, 2000b, pp. 171–7). The Jesus who appears through this reading is subversive of contemporary understandings of the kingdom of God (particularly apocalyptic ones). But to what extent is this perceived subversiveness the consequence of a stereotypical understanding of contemporary 'apocalyptic' expectation, with which Jesus' message is seen as necessarily contrasting, on account of the power of metaphor that Scott assumes is at work through his parables? (Cf. Horsley, 2012, pp. 15–25, discussing Crossan). My concern here is to see what may result if we suspend such assumptions and listen with more openness to how Jesus' hearers may have understood and responded to his stories.

Charles W. Hedrick does precisely this (1994; cf. 2004). He questions whether the assumption of a metaphorical force in the parables in fact obscures rather than clarifying their rhetorical operation. In a direct challenge to Scott's approach he states: 'The interpreter, therefore, should not assume that Jesus' stories are symbols that reference the kingdom of God or some other transcendental reality ... We must start with the story itself, for even that expression itself is a symbol' (p. 31). He approaches Jesus' stories as 'mimetic fictions', that is, as realistic reflections of the world around him, viewed through the prism of Jesus' own imagination, with the poetic potential 'of igniting the imaginations of those who consent to enter his fictional world' (p. 31). Quite rightly, Hedrick insists on the distinction between 'a story's *evoking* horizons more distant than the narrow confines of the world in the story and a story's deliberately *referencing* some other specific "thing" outside the story' (p. 33, his italics). Similarly:

> Any attempt to *force* meaning out of the story, whether figurative, moral or referential, in its own way consumes and dispenses with the story. Any one 'point' derived from the story simply cannot exhaust the story, as Luke's reading of the story of the Samaritan graphically attests. (p. 35)

This approach takes the narrativity of the longer parables more seriously than any surveyed so far, building on a summary of Aristotle's understanding of narrative (pp. 46–50). Hedrick also takes more seriously than most the stories' realism (pp. 39–43; cf. 2004, pp. 36–54). I identify three general weaknesses in his work.

First, while Hedrick (like Bailey) offers detailed analysis of the 'poetics' of the stories, drawing on Aristotle's *Rhetoric* to identify rhythm, periods, rhyme, assonance, consonance and euphony (introduced in 1994, pp. 59–72), this seems to me less crucial to grasping narrative force than the more central 'drivers' of a story – plot, character, point of view and setting. It also takes one further into the realm of speculation, because it is difficult to assess the extent to which patterns identified in the Greek text might mirror the Aramaic of Jesus' speech.

Second, and surprisingly, he states that 'the stories would have been grasped as affirmation, assault, or subversion of Judaism's shared "mental construct" about itself' (p. 53). This is a corollary of seeing the stories as part of a 'clash of fictions' (pp. 83–9). Imagining such a 'clash of fictions' is a fruitful way of thinking about Jesus' stories,[14] but Hedrick's lack of specificity about the elements of Judaism which were grasped as affirmed, assaulted or subverted reflects too monolithic a view of Judaism, as well as the Jesus Seminar's aversion to constructing too precise a picture of the interlocking logic of the different elements of Jesus' career. It tends to yield an over-generalized message, a besetting danger for parable scholars at least since Jülicher, as in this summary: 'it is in their nature to undermine paradigms, whether social, religious, or cultural' (2004, p. 103).

The work of those treated in the next and final section of this chapter forms a vital corrective to this, not least that of Herzog, who in the context of a critique of the standard 'criteria for authenticity' shows that the picture of Jesus as an individualistic subversive sage which emerges from the Jesus Seminar is too vague to be fully credible historically (Herzog, 2005, pp. 33–4):

> If Jesus had any credibility in the villages and towns of Galilee, it was because he articulated the meaning of Torah in ways that were congruent with this popular 'little tradition' and the Israelite folk traditions that shaped their lives. It is unlikely that a radical, individualistic voice would have been either valued or heeded in the village culture of Galilee.   (p. 34)

Third, and closely connected, Hedrick exemplifies in extreme form the tendency of some scholarship from at least the time of Bultmann through to the Jesus Seminar to discount the value of the Evangelists' framing of the parables for giving any clue as to how they might have functioned in Jesus' ministry. In his 2004 work, Hedrick introduces his guide to readers on how to place themselves 'in the audience at a parable's first audition' thus: 'All that is required of the reader is a little work and a willingness to set aside about two thousand years of Christian history, so as to hear the parable with a fresh naïveté' (p. 103). The reader's first step should be to 'separate the parable from its literary context' (p. 103). This approach is not only beguiling in its simplicity but also naïve in a less than helpful way, as I will seek to explain in Chapter 3. Hedrick himself acknowledged the critique of his approach (given before Hedrick published his 1994 work) by Amos Wilder, who argued that the original force of the parables 'continued in a kind of underground way in the memory of the community' (2004, pp. 87–8, citing Wilder, 1991, p. 128).[15]

Parables as signs of a prophet

A final group of scholars, diverse in some ways as were the previous groupings, are more open to Schweitzer's notion that, at least in some sense, Jesus entertained 'apocalyptic' beliefs about a divinely given order which would break in soon upon the world. Perhaps more significantly for us, they are joined by a conviction that Jesus acted in a way that evoked the stance and behaviour of a prophet, and that his parables, as stories, play a key role in this. Rather than being characterized as a speaker of isolated aphorisms – the tendency of the Jesus Seminar – he was a prophet who not only pronounced oracles but also led a movement of covenant renewal, like Moses or Elijah (Horsley, 2012, pp. 92–4, 115–17).

This group tends to be sceptical about the Jesus Seminar's scepticism. Recognizing the reality of 'layers' of 'tradition' of one kind or another, oral and/or written, between Jesus and the written Gospels, they also recognize the difficulty of coming up with adequate 'criteria of authenticity'. Rather than focusing on isolated sayings adjudged to be 'authentic' or otherwise, they seek a more holistic appraisal of Jesus' career. A key argument here is that of Richard Horsley (e.g. 2012, pp. 67–71) that the Gospels as wholes should be treated as sources, not merely as containers for sayings that are then abstracted from them. This does not mean uncritical treatment, but it does mean taking seriously the context of meaning for individual sayings which the Gospels imply. The words of Jesus do not stand alone, but are part of a profile which includes also his relationships, actions and experiences.

N. T. Wright offers a fuller rationale for Jesus' use of parable-speech as part of his deliberate praxis than many other historical Jesus scholars (N. T. Wright, 1996, pp. 125–31, 174–82). Wright views the parables as a symptom both of Jesus' prophetic praxis and his 'apocalyptic' outlook. They are not only words but also 'acts', which, like the classical prophets, make striking statements reframing Israel's self-understanding. As Judaism's 'apocalyptic' writers of the centuries around Jesus used highly symbolic language in which encouragements for Israel and warnings for their enemies were encoded, so, Wright argues, the veiled language of parable was a sign of Jesus' own expectations of coming judgement (pp. 177–8) – a judgement that would operate very differently from how other apocalypticists expected it would, in that Israel herself was indicted.

To some extent, as he recognizes (p. 144), Wright's approach does not quite tally with the distinction of Meyer (1979, see above, p. 32), who thought that the parables belong essentially to the 'public' speech of Jesus to the crowds, though their interpretations, insofar as they go back to Jesus, would have been given to the disciples alone. For Wright, the parables were 'essentially secretive ... Their import was so explosive that they could not necessarily be explained in public' (pp. 181–2). Three queries may be put to Wright's identification of the parables with the apocalyptic genre. First, this identification fits better with the rather mysterious story The Sower than with most of Jesus' other stories and shorter parabolic sayings – which appear more self-contained and transparent in their meaning, far-reaching though they may be in their implications. This is reflected in the fact that only The Sower and The Wheat and the Weeds are given explicit interpretations in the Gospels, making them, indeed, reminiscent of the visions that require angelic explanation in, for instance, Daniel 7—12, and *4 Ezra*. Second, apocalyptic was essentially a written genre, while the parables clearly originated as oral speech-forms. Third, the parables use an 'everyday' register of language, whereas apocalyptic literature employs sophisticated symbols from what we would call the realm of fantasy. Seeing them as 'ordinary' stories seems more natural, though Mark has undoubtedly cast the parables in an apocalyptic light in the way that he has set them in his overall narrative (see Myers, 2008 (1988), pp. 169–70, pointing to the parallels implied by Mark's structure between the discourses of Jesus in chapters 4 and 13).

However, this does not undermine Wright's key argument that we should hear Jesus, in his parables, retelling the story of Israel. Here he delineates, with more precision than Hedrick, 'the clash of fictions'. Of course, the extent to which the story (or particular stories) of Israel are being echoed and 'retold' in one of Jesus' stories is bound to be debatable, because of the very nature of echo. It is plausible to envisage a primary resonance of the parables in the conditions and events of Jesus' own time and place, with a natural secondary resonance in the stories which would have shaped his outlook. Sometimes this order might be reversed; the parables must be examined on a case-by-case basis before a judgement on this is made. Sometimes, however, Wright's interpretations of the parables as retellings of Israel's story may carry more weight as theological readings of the Gospel texts from our own standpoint, rather than as expositions of Jesus' purposes or how his hearers heard them.[16] And while acknowledging all sorts of echoes of Israel's Scriptures and story, we should not downplay the pressing immediacy of the socio-economic situation that must have shaped their understanding profoundly. Herzog comments on how Wright, as well as John P. Meier, 'tend to sublimate the political and economic dimensions' of the conflict with the authorities in which Jesus found himself 'in order to develop their theological readings' (2005, p. 198).[17]

A rather different but equally significant contribution to the debate comes from William R. Herzog II himself (1994, 2005). Herzog takes with full seriousness the stories' realism and therefore the economic and social matrix within which they make sense. Like Hedrick, he urges that we should imagine them being heard as fictions reflecting everyday life, rather than pointing away from themselves to spiritual or theological truth. Drawing on the pedagogical theory of the Brazilian liberationist educator Paolo Freire, Herzog sees the stories as 'encoding' the situation of the peasants and economically margin-alized, realistically portraying situations of oppression in order to raise consciousness and enable the poor to take ownership of their situation. Thus, for example, The Rebellious Tenants (1994, pp. 98–113) is as much about 'wicked landowners' who buy up the lands of the poor and provoke rebellion as it is about 'wicked tenants' (but see also his later, and in some respects more traditional reading, in 2005, pp. 199–204). The Labourers in the Vineyard is the story of an arbitrary employer taking advantage of the unemployed (1994, pp. 79–97; 2005, pp. 146–51). Jesus invites his hearers to see their own conditions of life and work in his stories and thus, implicitly, to do something about them.

For Herzog, Jesus in his parables is primarily 'pedagogue of the oppressed' (1994 *passim*; 2005, p. 16). This is not in contradiction to a 'prophetic' role (delineated in 2005, pp. 12–14, 99–124), but points to the local, small-scale, peasant environs in which Jesus characteristically worked (pp. 15–19). Herzog presents Jesus as an alternative to officially authorized rabbis, suggesting he may have told the story of The Widow and the Judge at a synagogue gathering (pp. 141–51). Herzog argues that three stages of Freire's pedagogical approach can be seen in Jesus' storytelling. First, immersion in the lives of peasant communities leads to a glimpse of the people's 'thematic universe', often one of passive acceptance of current, oppressive power-structures (pp. 17–18). Second, educators provide 'codifications' of this world, usually in visual form; through studying these, the peasants would become more conscious of the forces that actually controlled their lives (p. 18). Third, the people were encouraged to 'decodify' their world, removing 'the efforts to mystify the current arrangements', to 'problematize' it, turning a situation to be accepted into a problem to be solved, and to 'recodify' it, that is, to reimagine how, ideally, it might be.

Herzog's are some of the most refreshingly original readings of the parables in modern times. It is possible for a sociological model to be over-determinative, however, as Herzog himself no doubt recognizes, and while the model from Freire yields insights, there is a danger that it complicates efforts to imagine Jesus' storytelling and limits the possible range of immediate understandings, questions and responses it may have prompted.[18]

Similarly to Hedrick and Herzog, Luise Schottroff (2006) seeks to develop what she calls a 'non-dualistic' parable theory, in opposition to standard approaches in which the parable points away from itself:

> I call 'dualistic' those parable theories in which the content of the parable narrative, often called 'image' in contrast to 'substance', has no properly theological relevance; where the narrative, the 'image,' is thus regarded as merely an aid to clarifying the real 'substance.' But, in fact, the parables really talk about people's lives in the time of the Roman empire, and these depictions contain their own immediate message which needs to be heard. (p. 2)

Like Herzog's, Schottroff's understanding of specific stories in the light of her socio-historical analyses offers a useful contribution to the discussion about the precise nature of the 'real world' which Jesus' first hearers would have heard echoed in his stories. Other contemporary historians who emphasize the importance of this realistic setting of the stories, though without working through its implications in detail, include Sean Freyne (2004, pp. 58, 59) and Richard Horsley (2012, p. 125, calling The Unforgiving Slave and The Shrewd Manager 'slices of life').

In some contrast to these approaches, Dale Allison continues to advocate a Jesus who is focused on a coming apocalypse rather than being some kind of social prophet. His comments on the parables (2010, pp. 116–18) are brief, but important and revealing. He reflects on the way that the Jesus Seminar, in particular Funk, Crossan, Borg and Hedrick, see the parables as indicating a non-apocalyptic outlook, citing Funk's comment about their 'liberation of the Jesus of the parables and aphorisms from Schweitzer's eschatological Jesus' (Allison, 2010, p. 116). Allison says in response that the intrinsic polyvalence of the parables means that they should not be given such a controlling position in our construal of Jesus' outlook, but should defer to clearer sayings: and he points to the formidable array of 'clear' sayings pertaining to the imminent arrival of God's kingdom. (A similar argument is made by John P. Meier, 1994, p. 290). Thus, for Allison, the intrinsic malleability of the parables in the hands of interpreters should lead to caution in drawing historical conclusions from them (in an interesting parallel to Jerome, who in the fourth century had similarly argued that doctrine should not be founded on parables). Texts that open themselves to such a range of meanings should not, thinks Allison, be marshalled against those that admit of a far narrower range – those that clearly indicate eschatological expectation.

Horsley's critique of both the advocates of an 'apocalyptic' and a 'non-apocalyptic' Jesus is important here: both sides are working with an old scholarly construct of what first-century 'apocalyptic' beliefs really were (2012, pp. 9–64). Horsley argues that the main focus of apocalyptic texts was not a heaven-sent cataclysm, but rather 'the judgment of the oppressive empire' and '[t]he restoration of Judean society/Israel and of the people's independence in their land under God's direct rule' (p. 48). This in turn is an argument for paying more attention to the shape and detail of Jesus' stories, and allowing them more of a place in our construal of Jesus than Allison permits. If the focus of Jesus' words, like that of the apocalyptic texts, was more on immediate earthly circumstances than an imminent divine intervention, then the stories may turn out to be more transparent on those circumstances than opaque and deliberately secretive as Schweitzer (followed e.g. by N. T. Wright) took them to be.

Conclusion

In this chapter and the previous one I have tried to give, not a complete account of modern construals of either Jesus or his parables, but those key segments of this history which may shed light on our task of appraising his stories as a dimension of his activity. I am acutely aware of the incompleteness of this survey. I should note here that I have not dealt in these chapters with some major works on the historical Jesus (e.g. Meier, 1994; Dunn, 2003; Casey, 2010) and some major works on the parables (e.g. Hultgren, 2000; Snodgrass, 2008; Blomberg, 2012 (1990), together with the collections edited by Shillington, 1997; Longenecker, 2000; and Zimmermann, 2007). This is because the former deal only briefly with the parables, and the latter group are rather compendia for parable study than integrations of the parables into accounts of Jesus' ministry. My omission by no means implies a value judgement on these works in themselves.

We are now in a position, however, where we may outline positively the key elements in a fresh appraisal of Jesus as a storyteller which will guide the rest of this book.

3

Jesus' stories: tools for a fresh hearing

In the previous chapters I have tried to demonstrate that now is a time fraught with potential for a fresh appraisal of the stories Jesus told, but that we are also burdened with a history of interpretation laden with blindness as well as insight.

In particular, the scholarly study of Jesus' stories has been over-determined in three ways. First, through subsuming the stories within the category 'parable', their interpretation has been caught up in debates about what constitutes a parable, how a parable works and so on – debates which too often have simply ignored the accepted fact that the label 'parable' designates a range of rhetorical forms which cannot all be made to 'work' in one way. Some may function as similes, some as metaphors, some as proverbial sayings, and so on. Giving a story the name 'parable' does not tell us how to make sense of it; rather, it calls for attention as a story.

Second, and largely as a consequence, the stories' potential wealth of signification has been reduced. This has happened both with those approaches which, following Jülicher, have urged that they have just 'one point', and with those which continue to admit of a series of allegorical identifications in a parable (e.g. N. T. Wright, 1996; Blomberg, 2012). This is partly because of the ingrained bias of scholars away from taking seriously the stories' evocation of their own world, and towards finding in them encoded messages about another, or about a general existential demand. It has taken determination by scholars such as Hedrick, Herzog and Schottroff to stand out against the tide and bring to the fore the striking way in which the stories reflect, imitate and reshape the social setting of Jesus.

Third, and complicating matters considerably, scholars have drawn up criteria for getting back to what Jesus really said (in substance if not in exact wording) which have depended on tendentious prior assumptions about the forms and content of what Jesus could or could not have said, and about the purpose of the Evangelists in their use of the stories in their Gospels. There is no a priori reason why Jesus could, or could not, have employed language in a whole variety of ways, including allegorical narrative. The tactic of Hedrick, simply to exclude everything identified as interpretative framing by the Evangelists in order to hear the story afresh, replaces one kind of naïveté (equating the Evangelists' interpretations with those of Jesus' first hearers) with another (postulating a total disconnection between the two).

I propose to counter these 'over-determinations' in three ways, as follow treating the last first.

A two-level hearing

First, picking up the immediately preceding point, I offer 'hearings' of the stories on two levels, in two different parts of the book. First, in Part 2, we shall seek to hear them as 'performed' in the Gospels of Mark, Matthew and Luke. Then, in Part 3, we shall seek to hear them as Jesus' first hearers might have heard them.

By offering these 'hearings' separately, I aim to deconstruct the scholarly techniques which have in various ways polarized the Evangelists against Jesus. For example, it is often assumed that whereas the Evangelists' understanding and use of a pericope like a parable is 'obvious', we have to dig beneath that and exercise a lot more speculation to find out what Jesus 'really said' or 'really meant'. I dispute this distinction. Certainly, the Gospels give us the presenting evidence which must, like all evidence, be weighed carefully. Certainly, any attempt to reconstruct the Jesus 'behind' the Gospels entails speculation. But who is to say that the Gospel writers' own understanding of a parable is either obvious or monovalent? The Gospels are rich multilayered narratives whose various parts interlock in all sorts of ways (as demonstrated, e.g., in Tannehill, 1986). It is as reductive to speak of a single 'purpose' in a Gospel as it is to speak of a single 'point' in a story. Equally, the fact that the Evangelists have undoubtedly introduced, edited and interpreted Jesus' stories in various ways does not mean that they have obscured their original force to such an extent that we must ignore their interpretations in order to recover it.

Thus while affirming that the stories as we have them display traces of adaptation to the context, language and concerns of the Evangelists and their putative predecessors who transmitted them, I want to show in Part 2 that, far from reducing Jesus' stories in this process, the Evangelists preserve them as 'actions' which play a crucial role in advancing their narratives. That is, they have not turned the stories into allegories, or thematic teaching, or any other kind of rhetorical form; they have left them as stories. While naturally expecting that the stories will have some impact on their own readers, we shall see that they construct their larger narratives of Jesus' life with a desire that they be transparent upon the original impact of the stories on Jesus' hearers. Such a hearing of the Gospel narratives would entail, ideally, a detailed account of the multidimensional way the narrative of each Gospel unfolds. That is not possible here, but I hope to sketch enough of this overall movement to clarify the place and function of the stories of Jesus within it, without reducing the multiple intersignifications of different parts of the whole Gospel. In sum, I believe that neither the thrust of the stories within the Gospels nor their thrust within Jesus' activity is either wholly obvious or wholly opaque. My 'hearing' in both Parts 2 and 3 aims therefore to be appropriately tentative.

Similarly, it would be much too easy to fall into the trap of polarizing the 'literary' or 'theological' dynamics of the stories in the Gospels against the 'social' dynamics of the stories as Jesus told them. Thus although Part 2 essentially focuses on the 'literary' setting of the stories in the Gospels, it is important not to forget that the Gospels had 'social' settings just as Jesus' activity did, and that many aspects of these settings were similar to those of Jesus' own immediate environs. And although Part 3 essentially focuses on the 'social' setting of the stories, this encompasses people's world of thought and belief, and the texts which populated their mental universe, as well as their material circumstances. The Gospels, like Jesus, were heard in the overarching atmosphere of Roman hegemony. Matthew, surely, was in addition particularly close to Jesus' own Jewish setting and heritage; Mark and Luke, though probably composed at more of a distance from Judaism's heartland, were very far from being unfamiliar with it.

I note here that Gospel commentators who take seriously the narrative form and shape of the Gospel do not thereby lose interest in the sociological dynamics of the ministry of Jesus implied by that Gospel. An outstanding example of this is Joel Green's commentary on Luke (1997). Green traces with great sophistication the way in which Luke's literary narrative unfolds, while giving close attention to its social resonances not only for Luke's own hearers but also as reflective of Jesus' own immediate context. He is concerned with both 'the world to which [Luke's text] gives witness' and 'the world in which [it] was written' (p. 14). While emphasizing that Luke as a narrative theologian does not straightforwardly represent 'reality', but rather seeks to provide an alternative view of it for his readers (p. 12), he does not pit Luke against Jesus as if Luke's theological reordering of society's priorities was quite discontinuous from that of Jesus. For instance, in discussing The Great Banquet (pp. 554–63), he first notes the way in which Luke has carefully 'stitched' the story 'into its co-text' of the meal scene (Luke 14.1–14), before going on to outline the Mediterranean dining protocols which enable us to feel the story's impact (p. 555). But this does not lead to an automatic acceptance of the traditional reading of the story as expressing, in its current form, Luke's theology of salvation history in which the Gospel is first rejected by Jews and then accepted by Gentiles. Precisely for Luke (and not only in a putative context in Jesus' ministry) the story itself with both its narrative shape and its social resonances poses problems for such a reading, as Green shows (pp. 556–7), not least because it suggests that the inclusion of the 'poor' (or, in an allegorical identification, the Gentiles) was a kind of afterthought into which God had been impelled. In short, Green's approach 'necessarily blurs the distinction between the world *of* the text and the world *behind* the text' (his italics), 'in part because we believe Luke has himself invited this form of enquiry and engagement' (p. 19). In other words, Luke is interested neither in historical events per se nor in theology per se. His theology is done in keen awareness of the historical events on which it is based while his historiography is shaped by theological concerns. Green's simultaneous sensitivity to Luke's narrative theology and the social resonance of the words and actions of Jesus in which it is embedded has been programmatic for my own thinking about how to overcome the too-easy polarity set up by much twentieth-century scholarship between the Evangelists and Jesus.

It is as fallacious, therefore, to exclude social dimensions from our hearing of the Gospels as it is to exclude theological dimensions from our hearing of Jesus. Other good scholarly examples can be given. Robert C. Tannehill, whose focus is specifically on the narrative strategy and unity of Luke–Acts, points to the close connection between the social reversals seen in some of Jesus' parables (1986, pp. 109–10) and Luke's portrayal of Jesus' ministry to the oppressed (pp. 103–9). Ched Myers's 'political' reading of Mark (2008 (1988)) likewise combines literary and social analysis in a sophisticated way, even if the interpretation that emerges has remained a minority one. The combination is illustrated by Myers's comment on Mark's parables. In contrast to the popular notion of parables as 'earthly stories with heavenly meanings', Myers stresses that 'they are perfectly consistent with Mark's overall strategy of realistic narrative, in which any and all apocalyptic symbolics are kept "grounded"' (p. 173). And Warren Carter's 'sociopolitical and religious' reading of Matthew (2001) remains one which interprets the Gospel as a 'counter-narrative' (p. 1), that is, a literary construction which invites a theological reframing of the hearers'/readers' world.

All this means that the logic of the movement from Part 2 to Part 3 of this book is not the traditional 'stripping away of layers' from the Gospels to uncover a supposed 'original', since I do not believe we have the reliable tools or precise criteria to do this. I seek to be sensitive to the possible mechanisms of the stories' transmission, as the next section will show. But I will leave aside the old discourse of 'authenticity' in order to permit genuine openness to hearing at least echoes of the performances of both the Evangelists and Jesus himself. I will simply lay my hearings of the Gospels and of Jesus beside one another and invite the reader to judge them on their own terms.

The dynamics of storytelling

Second, in reaction to the over-determination of the stories' 'meanings' noted above, I will focus on the processes of understanding and response which take place in the hearer of a story. Narrative immediately invites the use of the imagination, though it does not predetermine whether the events to be recounted will be 'fact' or 'fiction'. It sets in train complex mental and emotional processes in the hearer. This provocation of hearers through inviting them into a narrative world does two things. It both calls for their participation (thus rendering the story on its own ambiguous, because it is incomplete without its recipient) and offers them a series of clues out of which they are to fill in the details of that world and start thinking about it.

The use of the familiar past-tense story form in the tradition of Jesus' sayings suggests two things: one, that the storyteller wanted his hearers' participation to fill out and complete whatever it was he was saying to them and, two, that he did not leave them without clues as to the basic outlines of that imaginative world he was calling them to enter. At once this suggests a more helpful and plausible solution to the double-sided character of Jesus' parable-speech (veiling and concealing) than the extremes offered by parts of the tradition (Jesus was uttering obscure things accessible only to the elect, on the one hand, or Jesus was uttering things so plain as to be immediately accessible, to an almost platitudinous degree, on the other). My guess is that Jesus was, indeed, using an indirect form of speech: not to be deliberately puzzling, but precisely to invite his hearers to make this imaginative world their own. This naturally called for an initial willingness, at least, by those hearers to 'play the game', to start to enter and explore the imaginative world, to fill in its gaps.[1] As they did so, they could, of course, be taken far beyond the setting portrayed in the story, and the immediate circumstances of their lives.

I fully agree with Hedrick (1994, 2004, *passim*) that this does not mean that the story becomes a 'metaphor' for something else. The story is only a 'metaphor' in the sense that the hearers come so to recognize its world, identify with its characters and engage emotionally with the logic of its plot that the story becomes a metaphor for a wider sweep of reality (cf. Ricoeur, 1975, pp. 96–100). Because of the power of metaphor to 'work both ways', hearers' own imagination helps to make sense of the story even as the story reshapes the way they view the world. Hedrick's comment that 'the realism of the story automatically eliminates any secondary plane of reality' (2004, p. 44), however, needs nuancing. In its multiple possible evocations of different elements of a hearer's mental and material world – fully recognized by Hedrick (2004, pp. 84–5) – it surely may take him or her far from the original scene that the story paints.[2]

To explore the way in which Jesus' hearers may have received his stories, started to enter the world they evoke and handed them on so that in due course they found a place in our Gospels, I will draw on several areas of current scholarly theory and interest: orality, memory, testimony, perform-ance, reception history and narrative criticism.[3] This will be done in a suggestive rather than a definitive manner, in recognition of the vast fields of possibility they open up. Claiming a degree of uncertainty regarding our knowledge of historical events, particularly ancient ones, is both common-place and prudent. (For a recent example see Le Donne, 2011, p. 74). Those who – for religious or other reasons – still hunger for the kind of historical certainty sought by the Enlightenment and its followers seem destined for disappointment. Since we are dealing here with highly individual speech-forms, it should be obvious that claims to 'know' either Jesus' aims in telling stories or his hearers' responses to them should always be shrouded in modesty.

Oral communication

One of the most important elements of contemporary Gospels research concerns the dynamics of orality. The implications of the fact that the culture in which Jesus lived and worked was predominantly an oral not a literate one have started to be taken with real seriousness (see e.g. Horsley, 2008, pp. 12–16, 56–108). It should not be overplayed: Jesus himself, and other well-taught Jewish men, knew the written Torah (Casey, 2010, pp. 160–2, gives the evidence). Yet we must reckon with the implications of the facts (1) that Jesus told his stories, he did not write them down, and (2) that they would initially have been transmitted by oral means, even if written collections of sayings started circulating quite early, and would have continued to be 'told' in various settings even when they existed in writing. The Gospels themselves would have been encountered by many as they heard them read aloud in the early Christian assemblies, rather than in written form.

The orality of the stories is important. To modern readers schooled in literacy and private modes of encountering texts, it takes an effort of imagination to reinhabit a world where, by and large, you heard stories, in the company of others, without either reading them or watching them on a screen. I touched on some of the dynamics of orality, especially the way in which it provokes lively figurative associations in hearers, in my earlier work (S. I. Wright, 2000b, esp. pp. 53–4). Jesus' first hearers would not have had opportunity to go back over the stories and pick apart their literary structure or allusion to old texts. They would have encountered them in their raw immediacy, their language and movement triggering all kinds of associations, and maybe confusions, and been left to process these individually or together. Yet we should not fall into the trap of equating orality and polyvalence and pitting them against writtenness and fixed meaning.[4] Jacques Derrida was convincing in undermining this traditional opposition, showing how the presence of a speaker can actually limit and control meaning, whereas a written text set loose from its authorial moorings can give birth to multiple meanings. Recognizing the oral nature of Jesus' stories and the consequent confusion of resonances they might have had does not imply that hearers could pick up no direction or controlling thrust. Nor does it imply that the Gospels' presentation of the stories inevitably closed down meaning rather than multiplying it.

As for orality in the stories' transmission, James Dunn argues that the degrees of variation yet commonality between the Synoptic Gospels are not sufficiently explained through hypotheses of literary dependency but reflect a lively and continuing oral tradition (2005; 2011, pp. 22–44). This assumption, though it remains disputed, may help (for instance) to make sense especially of the two stories which appear, with variants, in all three Synoptic Gospels, as well as the *Gospel of Thomas* (The Sower and The Rebellious Tenants), without denying elements of literary dependence also.

Memory and testimony

A corollary of the oral nature of Jesus' culture was people's dependence on memory for the transmission of important stories and sayings. This forms the organizing principle for Dunn's major work on Jesus (2003). Before they were written down, they had to be remembered. There are, of course, analogies to this today, in the need for careful retention of a story (or perhaps joke) one wishes to relay to others. The big difference from today, however, is that almost certainly one will be able to seek and find the story or joke in 'written' form, before very long, whether in print or on screen. Fewer and fewer sayings remain confined to private oral space, and much that is memorable or amusing (along with a good deal that is certainly neither) is likely to appear very soon on YouTube® or Facebook®. Although archaeological evidence suggests quite widespread literacy in the Roman Empire, the absence of means of mass distribution as well as the poverty of the peasant culture in which Jesus lived meant that the faculty of memory assumed much greater importance.

This does not mean that first-century people had 'perfect' memories. Nor does it mean that their memories were not 'distorted' or, in Anthony Le Donne's helpful term, 'refracted' (2011, pp. 106–9). This is, as Le Donne shows, the essence of all memory: that it presents the past to us in a focused, selected and interpreted form. The implication is that we need to take seriously the way in which disciples' memories have retained and shaped the stories of their master, because for a good many years those memories may have been the stories' sole repository. The transmission of the stories by the Evangelists needs to be appraised, therefore, not simply as the 'editorial' 'redaction' of earlier 'material' – all of which terminology suggests mainly the use of scissors-and-paste on material artefacts – but as the reproduction of tales that had been remembered and, in the very act of remembering, interpreted. Le Donne offers helpful clues as to how this may have happened – for example, the use of typology as 'both a memory-shaping filter and a literary device' (p. 90). Perhaps this is a clue to the way in which The Rebellious Tenants, which plays on the typology of Israel as a vineyard, was recalled.

Who was it, then, who remembered not only what Jesus had done but also the stories he told? The role of eyewitness testimony in the process which led to the writing of the Gospels has been argued for convincingly by Richard Bauckham (2006) against an earlier consensus which more or less discounted it. The Gospels are not simply the product of a very lengthy process of tradition, oral and written. They often display the marks of remarkably direct eyewitness accounts – for example, the use of personal names such as Bartimaeus (Mark 10.46) or Simon of Cyrene (Mark 15.21) suggests that there were individuals known or known of in the Christian community who were the eyewitness sources for particular stories (Bauckham, 2006, pp. 40, 51–3).[5]

How might the premise that there were eyewitnesses (or more accurately 'earwitnesses') who heard a story of Jesus, on one or more of the possibly many occasions on which he told it, help to explain one or more features of it as it now stands in our Gospels? The process of how a longer stretch of discourse, in particular, is heard 'live', then retained and communicated, is likely to be distinct in some ways from the process of how an action is seen, remembered and reported, the main focus of Bauckham's book.

Though I have no particular theory to advance here, it is fruitful to ponder possible implications of seeing the reproduction of Jesus' stories as an act of testimony. On the one hand, it seems very unlikely that their preservation is a result of purely individual encounter with Jesus. Though two of them are recorded as told in response to individuals (The Good Samaritan and The Rich Fool), the Gospels give a very plausible picture of the audiences of the stories as being groups of people, whether crowds, disciples, opponents, or combinations of different groups. In the two cases mentioned, Jesus tells The Rich Fool to 'them', that is, the crowds around him, not just to the man who had asked for his advocacy (Luke 12.16); and The Good Samaritan sounds the kind of story that could easily have been told in a number of settings, not least because its extant ending ('Who was the neighbour?') does not match the question which prompts it ('Who is my neighbour?'). Jesus' stories, in other words, are much more likely to have been handed down through shared occasions of retelling than through the witness of a single individual.

On the other hand, the preservation of their narrative form suggests that they have not been greatly adjusted by the desire of early Christian witnesses to say something clearly about Jesus and his effect on their lives. In other words, if you wanted to give a plain account of the evangel you believed Jesus had announced, you would probably not have done so in the form of a story such as The Shrewd Manager or The Wedding Feast. As they have come down to us, Jesus' stories look much more like attestations of what Jesus said than of what early Christians believed. And it is striking that nothing like these stories appears in the rest of the New Testament. In that sense they seem to be a key part of the corporate testimony to what Jesus actually said and did, refracted through shared memory in various ways, to be sure, but far from being the coded expressions of early dogma to which many interpreters ancient and modern, 'conservative' and 'liberal', have effectively reduced them.

Performance

A third area of theory closely related to memory and testimony is performance. If, indeed, '*there were no original manuscripts*' (Le Donne, 2011, p. 75, italics his; see also Dunn, 2011, p. 39), then it is fallacious to think of particular renderings of stories about Jesus or stories by Jesus, such as those in the Gospels, as adaptations of or deviations from some standard perfect form. Each telling of such a story is a 'performance', and it is entirely likely that Jesus himself 'performed' his own stories on more than one occasion. As others passed them on, they would have done so with that stability yet diversity of content characteristic of an oral culture (on which see Dunn, 2011, p. 38; Le Donne, 2011, pp. 67–71).

Here an important distinction is to be made: that between language itself as performative and the 'performance' of already written texts. As we have seen, the recognition of the parables as performative language went back to the New Quest and New Hermeneutic of the 1960s. We need to think about what Jesus' stories 'did' as well as what they 'said', about the impact on his hearers as well as the 'meaning' of his words (Thiselton, 1985).

The other sense of 'performance', relating to already written texts, clearly does not apply to Jesus; there is no evidence that in his storytelling he was working from physical scripts! However, it is extremely important when it comes to appraising the character and testimony of the Gospels. Scott (1989) deployed this concept extensively, to stress that each version we have of a parable in the various Gospels should not be seen as a merely literary 'edition' but rather a fresh 'performance' for a new audience.

The discipline of 'performance criticism' has been further applied to the Gospels since then. A number of writers have argued that if we take the low levels of literacy in first-century Palestine as well as the wider rhetorical practices of the time seriously, we should study the Gospels as texts which were to be performed, not just texts to be read (e.g. Horsley, 2008, pp. 56–108). In a politically repressive atmosphere, such performances would perhaps be ' "closet" dramas' in private homes (Ward and Trobisch, 2013, p. 32). Part of the ethos of performance of texts in this period was expressed by the Roman writer Quintilian:

> Impersonation of a character was a highly valued rhetorical device ... Speakers in all genres were encouraged by their teachers to 'display the inner thoughts of adversaries and to introduce conversations between themselves and others' ... To 'play' a character, the performer would take the character's fortune, social rank and achievement into account. Then the performer would communicate these elements by means of suitable gestures and vocal intonations. What the performer sought in a study of the character was a sense of the character's passion.
> (Ward and Trobisch, 2013, pp. 15–16, citing Quintilian, *Institutio Oratoria*, 9.2.391, 3.8.505–7, 6.2.417)

It may be that to apply this kind of ancient performance advice to our understanding of how the Gospels were communicated is to exaggerate, and that a model of 'public reading' is more accurate than 'public performance'.[6] But if any 'performance' element is allowed, it helps to explain why the Gospels seem to have preserved many vivid indicators of the original realistic stories of Jesus.

As with studies of orality, memory and testimony, the study of performance helps us to reconceive the process of handing on traditions about Jesus as a more flexible yet stable process than it has often been imagined to be. Each performance of a story is fresh, and tailored to a particular audience, but the basic structure of the story, especially one told by a highly influential leader, tends to remain intact. It can also help us to reconceive the stories' dramatic quality and listen out more carefully for tone of voice, implied gesture and so on – on the level of both the Gospels and Jesus. When heard as 'performed', they come close in character to his symbolic actions, such as healing in a synagogue on the Sabbath (Luke 13.10–17) or overturning tables in the Temple (Mark 11.15–19).

Reception history

It is a commonplace today that different contemporary hearers or readers respond differently to written texts, especially multivalent ones like stories, sometimes in fundamental ways. 'Reception history' has become an illuminating discipline, studying the way in which texts have been received through different periods of history. It is a reminder that texts have the potential to be interpreted, and to exercise influence, in a number of different directions. Historians seeking to establish how sayings of Jesus were originally intended or heard should be cautious about trying to pin them down to a single meaning.

At the same time, reception history alerts us to exercise a degree of suspicion in our evaluation of different interpretations. Awareness of a scholar's own standpoint, strategy and agenda (hidden or open) is useful. I have studied elements of the reception history of some of Jesus' major stories elsewhere (S. I. Wright, 2000b, esp. pp. 62–181). Recent studies highlight specifically the way in which research into the historical Jesus is shaped by contemporary cultural forces (Moxnes, Blanton and Crossley, 2009). Although in this book elements of reception history are largely limited to the survey in Chapters 1 and 2, and to the discussion of interpretations which I have found particularly insightful during my detailed study of the stories in Chapters 4—10, one recurring element will be important. Some approaches to Jesus' stories in the past and even the present operate with crude stereotypes of the 'Judaism' within which Jesus grew up and lived. Of course, identifying the background or worldview of a scholar does not in itself lead us to reject their insights. The fact that (say) a Lutheran scholar reads the parables in a way that makes them yield a Lutheran message, or a political radical reads them in a way that makes them yield a politically radical message, should not in itself lead us to conclude that this was not in fact Jesus' message. But understanding a writer's perspective may undoubtedly be a significant factor in weighing the validity of their arguments, and a sense of reception history is an important counter-weight to the over-simple instruction of Hedrick that the parable-reader should be willing 'to set aside two thousand years of Christian history' (2004, p. 90). Willing to gain fresh and disturbing understanding, certainly, but to ignore the history of interpretation is simply to privilege Enlightenment individualism (cf. my closing comments in S. I. Wright, 2000b, p. 250).

The shape and power of narrative

I have left till last the most important analytical lens for studying Jesus' stories, that of narrative criticism. It is surprising that this has been used in such a patchy and piecemeal way with the parables in the past, given that it has been applied in detail to a range of biblical material, especially the Hebrew Scriptures.[7] The main reason, probably, is that narrative critics have focused on the Gospels as a whole as narratives, and that focus has yielded rich insights (see e.g. Tannehill, 1986).

I have found particularly useful the introductions by Powell (1993), Marguerat and Bourquin (1999) and Resseguie (2005) to the discipline in general. Narrative criticism, with its detailed focus on the way that the rhetoric of stories works, will not yield any greater degree of certainty than older historical criticism can (on this see Moore, 1989). While the structuralist understanding of narrative which became fashionable in the 1960s and 1970s seemed for a while to promise new confidence in parable analysis, it was limited by the fact that the theory focuses precisely on universal or timeless structures evident in cultures and literature, not specific instances of discourse in their peculiarity.[8] It was subsequently to be decisively undercut by deconstructionist awareness of the essentially shifting and unstable patterns of language, not least when they become encoded in writing. But the heuristic potential of a 'light-touch, low-theory' narrative criticism remains huge. Such an approach need not and cannot be separated from a historical one. The very phenomenon of written stories deconstructs such a separation, as we shall see in more detail shortly.

This potential is not to be achieved by trying to make a whole set of stories fit into a single shape or pattern, but rather by approaching them inductively, asking questions about the basic features common to all stories: in particular, setting, character, point of view and plot (following the order in Resseguie, 2005). Each of these features offers a rich range of possibilities to the storyteller. Though for the sake of clarity these features can be examined separately, the richness of narrative forbids rigid disjunction between them. It is precisely the way in which they work together that generates each story in its uniqueness.

To approach the stories of Jesus using this lens of narrative criticism has the crucial benefit of bringing out the inherent ambiguity of the texts. For instance, it exposes a range of possible responses to character, depending on the hearer/reader's point of view. Such ambiguity is not unlimited, not least because these are very short stories, not long novels in which 'meaning' multiplies exponentially; nor should it be exaggerated in the interests of highlighting their universal appeal. Thus – for the sake of argument – it may be reasonable to conclude in a particular case that there would be little ambiguity about how Jesus' hearers would initially perceive a particular character, and what sort of place he or she occupied in their society, but that there might be a good deal of ambiguity about how a range of hearers might evaluate that character's behaviour in the story, and what degree of sympathy the character might evoke. Thus the 'shrewd' manager in Luke 16.1–8 would probably appear as a familiar middleman caught in a tight spot, but it is harder to predict what different listeners would have made of the decision he makes, or of the praise he finally receives.

How, then, may the classic categories of narrative criticism illuminate a study of Jesus' stories? First, it is crucial to identify the settting which they imply. Although there may be few clues to it in a short story, the storyteller assumes a whole environment with which his hearers will be familiar. Setting, therefore, provides the irreplaceable link between a literary and a historical appraisal of stories. Literary criticism cannot escape from thinking about the *realia* of the world within which the narrative makes sense. Historical criticism cannot escape from entering imaginatively into the narrative and reconstructing the world into which it beckons the hearers, on the basis of the clues it gives.[9] We need to imagine all that has brought characters and events to the point of the beginning of this narrative. In the words of Richard Q. Ford (1997, p. 6), 'the true beginnings of these stories may be as distant as the origins of those entrenched social roles endemic to the ancient imperialisms that invaded Israel at least since the time of Alexander the Great'.

Making the wager that the stories are realistic, then, their broad setting is first-century history, and, more narrowly, the situation of Jewish people in Palestine of that period, under Roman rule. Further, as Michael Wolter points out (2009, p. 129), they are located at the 'meeting-point' between this general cultural context and the specific historical context of Jesus' ministry. They are now overlaid to some extent by the setting of the Evangelists who incorporate them into their Gospels, which would have been different to some extent (esp. for Luke). This means that their scenery, characters and logic must have made sense to hearers within those contexts. There will be, of course, a variety of ways in which to restate the 'sense' which they made. And the fact that they made 'sense' does not at all mean that the events they narrate have to be trivial or 'normal'. The driving interest of a realistic story is precisely the way in which specific, unique events are narrated against a backdrop of the world that the hearers know.

The situation of Palestinian Jews in the first century and that of the Gospel audiences includes their social, economic and political status and conditions, on which many scholars today, such as Horsley and Herzog, are able to shed so much light. But it also includes the traditions, beliefs and stories which shaped them. These would have formed part of the oral ether within which Jewish people grew up, as texts read and discussed in their synagogues, and retold for edification, encouragement and no doubt entertainment in the home,[10] though the vast majority would not have had access to them in writing (Horsley, 2012, pp. 87–8). As for the Evangelists, they were clearly literate, and thus may have had access to written texts, such as the Hebrew Scriptures in its Greek version (the LXX). We would expect, then, to find traces of literary quotation and allusion in Jesus' stories in their present form. But sorting out verbal allusions imported by Evangelists from those that may have been present to Jesus' hearers is, in my view, a well-nigh impossible task, not least since Jesus spoke Aramaic and the Gospels are written in Greek. (This is not to disparage the efforts of those such as Matthew Black (1946) and Maurice Casey (2002) who have attempted reconstructions of Jesus' Aramaic, but to recognize the inherent inaccessibility of the original moments of communication.) One uncertainty is the extent of access for Jesus' contemporaries to the books that are included in the LXX but not in extant Hebrew versions (see Goodman, ed., 2012 (2001), pp. 2–4). It seems clear, however, that Sirach and some other books from our 'Apocrypha' were already considered sacred texts in their original Hebrew by Jews in Jesus' time (Casey, 2010, p. 124). Certainly, whether specific texts were known in written form in Jesus' time or not, the 'big picture' the 'Apocryphal' texts yield, of the atmosphere of the period and the powerful traditions through which Jewish people saw their world, offers plenty of positive illumination.

Thus, for example, the chronicles available to us of the couple of centuries before Jesus, in the books of the Maccabees and the writings of Josephus, offer a splendid backdrop against which we can hear the resonances set off by the stories of Jesus, a hearing which does not depend at all on the identification of verbal parallels. The Maccabean tales would surely have been the stuff of 'live' folklore in Jesus' time. They are rife with fickle tyrants, heroic underdogs, fearful rebels, taxes and debts and tributes and rents – the very stuff of Jesus' stories (see e.g. 1 Macc. 11). They offer a window on the political realities which would have conditioned both the invention and the hearing of those stories. No doubt, on occasion, themes and motifs entered in via the wider Hellenistic culture too.[11] In addition, some stories would have resonated with what we call 'news': recent or contemporary events which might be thinly dressed up as fiction, but which provided examples for the present, the more powerful because of the shared knowledge of the fact on which they were based (see especially The Pounds).

To study 'setting', then, involves a grasp of the historical circumstances in which the stories were told and retold, and the resonances they would have set off with Jewish tradition and popular folklore. To identify the setting of the stories as a 'realistic' one is to say that the 'world' into which Jesus' stories invite hearers is a version of this world, rather than some other sphere (cf. Hedrick, 1994, 2004; Herzog, 1994, 2005; Schottroff, 2006; S. I. Wright, 2000b, pp. 182–207). We should note, however, that this world, for Jesus and his Jewish hearers, is unquestionably God's world. The realism and apparent 'secularity' of the stories does not, therefore, mean that God is excluded from their sphere of meaning.

Character is the next important narrative element (for what follows see Resseguie, 2005, pp. 121–32). In the same way as setting, it tends to be evoked more than it is spelled out, 'shown' rather than 'told' (Resseguie, 2005, pp. 126–30). Hearers must listen out for clues to character in the speeches, actions, appearance and so on of the figures portrayed. Characters are in relationship with each other, and listeners to stories are on the alert for signs of social status as well as the nature of moral choices being made and interactions between different characters. They are 'major' or 'minor' depending on the role they play in the story. They are 'round' or 'flat' depending on their complexity and depth. They may be 'stock' characters, like the heroes and villains of a pantomime. Sometimes a character is a 'foil', existing only to point to the qualities of another by contrast. There are 'walk-ons' who are really just part of the scenery. And there are 'dynamic' characters, who develop, and 'static' ones, who do not. These are all heuristic labels developed by narrative critics to name what is going on in a narrative's characterizations and a hearer/reader's experience of it. Discerning explicit or implicit traits in the characters who people Jesus' stories is critical to capturing their thrust. As with setting, a grasp of historical background is vital in the appreciation of characterization, just as sensitivity to a storyteller's strategy is vital for historical appraisal of the story's significance. Moreover, it is precisely through identification with one or more of the characters that the world of the story intersects with the world of the hearer, such that new insight ensues (see Hedrick, 2004, p. 64, drawing on Funk, 1982, p. 34).

The next key feature of narrative, point of view, is the perspective from which the story is told. Point of view may be expressed in four different 'planes': phraseological, spatial–temporal, psychological or ideological (Resseguie, 2005, pp. 169–73, following Boris Uspensky). The phraseological plane involves specific clues in the language as to how the narrator sees things. The spatial–temporal plane concerns 'where' the narrator is in relation to a story. Is she, for instance, always alongside a particular character, seeing things as that person sees them, or does she move between different locations, allowing hearers to eavesdrop on a number of conversations happening in different places? And what is the time distance between the narrator and the narrated events? In the psychological plane, the narrator is inviting hearers into a character's inner world, as happens sometimes in Jesus' stories when we 'overhear' someone's interior thought processes. The ideological point of view may be discerned via the other planes, and concerns the attitudes or beliefs that the narrator seems to be either supporting or opposing. Attention to point of view is essential if we are to gain a sense of Jesus himself as a storyteller. Again, it is always possible that from time to time the point of view of Jesus as narrator is refined by or in tension with a different point of view expressed through the story by the second-level narrator, that is, the Evangelist.

Finally, there is the plot (for the following, see Resseguie, 2005, pp. 197–211). To focus on plot is to focus on the inner logic of the story, the reasons why events are connected and things happen as they do. Characters' decisions and actions may propel events forward, but so may good or bad fortune. A good plot is a unified whole (Aristotle, *Poetics* 8) and normally entails elements of conflict, suspense and surprise. 'Masterplots' are plots with universal human resonance. Plots may have different shapes, in particular 'comic', with a happy outcome (U-shaped – down then up), and 'tragic', with an unhappy one (an inverted U – up then down). Narrators may vary the order of narration of events so that the order in which things are told is not the order in which we are asked to believe they happened. The outcome of a plot may be 'resolution' (i.e. the solving of a problem) or 'revelation' (i.e. the disclosure of a truth) (Marguerat and Bourquin, 1999, pp. 56–7). Perhaps, when scholars have reductively argued that all Jesus' parables have just one 'point', the germ of truth they were striving for was that his (story) parables have a connected and coherent plot. Discerning the plot is another indispensable move in grasping what Jesus was saying and doing. Attention to plot invites observation of 'nodal points' at which events could take more than one different direction, confirming or contradicting listeners' expectations (Wolter, 2009, pp. 129–34).

In addition to these four central features of setting, point of view, character and plot, Resseguie also outlines some of the many rhetorical techniques that storytellers, in common with speakers or writers of all kinds, use as part of the very texture of their narrative art (2005, pp. 41–86). He groups these under the headings of repetition, framing narratives, and rhetorical figures (of speech or thought). We will not detail these here, for many are familiar, but we will be attentive to possible rhetorical features as we seek to rehear Jesus' stories in the following chapters. Most important of all for our purposes, the discipline of narrative criticism works with the notion of the 'implied speaker' (or 'author') suggested by the story she or he tells, and this will be crucial to my summary assessment of what the stories may tell us of Jesus himself, in Part 4.

Building on a shorter overview of the stories as part of the wider narrative of the Gospels in Part 2, we will bring into play the four main categories of narrative criticism in Part 3, as the organizing keys of a more detailed hearing of each story as Jesus' hearers might have heard it. Since, as we saw, setting, character, point of view and plot mesh together very closely to create a story, these sections will not be too sharply demarcated. For each story, I aim for a sense of a 'cumulative' hearing, culminating in a section of overall reflection on the story.

Identifying the stories

My third and final response to the 'over-determinations' of scholarship identified at the beginning of this chapter relates simply to my selection of texts. I will deal in detail only with those stories ascribed to Jesus which have come down to us in indisputably narrative form. The use of a series of simple past tenses, recounting events connected by patterns of causation, involving the thoughts, actions and experiences of one or more human characters, delimits for us the group of texts to be studied. Such series are basic to normal understanding of what a story is. This means that we exclude from focal consideration here those shorter parables in which there is no discernible 'plot' or any real opportunity for display of character, but only one or two events (e.g. The Treasure in the Field) and/or only verbs in the present or future (e.g. The Merchant in Search of Fine Pearls). The four parables found only in the *Gospel of Thomas* seem to fit into this category of shorter similitudes, and so are not considered here. This is not to discount the interest or importance of such shorter parables, nor the presence of an 'implied' narrative in many of them, but to protest against their being lumped too regularly with their longer neighbours, and to give those neighbours a chance to stand out on their own terms. Inevitably I have had to make some choices about what constitutes a genuine story in this sense and what does not, but my argument in no way depends on the precise categorization of all Jesus' sayings – the very pitfall I identified near the beginning of the book.

At first sight this selection of 'obviously' narrative segments of discourse put in Jesus' mouth may seem to fall foul of the danger we have seen in Hedrick's work, of simply abstracting the narratives from their evangelistic frames – stripping away, for instance, those introductions which suggest a comparative force, such as 'The kingdom of God is like'. I hope to show throughout the rest of the book, however, that such introductions and conclusions, though often clearly indicators by the Evangelists of a particular interpretative direction, do not cancel out the force of the stories considered as stories. In other words, my selection is for the simple purpose of highlighting the clear dynamics of narrative on the lips of Jesus, not for lifting them out of their frames. I trust that the continuity yet distinctiveness between Parts 2 and 3 which now follow will make this clear.

Part 2

HEARING THE STORIES
THROUGH THE GOSPELS

4

Hearing the stories through Mark

Mark tells us that Jesus told numerous parables, in the broad sense of the word (4.33, 34); but he only records for us two full-blown stories of Jesus, The Sower (4.3–8) and The Rebellious Tenants (12.1–11). (I exclude from consideration the short parable The Seed Growing Secretly in 4.26–29, since it depicts a common scene rather than a specific event, though it can be regarded as an 'implied story'.)

John Drury comments that it is 'their dramatic, their narrative context which gives Mark's parables their power' (1985, p. 42). This emerges straightaway with The Sower, which is immediately followed (4.10–12) by Jesus' citation of Isaiah 6.9–10, through which he clearly aligns himself with the prophets who faced resistance to their message. Storytelling to a crowd is immediately followed by observation, to the inner circle, of human resistance to divine communication.

The Sower is set by Mark within Jesus' Galilean ministry. The scene is striking. A 'very large crowd' gathers around Jesus, and he uses a boat on the lake of Galilee to step back from them sufficiently to teach without being overwhelmed by the throng (4.1). This seems to be, for Mark, a typical scene of Jesus' public activity. It is therefore interesting that he does not place it earlier in his narrative. Before it comes a succession of stories in which Jesus' actions arouse amazement, misunderstanding and suspicion, and in which not only the content but the very fact of Jesus' teaching arouses controversy. The way in which one event is quickly added to another is typical of oral performance (Horsley, 2008, p. 103). But there are also many connections between events; later ones recall earlier ones, not only assisting memory but adding to the richness and intensity of the drama (Horsley, 2008, pp. 97, 105, drawing on Dewey, 1994, and Havelock, 1984, pp. 182–3). We will follow the performance of the first four chapters, at some speed, from the start.

Following Mark's summary of Jesus' proclamation (1.14–15), he immediately shows us Jesus in action, walking along by the lake and calling fishermen to follow him (1.16–20). These are men whom, along with others, he would in due course send out with the authority to do and say the things that he has been doing (3.13–19). Part of the sequel to this is the attempt by Jesus' own family to 'reclaim' him (3.21, 32) and Jesus' own explicit redefinition of his 'family' (3.34–35). This sequence in 3.13–35 is therefore a typical reprise, reawakening the memory of the earlier episode of the fishermen's calling: it will lead straight into Mark's account of Jesus' telling of The Sower from the boat on the lake from 4.1.

Between these episodes about Jesus' followers, the remainder of this opening segment of Mark, 1.21—3.12, communicates a sense of intensifying controversy. It is a tightly structured section using rhetorical patterns such as chiasm (see Horsley, 2008, pp. 106–7). In the Capernaum synagogue Jesus' teaching carries an authority which provokes an outcry from a man with an unclean spirit, whom Jesus then exorcises; the people were amazed at a 'new teaching' which carried such power (1.21–27). Jesus' reputation then spreads like wildfire, which leads to crowds gathering about the door of the house where he was staying, but his very healing power is inherently controversial, as it entails the casting out and silencing of 'demons' (1.28–34). The (unwitting) contribution from ordinary human sources to this conflict, on the wrong side, is strongly hinted at in the next section (1.35–45), in which first the disciples disturb Jesus' solitary prayer because people are searching for him, and he then leads them away from those crowds to other towns 'that I may proclaim the message there also; for that is what I came out to do' (1.35–38). Then, as his powerful speech and activity continue (1.39), a man with leprosy comes to him, whom he heals out of compassion, but urges to keep quiet, show himself to the priests and offer the usual sacrifice for cleansing (1.40–44). The man's disobedience to this command further restricts Jesus' movement (1.45).

The next episode adds a comic dimension to this picture of a huge upheaval in the little area of Galilee (2.1–12). When word gets out that Jesus is at home again, the crowds are so tightly pressed around the house that an ingenious group have to remove the roof to let down a paralysed man inside the house. Jesus, far from seeking to defuse a situation that threatens to get out of control, provokes further controversy by announcing that the man's sins are forgiven, arousing the ire of some scribes.

The section from 2.15—3.6 portrays a running and deepening conflict with figures of authority within the community, even as crowds continue to gather around Jesus (2.13, 15). Scribes and Pharisees object to Jesus' convivial association with the unclean and disreputable and to his apparent disregard for the application of laws concerning the Sabbath. The culmination is an unholy alliance of Pharisees and Herodians who plot his destruction (3.6). Once more Jesus withdraws with his disciples (3.7; we notice a pattern of escape from the crowds into their company in 1.29, 38; 2.1, 15). Once more, however, the crowds are after him (3.7–8), this time from an area far wider than Galilee. At this point, for the first time, we read of him retreating into a boat (3.9), to avoid being crushed, even as the narrative portrays the conflict with unclean spirits continuing (3.10–12).

At 3.13–19, with the appointment of the Twelve, we have reached a key narrative moment in which Jesus begins to delegate his authority, partly at least in view of the extreme pressure he was under himself. Mark's note of the purpose of this appointment is significant: the Twelve were 'to be with him, and to be sent out to proclaim the message, and to have authority to cast out demons' (3.14–16). We have already seen the disciples being 'with' Jesus, in those moments of (attempted) escape from the crowds, in their shared meals with Jesus (2.15, 18) and walking through the grainfields (2.23). From this point on, the Twelve are also commissioned to go out, although we do not see them doing this till 6.7–13.

Another return 'home' (3.20) heralds the raising of tension to fever pitch. The crowds prevent Jesus and the disciples even from eating (3.20), Jesus' family try to seize him for his own protection (3.21), and the Jerusalem scribes accuse him of being possessed by Beelzebul (3.22). Jesus' response, too, raises the stakes: blasphemy against the Holy Spirit – speaking of God's work as if it were his enemy's – is 'an eternal sin' (3.30).

For Mark, then, the telling of The Sower, when we get to it in 4.2–9, is far from being a scene of relaxed entertainment. It continues Mark's energetic dramatization of Jesus' intense activity that has already aroused such attention, opposition and misunderstanding. The tactical retreat into a boat is seen as part of an emerging pattern (note 'again', 4.1): for Jesus, it is essential that he has the time and physical space to teach, and not be overwhelmed by the crowds' obsessive attentions.

The teaching with which Mark follows The Sower underlines the impression that, as has often been noted, this is a 'parable of parables'. It concerns the very hearing of the 'word' (God's word) that Jesus is speaking (4.11–32). In Mark's performance it reflects, explains or somehow provokes thought about the situations of crowd hysteria and fierce conflict which have beset Jesus' proclamation of God's kingdom. After the lakeside teaching scene is over in 4.34, the drama continues with Jesus and the disciples leaving the crowd and crossing the lake, only to be confronted by a great storm, seen by Jesus as a test of his disciples' faith (4.35–41), and then, on reaching the other side, by a fierce possessed man (5.1–20). The dramatization of different responses to 'the word' continues through the Gospel (Drury, 1985, pp. 51–2).

Returning to the immediate aftermath of the story, when Jesus is alone, the Twelve ask Jesus about 'the parables' (plural, 4.10), a clue that Mark sees this scene as epitomizing the public proclamation of Jesus and responses to it. Jesus first identifies the disciples (and thus Mark's hearers) as those who have been given 'the secret of the kingdom of God' (4.11a). For those outside, however, 'everything comes in parables' (4.11b). The fact that he rebukes the disciples for not understanding this particular parable (4.13), and goes on to offer an explanation of it, shows both that he does not regard his task as utterly hopeless (as the quotation from Isa. 6.9–10 in v. 12 might on its own indicate) and also that he recognizes the hard work that he is going to have even with those to whom he is closest. The implication is that it should not be hard to understand either this parable or others (4.13b). If there is misunderstanding, it is not because hearers lack innate capability to grasp them but because they have not applied themselves to the task. When Jesus says, 'for those outside, everything comes in parables' (4.11), Mark is not implying that Jesus deliberately wants to obscure truth from the crowds, but that those who will not take even the basic step of enquiring further as the disciples have done, dramatized in Mark's account as 'outsiders', cannot expect to hear anything beyond a 'riddle'.[1] The quotation from Isaiah in verse 12, by aligning Jesus with the prophets whose message was resisted the more it was spoken, communicates Mark's strong sense of a divine purpose in this unfolding drama.

The interpretation of The Sower which Jesus proceeds to give (4.14–20) elucidates it as an account of the way 'the word' is heard. Whose word is not specified, but Mark's lively narrative performance of Jesus' proclamatory activity in his early chapters means that this is naturally read as God's word through Jesus himself, though the references to 'trouble and persecution' (4.17) and probably 'the cares of the world, and the lure of wealth' (4.19) certainly sound like Mark's nods to a wider, post-resurrection audience. It is important, however, to note that this interpretation of the parable does not say what it is commonly, though carelessly, heard as saying. The equation of the seed with the word of God (explicit in Luke 8.11, but less so here in Mark and in Matt. 13.18–23) tends to lead interpreters to follow an allegorical logic by taking the various different kinds of soil as representing different kinds of hearer. But Mark's rendering, after the rather ambiguous 'The sower sows the word' (4.13), seems to identify the seeds themselves with the various types of hearers: 'these are the ones on the path where the word is sown' (4.15), 'these are the ones sown on rocky ground' (4.16), 'others are those sown among the thorns' (4.18), 'these are the ones sown on the good soil' (4.20). This reduces the sense of fatalism sometimes read into the parable, for though both 'seed' and 'soil' might be regarded as entities that cannot change themselves, the opposition between a given seed (the word) and a given soil (the human character receiving it) is removed. The implication, rather, is that the seeds grow into humans who bear more or less fruit. The different kinds of soil constitute part of the realistic setting of the story but are not allegorized as conditions of the heart. The interpretation is not a rationalization of the failure of the word by observation of unchangeable human natures but part of the challenge Mark wants to draw out from his story so far, expressed in 4.24: 'Pay attention to what you hear'.

The varied fortunes of the seed reflect the situations Jesus has encountered in Mark 1.14—3.35. Great crowds have pursued him, but the fact that they have often made it difficult for him to teach suggests that their response to 'the word' in him has been superficial, like those sown along the path or on the rock. In others, such as the scribes and Pharisees, 'the word' has been more or less stillborn, choked by the thorns of their outright resistance. The welcome Jesus has received among those living outside the pale of the law, however, represents a hopeful sign of fruitfulness. The implied challenge of Mark to his readers is the same as that implied as given by Jesus to his inner circle: that they too should be ready to embrace and nurture the word, allowing it to make them fruitful. Giving full and obedient attention to it is crucial (4.25).

The other sayings that follow The Sower and its interpretation also accentuate the urgency of a positive response, with their overtones of a time of revelation and judgement. Secrets will come to light; the true nature and character of people will be revealed (4.21–23). The coming of God's kingdom is mysterious and unseen, but there will be a harvest (4.26–29) and one day it will be all-embracing (4.30–32). The implication is clear: face up to all this, and be ready; or, in the words of 1.15, 'The time is fulfilled, and the kingdom of God has come near; repent, and believe in the good news.' The Sower, then, with its simple account of the fortunes of different seeds sown by a farmer, becomes in Mark's literary setting a narrative that dramatizes the very different responses that God's word in Jesus has been receiving, while pointing to the hope of a fruitful outcome, and inviting hearers and readers to make that a reality.

The Rebellious Tenants (Mark 12.1–12) occupies as important a place in the closing section of the Gospel as The Sower occupies in its opening one. Moreover, it dramatizes the conflicts and choices that have been emerging in the wider narrative, which is now approaching its climax.

The deliberate entry of Jesus into Jerusalem on a colt attracts crowds who hail this as a sign of the coming of 'the kingdom of our father David' (11.1–10). Subsequent events show, however, that Jesus himself had a darker perspective on the way things were unfolding. The account of Jesus cursing the fig tree, and its consequent withering (11.12–14, 20–22), frames the account of Jesus' prophetic action against the Temple (11.15–19), a typical Markan device inviting readers to interpret one event in the light of the other. Where the crowds had seemed optimistic, Jesus with prophetic insight sees the ungodliness at the heart of the 'holy' nation, and confirms it with a graphic sign of judgement against an unfruitful tree. The sayings about acting in faith in God, asking in prayer and forgiving others which Mark appends to this section (11.15–25) underline for the disciples the fact that Jesus' own authority has been shared with them (cf. 3.15). Thus Mark emphasizes that the prophetic persona of Jesus remains alive in his followers.

It is not surprising that the next incident (11.27–33) concerns Jesus' authority. Jesus refuses to respond to a question by leading Jews about who gave him authority to do what he was doing. Or rather, his response takes the form of a question which has an effect very similar to a narrative parable. He invites them to think about from whence John the Baptizer got his authority. Their unwillingness to commit themselves to an answer reflects not ignorance but cowardice, as Mark's account makes clear: if they answer 'from God', that automatically indicts them for their lack of response to John's preaching; if they answer 'from humans', they will court opposition from the people. Just as a parable (according to the teaching of Jesus in Mark 4.1–34) calls for great care in hearing if it is to lead to real understanding, so the leaders in Jerusalem needed to overcome this shallow cowardice if they were to discover the truth about Jesus' authority.

At this point, according to Mark, Jesus 'began to speak to them in parables', of which Mark gives just one example, The Rebellious Tenants. It is a story that has called forth a wide variety of readings and reconstructions, most thoroughly surveyed by Kloppenborg (2006). How, in its present form, does it fit into Mark's narrative?

It has been widely assumed that, whatever may have been the force of the parable on the lips of Jesus, for Mark at least it is an allegory of the rejection of God's word by Israel (his tenants) through the prophets (his servants) and ultimately by Jesus (his son), leading inexorably to the ejection of Israel from the place of favour (the vineyard) and her replacement by 'others' (Gentiles). This reading of the parable in Mark has been reinforced by the recognition of its echoes of Isaiah's vineyard song (Isa. 5.1–7), a parable of judgement on Israel; by the phrase 'beloved son' in Mark 12.6, echoing the words of God about Jesus at his baptism (1.11) and Transfiguration (9.7); and by the appending of the words about the rejected stone from Psalm 118.22–23 to the conclusion of the story in Mark 12.10–11.

Unlike The Sower, however, The Rebellious Tenants receives no explicit interpretation in the Gospel; all detailed interpretations are those given by the Church, from early times onwards (or, more recently, scholars from a Jewish or non-religious background). We should be cautious, then, about reading it in Mark as 'obviously' allegorical. Mark's note about the Jewish leaders' perception that Jesus 'had told this parable against them' (12.12) need not imply that, in Mark's view, they immediately equated Jesus with the son, and themselves precisely as the tenants on course to slay him. Given Mark's portrayal of the leaders' resistance to God's word and consequent blindness and lack of understanding, it is unlikely that he would have ascribed to them such penetrating insight into his meaning. The leaders' reaction, for Mark, is more probably a realistic response to the words about judgement and reversal which bring the story to a climax, reinforcing their mounting sense of Jesus' antagonism towards them, which would have been increasingly clear from his demonstration in the Temple onwards.

The closing words of the story about the vineyard being given to others (12.9) sound, in Mark's account, like a prophetic indictment of Israel's leaders in the style of a Jeremiah (see e.g. the denunciation of the people of Judah in the Temple gates in Jer. 7.1—8.3, with the warning that God would cast them out of his sight for their evil ways (7.15)). It is hardly surprising that this should have been a significant moment in those leaders' growing determination to do away with Jesus, just as Jeremiah was opposed by the rulers of his time. But it is as much in the mood and thrust of the story, its rhetorical action, as in any specific metaphorical identifications of its elements, that its significance in Mark's narrative lies. This is why I disagree with Drury's fully allegorical reading (1985, pp. 64–7): Drury rightly integrates the story very closely into the unfolding events of Jesus' suffering in Mark, but sees the links as made in the plane of allegorical identifications within a piece of literature rather than the tone of an oral performance:

The congruence of the *vineyard* parable with the passion story is a vivid instance of the function of a parable within narrative. Like a programme note to a drama, it outlines the points in it which are most integral to its meaning. It points to its symbolic values. But it prefers to do so by keeping to narrative form rather than discursive argument. So another form than the directly historical is required ... which relates its own masked characters and events to the real characters and events of the larger historical tale which it explicates. It is allegory. (1985, p. 66)

Much more satisfactory is Myers's hearing of the story in Mark as a mixture of realism and allegory which still allows us to pick up the allusion 'to the greed of the ruling class – which Isaiah's vineyard song also condemns (Isa. 5.8)!' (2008 (1988), p. 309). There is no need for a direct identification of the vineyard-owner with God, for his action in 'destroy[ing] the tenants and giv[ing] the vineyard to others' (Mark 12.10) would resonate equally, for Mark's hearers, with the overweening Roman power and its clients, at whose behest smaller fiefdoms rose and fell.

The links between the story of the tenants and the immediately following account of the attempt to trap Jesus through a question about paying tribute to Caesar (12.13–17) are important. The trap is laid by Pharisees and Herodians, the same pairing who were plotting against Jesus following his provocative act of Sabbath healing in 3.6. The Pharisees and Herodians were representative of the priestly and royal agents of Rome in ruling the people of Judea and Galilee (Horsley, 2012, p. 144). In his gnomic response, 'Give to the emperor the things that are the emperor's, and to God the things that are God's' (12.17), Jesus refuses to encourage his hearers to withhold imperial tribute. But he also draws attention to the blasphemous overtones of imperial coinage (which his questioners clearly possessed) with its exaltation of the emperor to divine status (Casey, 2010, p. 423). In similar vein, The Rebellious Tenants might then constitute, in Mark's narrative, not only (in the tenants' behaviour) a stark warning to any who would violently oppose imperial power, perhaps in the misguided belief that in doing so they would bring near 'the kingdom of our father David' (11.10), but also an observation (in the owner's behaviour) of the leaders themselves whose blasphemous and oppressive rule over the people, effectively siding with the empire, both provoked violence and violently retaliated against it. The story would thus function (like The Sower) as an implied indictment of both groups: the hard-hearted, ruthless rulers and the crowds with their superficial enthusiasm and dangerous aspirations.

From the very beginning, Jesus' words and actions in Mark have been an implicit or explicit indictment of the attitudes and behaviour of the current powers within Judaism (see Horsley, 2012, esp. pp. 134–49), leading inexorably to conflict. A story like The Sower, with its mood of hope, may not have sounded as immediately threatening as The Rebellious Tenants, notwithstanding the implied challenge it contained. But even The Sower, as Herzog shows (2005, pp. 28–30), has overtones of violence, in the predatory birds and the devouring thorns (4.4, 7). In The Rebellious Tenants, violence becomes explicit. Without any 'decoding' of different elements, but an identification of the scene as a realistic reflection of the violent tensions pervading first-century society in Palestine (and, for Mark, the wider Roman world), it carried a clear warning in Mark's performance. As Drury says (though not quite in the way that he means: see above), 'The parable alerts the reader to the significance of what has happened and what will happen on either side of it' (1985, p. 66).

Mark's hearers would not be at all surprised at the discomfiture of the leaders at the end of the story. As a largely Gentile Christian congregation, they would see themselves as beneficiaries of the reversal announced in 12.10–11. Moreover, they would already know at least the basic facts behind the end of Mark's Gospel narrative. They believe that, in the resurrection, God vindicated Jesus and his followers, and put his opponents to shame. Thus the phrase 'beloved Son' (12.6), with its echo of the scenes of the baptism (1.11) and Transfiguration (9.7), would function as a rhetorical nod to Mark's hearers, signalling shared knowledge of the real stumbling-block against which the leaders fell: Jesus himself. Nor will the deep irony have been lost on them, that the violence graphically exposed in the story is soon directed on to the storyteller.

Thus both The Sower and The Rebellious Tenants are caught up in Mark's dynamic performance, reflecting the 'agonism' noted by Dewey (1994). They are not static revelations of abstract truth, but acts which propel the narrative forward, highlighting the intense conflict in which Jesus was caught up and the responses, allegiances and alliances this both emerged from and provoked.

The fact that these are the only full stories told by Jesus that Mark includes prompts questions about Mark and his concerns. Is the small number simply a function of Mark's general brevity and concentration on Jesus as a man of action and suffering, rather than on what he said? Did he not know of any more stories? Is it significant that the two stories he does record are the two which have been most regularly heard and read in an allegorical fashion – and, if so, is this because he has no time (or space) for Luke's more leisurely and less easily allegorized stories within his tight performance? Did they particularly suit his apocalyptic outlook? As we have seen, the notion that Mark 'allegorizes' these stories (even that of The Sower) must be qualified considerably. He allows us to hear them in the suggestive, provocative form of story. Perhaps the key to the inclusion of these stories in Mark (and their retention in both Matthew and Luke) is their deep connection with the career of Jesus himself. And, I would argue, their connection with that prophetic, conflict-ridden career is better traced through the lens of dynamic performance than that of static allegorical correspondence.

5

Hearing the stories through Matthew

As a text for possible performance, Matthew is more measured than Mark; what it lacks in immediacy, pace and bluntness it makes up for in order, organization and a didactic eye. The difference is seen immediately when we note Matthew's setting for The Sower.

Rather than following on the heels of an account of Jesus' hectic and conflict-ridden early activity in Galilee, as in Mark, The Sower is placed by Matthew at the beginning of a thematically arranged chapter (13) in which he has assembled seven parables, including two full-blown narratives (The Sower, and The Wheat and the Weeds). This makes up one of Matthew's five long discourses of Jesus, which seem clearly constructed as topical collections of Jesus' teaching designed for ready memorization by a performer and assimilation by audiences in early Christian assemblies. Interestingly, however, Matthew preserves the physical Markan location of The Sower as told from a boat to crowds on the lakeshore (13.1). He also precedes it with some of the same stories as Mark, illustrating Jesus' conflict with the Jewish leaders (12.1–45; cf. Mark 2.23—3.6, 20–30) and his redefinition of family (12.46–50; cf. Mark 3.31–35). The atmosphere of conflict in Matthew is further heightened by the accounts of Jesus' rejection in 'his own country' immediately after the collection of parables in 13.53–58, and the killing of John the Baptist in 14.1–12. In the background of this conflict we must recognize not only the situation of Jesus but also the situation of Matthew, who was surely writing in similarly tense times, within a similar social setting (on which see Carter, 2001, pp. 1–49).

The interpretation of The Sower in Matthew (13.18–23) thus retains the resonances with the wider narrative that it had in Mark: Matthew, too, has narrated a range of responses and potential responses to God's word as Jesus has gone about in Galilee. In addition, Matthew, like Mark, includes before the interpretation Jesus' explanation of why he speaks in parables (13.10–17). A significant difference here is that in Matthew Jesus pronounces a blessing on the disciples for the privileged insight they have been given (13.16–17), whereas in Mark he had rebuked them for their lack of understanding (4.13). The point is underlined at the end of the discourse in Matthew, where the disciples answer with an unambiguous 'yes' to Jesus' question, 'Have you understood all this?' (Matt. 13.51), and are affirmed by Jesus as scribes 'trained for the kingdom of heaven'. This is a good illustration of one of Horsley's points about the Gospels as performances. If he is right that the negative portrayal of the disciples in Mark reflects conflict between the actual hearers of the Gospel and the original disciples (Horsley, 2008, p. 97), then we may hear in Matthew's more positive portrayal of the disciples the awareness of (or at least a strong desire for) a shared identity between Matthew's hearers and Jesus' first followers. Indeed, as Jack Dean Kingsbury demonstrated (1969, p. 130), this chapter is the great 'turning point' of the Gospel. Events thus far have shown increasing division between those who gladly receive Jesus' powerful words and actions, and those who are resistant to them. In this chapter the distinction is dramatized and confirmed, as the disciples are revealed as those who see and understand (13.15–17, 51–52) while the resistant are characterized as those like the people of Isaiah's time, whose heart has grown dull, their ears hard of hearing, and who have shut their eyes (13.15). However, in saying that Jesus 'turns against the Jews' in chapter 13, Kingsbury unhelpfully goes further than Matthew himself (1969, p. 130).

This shared identity between his own hearers and the disciples is also reflected in Matthew's apparent desire to be much fuller about the content of Jesus' teaching than Mark. He wants his hearers not only to experience Jesus in his regularly conflicted encounters with his audiences, as Mark does, but also to draw more explicitly on the pictures Jesus gives of God's kingdom, to strengthen their sense of their own place in it. Highlighting the political dimensions of this, Carter writes that Matthew 13 'explains to the gospel audience' that the lack of receptivity to Jesus' message 'derives not from Jesus' or God's failure but from human sinfulness and Satan's activity. On the other hand, the chapter affirms the audience's welcoming experience of 'the empire of the heavens' (2001, p. 280).

So, in this chapter, Matthew includes another full-blown story, The Wheat and the Weeds (13.24–30), together with an explanation to the disciples (13.36–43). By the very inclusion of this private explanation he dramatizes further his picture of the disciples as those with privileged insight. Furthermore, just as his presentation of The Sower and its interpretation portrays the disciples as the privileged recipients of revelation (13.16–17), and thus representatives of those who are sown on good soil and 'understand' the word (*sunion*, 13.23; Mark 4.20 has 'accept', *paradechontai*), so his presentation of The Wheat and the Weeds and its interpretation invites the identification of the disciples with the 'good seed', the 'sons of the kingdom' (13.38). The interpreted parable thus functions for them as part assurance of final judgement on the 'sons of the evil one' (the main emphasis of the interpretation), and part warning against judging such in the present (the main emphasis of the parable itself). Within the performance of the Gospel as a whole, this solidifies the identity and hope of Matthew's hearers as 'sons of the kingdom', the righteous (13.43), and also chimes with plainer teaching about not judging (7.1–5), winning back a lost member of the fellowship (18.10–20), and the often hidden nature of righteousness and unrighteousness in the present, to be revealed on a future day of reckoning (25.31–46).

Before the interpretation of The Wheat and the Weeds, Matthew inserts the short parables of The Mustard Seed and The Leaven (only the former of which is in Mark). After the interpretation, he adds those of The Treasure in the Field, The Merchant in Search of Fine Pearls, and The Net. Structurally this enables Matthew to suggest that the shorter parables, too, are told to the crowds. He specifically says in verse 34, after the parables of The Wheat and the Weeds, The Mustard Seed, and The Leaven, 'All this Jesus said to the crowd in parables'. Although he then 'left the crowds and went into the house' (v. 36), where he explained the parable of The Wheat and the Weeds to the disciples, it is likely that the final three short parables in verses 44–50 are also to be heard as addressed to the crowds, before Jesus finally turns to the disciples in verse 51 and asks if they have understood 'all this'. Matthew does not seem too fastidious about noting changes of audience (see Drury, 1985, pp. 85–6). He does not signal any change after the private explanation of The Sower between verses 23 and 24, despite the fact that verse 34 indicates that the three parables in verses 24–33 were addressed to the crowds, so it would not be surprising if there was again an unsignalled change of audience between verses 43 and 44. Perhaps the body language of performance (cf. Horsley, 2008, p. 108) would have supplied the change of focus lacking in the text? Matthew does, however, take pains to make it clear that though Jesus' parable-speech is open, proclaiming 'what has been hidden from the foundation of the world' (13.35, citing Ps. 78.2), it is the disciples who understand (Matt. 13.51).

It is Matthew's hearers, then, identifying with the disciples, who are expected to see in these short parables, like the full-blown stories, their place in the kingdom of heaven, and to react accordingly. The thrust of the interpretations of the stories does duty for unfolding the meaning of these short parables too. In this context, the parables of The Mustard Seed and The Leaven underline the reality of present insignificance contrasted with future breadth of embrace. Hearers are to take courage from this; small numbers of Jesus-followers in the present should not lead them to doubt that the kingdom of heaven has indeed been planted on earth. The parables of The Treasure in the Field and The Merchant in Search of Fine Pearls remind Matthew's hearers that though they may have given up much to follow Jesus and live the life of God's kingdom, it is abundantly worth it. The parable of The Net is a final assurance that God will ultimately exercise decisive judgement on a deeply mixed-up world.

The implicit message of this parable-chapter for those who identify themselves as 'sons of the kingdom', that they should not be surprised by the present mixed fortunes of God's kingdom or tempted to pass judgement on others before God's final judgement, is made more explicit in the next full-length story of Jesus in Matthew, The Unforgiving Slave (18.23–35). Like the stories of chapter 13, this is part of a block of teaching (18.1–35). The focus of this teaching is avoiding causing others to sin; in this case, the story comes at the end of the block, not the beginning. The other side of the coin of being self-consciously 'sons of the kingdom' is huge responsibility, and the discourse reflects the fact that the disciples' understanding of the nature of the kingdom remains at a shallow level (18.1).

Thus Matthew's hearers are reminded of their calling as a community to reverse the normal power structures of the day. Instead of grabbing honour and exercising power over those who have less or none of it, they are to be like children, receive children in Jesus' name, and strenuously avoid all careless behaviour which might lead children or other vulnerable people into the destructive patterns of sin (18.1–9). They are to go out of their way, in accordance with their Father's will, to win back to the fold of discipleship those who have gone astray (18.10–20). And they are to persist in indefinite forgiveness (18.21–22). At this point Matthew attaches The Unforgiving Slave.

I have argued briefly elsewhere that Matthew preserves the realism of the story (S. I. Wright, 2009, pp. 15–18). It concerns a human king who has just the same kind of power over his inferiors as the Herods who appear in Matthew's Gospel (2.1–23; 14.1–12). The indebtedness of the servant is unusual but not unheard of: ten thousand talents was extracted from Judea by Pompey in 63 BCE (Josephus, *Antiquities* 14.78; see Carter, 2001, p. 372). The king is unpredictable and impetuous in both his act of mercy and his act of punishment. His generous, but one-off act of forgiveness is nothing like (and was surely meant to be nothing like) forgiveness 'seventy times seven'. He is not God and he does not represent God. But the conclusion of the story turns it into a warning about God's judgement on the unforgiving: 'So my heavenly Father will also do to every one of you, if you do not forgive your brother or sister from your heart' (v. 35).[1]

Matthew's hearers, unlike some literal-minded readers in later times, were surely alive enough to figurative language, and to the heart of the gospel, to know that this sentence was never designed to imply that God the Father had torture chambers ready to receive those he earmarked as hard-hearted. Nonetheless, the story functions as a warning for them, similar to those of 24.36–44: final judgement will be sudden, and there is never a time to be off-guard or unprepared. And the particular danger of which the hearers were being warned is that of unforgiveness, the kind of unforgiveness which excludes people from the blessings of the kingdom and refuses to let them start on the kingdom's way again when they have veered off the path. In its place in Matthew's performance, the story harks back to the petition about forgiveness in the Lord's Prayer (6.12) and the statement which follows it (6.15). It is a sharp admonition to the 'children of the kingdom' to beware of the complacency and pride which is happy to receive the blessing, privilege and acceptance of God's kingdom but is unwilling to behave in such a way as to extend those to others. The story thus resonates not only with The Wheat and the Weeds, with its implicit warning against premature judgement, but also with the positive commission of 28.16–20 that the disciples should go and make disciples (rather than remain in their own self-satisfied côterie). The radical self-perception this calls for in the 'sons of the kingdom' is underlined in Matthew's next scene, where, in discussion of divorce, it is the Pharisees who are accused by Jesus of 'hardness of heart' (19.8) – the very thing that the disciples themselves are being warned of in chapter 18.

Another story unique to Matthew, The Labourers in the Vineyard, is found in 20.1–15. This, too, functions as reinforcement of Matthew's repeated admonitions to his hearers not to let their privileged position in God's kingdom go to their heads. It is framed by the nearly identical sayings in 19.30 and 20.16 about the first being last and the last first. Jesus has just challenged the disciples' standard belief in the intrinsic blessedness of being rich (19.23–26). In response to Peter's reminder to Jesus (!) of how much they had left to follow him, and question 'What then will we have?' (19.27), Jesus points firmly to a time in the future, in 'the new world' (*palingenesia*), as the point where all his faithful followers will inherit glory (19.28–29). But, in the meantime, there is no millimetre of room for self-inflation: 'many who are first will be last, and the last will be first' (19.30).

As with The Unforgiving Slave, The Labourers in the Vineyard remains transparently in Matthew a realistic tale which needs no direct or allegorical reference to God to grant it integrity or meaning. It is an invitation to imagine a new order of compassion and concern for human need (as opposed to the demands of strict fairness). The owner provides for the needs of the day-labourers, even those who have only worked for an hour at the end of the day. In its place in the Gospel, it reminds Matthew's hearers of that new order, so that they may practise it without delusions of superiority or grandeur. Once more, the message is reinforced by what comes immediately afterwards in the narrative: Jesus' reminder that the Son of Man (a glorious figure in Jewish literature, Dan. 7.13, 14) was on his way to condemnation by both Jews and Gentiles, and thence to cruel torture and death (Matt. 20.17–19). The birthpangs of this new order are to be painful in the extreme. Jesus then needs to labour the implications yet again, as the mother of James and John asks him for special favours for them, and he has to point out that the Son of Man's way of service must be that of his disciples too (20.20–28).[2]

Matthew uses Mark's second story, The Rebellious Tenants (Matt. 21.33–43), and he repeats the comment that the chief priests and the Pharisees perceived that Jesus was speaking about them (21.45). As in Mark, their response is not understanding and repentance but an attempt to arrest Jesus, aborted by their fear of the crowd (21.46). Matthew says this was in reaction to 'the parables' generally. This reflects the fact that, as in chapter 13, Matthew augments Mark's bald presentation with extra material, in this case two more stories, one immediately before The Rebellious Tenants (The Two Sons, 21.28–32) and one immediately after (The Wedding Feast, 22.1–14).

All three stories dramatize indictments of the Jewish leadership. Jesus explicitly identifies the chief priests and elders with the son in the first story who said he would do what his father wanted and did not – in contrast with the toll-collectors and prostitutes, identified with the son who said he would not do the father's will yet ended up doing it. This resonates closely with 7.21:

'Not everyone who says to me, "Lord, Lord", will enter the kingdom of heaven, but he who does the will of my Father who is in heaven.' The Rebellious Tenants speaks, as in Mark, of the 'vineyard' being let out to other tenants (21.41), and, more explicitly than in Mark, is followed by Jesus saying directly to the leaders 'the kingdom of God will be taken away from you' (21.43). (In Matthew, Jesus leaves them in little doubt that he is 'speaking about them'!) The Wedding Feast also points starkly to an atmosphere of violence, in which a repressive system produces violent response followed by violent retaliation. Those who decline the king's invitation, some of them violently, are killed (22.7). While others of all kinds are gathered in (22.10), a man who refuses to wear the right garment is consigned to torture (22.13). As in Mark, however, we should see not just the subordinate figures (the tenants of the vineyard and the wedding guests) as implicated in violence, but the dominant figures too (the vineyard owner and the king). The Jewish authorities are to see the entire scenes as reflective of the political atmosphere. As in Mark, there is no hint that those leaders are convicted of their own violent tendencies, nor even that they understand what Jesus is saying. For them, the stories achieve nothing; they stand in prophetic judgement against them.

For Matthew's hearers, however, the 'sons of the kingdom' who 'understand', there is, as in chapter 13, a message about their own status and responsibility. If they, now, are those who have agreed to go in the way of righteousness (21.32), obeying the 'father', they should take heed that they actually do what they have said. If they are those who have now inherited the 'vineyard', they should take care to yield up its fruits (21.43). The theme of fruitfulness has been heard previously in the Gospel (7.16–20), and earlier in this same chapter Jesus has cursed a barren fig tree (21.18–22). Now, in Matthew's performance of The Rebellious Tenants, he inserts 'fruit' three times. The owner sent his slaves 'when the harvest time [lit. 'time of fruits'] had come' (21.34). Jesus' hearers themselves say, in response to his question about what the owner will do, that he will 'lease the vineyard to other tenants who will give him the produce [lit. 'fruits'] at the harvest time' (21.41). And Jesus presses the point home: 'the kingdom of God will be taken away from you and given to a people that produces the fruits of the kingdom' (21.43). The implication is clear: the new tenants will fare no better than the old, if they do not come up with the fruit. Finally, if Jesus' hearers are those who have responded to the invitation to the 'feast', they should take care to wear the proper attire (22.11–14).

Like Matthew's previous stories, all these are transparent upon a realistic setting, making sense in their own, this-worldly terms, recording the tale of Jesus' stand-off with the authorities. But they are also co-opted by Matthew into his didactic purpose of prompting the members of the Christian community, who have inherited such privileges, to think seriously about their responsibilities, and Carter points to various ways in which they are woven thematically into the Gospel and echo biblical themes (2001, pp. 426–31,

432–7). For example, he suggests a link between the suffering slaves who go to collect the fruit and the persecuted prophets mentioned by Jesus in 5.12 (p. 428), and between the 'unworthiness' of the guests in 22.8 and John's call to the leaders to bear fruit 'worthy of repentance' in 3.8. The woes pronounced on the scribes and Pharisees, the authoritative agents of the priestly hierarchy, in 23.1–36 (but addressed to 'the crowds and his disciples', 23.1) reinforce Jesus' opposition to the Jewish leaders in a different rhetorical vein, while similarly reminding Matthew's Christian hearers of the dangers to avoid. Again, we should connect his words about the scribes and Pharisees being 'descendants of those who murdered the prophets' (23.31) not only to the rebellious tenants themselves but also to the policemen of the murderous system, epitomized in the owner of the vineyard – even though on another plane, the owner can be read as the God who gave the land to Israel's leaders to steward wisely for the good of all.

A final pair of stories in Matthew, The Ten Bridesmaids (25.1–13) and The Talents (25.14–30), is found, like the stories of chapters 13 and 18, as part of a longer discourse (24.4—25.46). In this case, they are preceded by Jesus' warning to the disciples of the destruction of the Temple, tribulation to come, and the coming of the Son of Man – with the urgent consequence that they should be ready at all times (24.2–51). The two stories then follow, with the vision of the final separation of the righteous and the wicked on the basis of their response to Jesus' 'brethren' concluding the discourse (25.31–46). Together with that final 'parable' of The Sheep and the Goats, the two stories thus constitute a significant addition by Matthew to the apocalyptic discourse found in Mark 13.1–35. (Matthew has also added 'Q' material in 24.37–43; it is questionable whether the story of the talents in 25.14–30 is 'Q' material, since it contains many differences in wording from The Pounds, found in Luke 19.12–27).[3]

Once again they are realistic stories, which relate to marriage, trading customs and the socio-economic hierarchy. They are set by Matthew in the context of warnings about final judgement, and 'unrealistic' language surfaces which demonstrates that he wants them to reinforce this message ('As for this worthless slave, throw him into the outer darkness', 25.30; perhaps also 'enter into the joy of your master', 25.23). The conclusion to the story of the bridesmaids, 'Keep awake therefore' (25.13), echoes the warning of 24.42. There is no need to imagine, however, that Matthew has therefore 'allegorized' the stories. The echoes of biblical language (marriage feast, bridegroom, master) remain suggestive without becoming dominant. The bridegroom is not God, or Christ; nor is the master, in anything but an oblique way. For Matthew and his hearers, they are stories about moral preparedness, which resonate with all the other material he has included on this topic in his Gospel.

Unlike the stories in chapters 21 and 22, set by Matthew as directed to the Jewish leaders, though with an implied message for his own hearers, there is no audience in view here other than the disciples. It seems clear that Matthew is inviting his Christian readers to place themselves as those who will be answerable, along with all others, for their conduct on the day of judgement. It is a further challenge to complacency, stronger than any that have preceded it. The consummation of the kingdom is not yet; so, in the intervening time of threat and danger, the children of the kingdom must be perpetually watchful, and active in the king's service. But those sharp angles of the story that betray their realism are allowed to poke through the Gospel surface, and we shall explore them further in Chapter 10.

Matthew, thus, repeats and extends Mark's dramatic portrayal of Jesus as the teller of two main stories, which echoed and also prompted misunderstanding and resistance. But he also expands this portrayal by underlining the resonance these stories should have with the children of the kingdom, warning them not to rest complacent in that self-identification, and adding other stories which in a variety of ways communicate the same thrust and remind hearers of the judgement that had come upon those who had fallen into that trap.

6

Hearing the stories through Luke

Luke recounts more stories from the lips of Jesus than either Mark or Matthew. Most of these occur in the 'travel narrative' of Jesus' journey to Jerusalem in 9.51—19.27. Whereas Mark gives us his two stories as part of the raw drama of Jesus' constant engagement with crowds, disciples and opponents, and Matthew performs these two and others in such a way as to draw out their didactic implications for his hearers, Luke deploys Jesus' stories as part of his own more subtle and sophisticated narrative pattern.

The false polarity we noted in Chapter 3 between 'social' and 'theological' emphases in reading the Gospels is well exposed by Green in Luke's case, with reference to Luke's pervasive theme of God's salvation: 'The Third Evangelist knows nothing of such dichotomies as those sometimes drawn between social and spiritual or individual and communal. Salvation embraces the totality of embodied life, including its social, economic, and political concerns' (1997, p. 25). For Luke, the activity of Jesus and the stories he tells repeatedly intertwine with one another and mirror each other (cf. Tannehill, 1986, pp. 103–39). The interconnections can be demonstrated on the level of individual words as well as wider themes (Wright, 2000b, pp. 30–61). This 'intratextuality' embraces also the book of Acts, though space forbids widening this chapter to Luke's second volume too (but see Tannehill, 1990).

The Sower in Luke (8.4–8) has lost its lakeside setting. It follows immediately a summary account of Jesus' itinerant preaching, accompanied by the Twelve and some women (8.1–3). The episode of Jesus' mother and brothers coming to him occurs soon afterwards (8.19–21) rather than immediately before, as in Matthew and Mark. Like the others, Luke includes Jesus' explanation of his parable-speech, drawn from Isaiah (8.9–10), and an interpretation of the parable (8.11–15). Like Mark, he follows this interpretation with Jesus' words about lighting a lamp, the certainty of secrets becoming open, and the injunction 'take heed how you hear' (8.16–18).

As in Matthew and Mark, the story with its interpretation resonates with the accounts of actual individuals and groups who respond aright to Jesus (such as the women in 7.50—8.3) or do not (such as Simon the Pharisee in 7.39–47). The interpretation in Luke, however, widens the application of the story further. Unlike the other versions, it begins unambiguously: 'The seed is the word of God' (8.11). This locates the parable in the broad sweep of Luke's salvation-historical concerns. What is happening in Jesus' ministry is but a focal instance of what has happened down the ages, particularly within Israel, and what will continue to happen when Jesus is no longer physically present: God's word comes to people and meets with varying responses.

The great stories reproduced in Luke's narrative of Jesus' journey to Jerusalem demonstrate Luke's artistry in performance and also highlight Jesus' own insight into the human heart and condition (Sellew, 1992). Snatches of dialogue bring the scenes to life, while internal monologues demonstrate the penetration of Jesus' vision (12.17–20; 15.17–19; 16.3–5; 18.4–5, 11–13; cf. also the monologue Luke inserts into The Rebellious Tenants, 20.13: 'What shall I do? I will send my beloved son; perhaps they will respect him'). The 'way' to Jerusalem for Jesus is turned by Luke into a narrative construct expressing the 'way' of disciples in his own time. The stories take their place within the careful structuring of this section (on which see Blomberg, 1983). As 'stories within a story', they exemplify the motif in different cultures of narratives told on a journey or pilgrimage for entertainment and edification (compare Geoffrey Chaucer's fourteenth-century *Canterbury Tales*). As well as purporting to report the teaching of Jesus, they carry forward Luke's own narrative in an engaging manner, presumably captivating his audience, as well as serving his wider purposes of nurturing disciples in his own setting.

Just how they serve those purposes is a matter of interest. Drury (1985, pp. 112–13) argued that the Lukan parables have a central turning point, which represents in microcosm the 'turn of the ages' which Luke in his two volumes of salvation history narrates. Certainly these stories have a characteristically Lukan focus on the individual and his or her wise or foolish response to circumstances. They instantiate aspects of the gospel of God's kingdom through dramatizing individual human responses to it (S. I. Wright, 2000b, pp. 30–61). Mostly, they have a positive, hopeful tone, contrasting with the darker stories peculiar to Matthew. While reflecting Palestinian cultural features, the range of situations portrayed is recognizable more widely and they are thus well suited to Luke's project of presenting Jesus as the culmination of Israel's story and the point at which that story opens up to embrace the nations. They deal with very practical realities, especially concerning wealth and poverty, and while Luke Timothy Johnson is right that for Luke wealth is closely associated with a negative response to the message of Jesus (Johnson, 1977), this does not mean that Luke is unconcerned with the question of material goods in itself, treating it as a mere cipher for the question of unbelief or belief. On the contrary, he surely sees this element of life as precisely one of the most important practical areas in which the gospel could be demonstrated in the Gentile churches for which he narrates the story of Jesus.

We may best outline Luke's performance of these stories by noting the way he has woven them into his travel narrative as explanations, illustrations, clarifications or expansions of teaching and situations that arise 'on the way'. Interaction with others is a constant. The Good Samaritan (10.30–37) is told to blow apart a lawyer's narrow conception of 'neighbour'. Moreover, it is immediately followed by the story of Jesus' visit to the house of Mary and

Martha (10.38–42). The two scenes side by side form, as Donahue says, 'a twofold parabolic illustration of a single command', the injunction to love God and neighbour as stated by the lawyer in verse 27 (1988, p. 136). As often in Luke's performance, this is a case of story being quickly mirrored by action. The Rich Fool (12.16–21) serves as a warning against covetousness to a man who is overanxious about his property rights. The Barren Fig Tree (13.6–9) encapsulates the situation of Israel, whose people are still called to repent (13.5), and to avoid being diverted from this by projecting their own sinfulness on to the victims of a ruler's atrocity or a natural disaster (13.1–4).

The Great Banquet (14.16–24) is appropriately set at a dinner table (14.1). It follows Jesus' justification for healing on the Sabbath (14.5), his warning to his Pharisaic fellow-guests about seeking places of honour (14.7–11), and his advice to the host about inviting those who are not in a position to return the favour (14.12–14). The story thus seeks to prise open the Pharisaic world-view by pointing to the logic of inviting to the 'feast' people of all kinds who are willing to come – as well as hinting that the Pharisees themselves might be in danger of missing out on the feast of God's own banquet. The realities of economic and social life in Palestine are fused with Graeco-Roman understandings of honour and shame and the Israelite tradition of the Messianic banquet in a suggestive story which both reflects what is happening in Jesus' own ministry (outcasts tasting a 'banquet', literally and metaphorically, 5.29, 15.1–2), and points prophetically (for Luke) to the shape of the renewed 'Israel' manifest in the early Christian gatherings (Acts 2.44–47). Donahue is not far off the mark: 'Luke makes the parable an exhortation for the community to become inclusive' (1988, p. 146).

The Prodigal Son (15.11–32), following on the short comparisons of The Lost Sheep and The Lost Coin, functions as part of Jesus' response to those who complain at his welcome of 'sinners' (15.1–2) and thus links closely with the banquet theme of 14.1–24. The Pharisees and scribes are enticed to contemplate the beauty of forgiveness, and in the process, perhaps, to wonder whether they themselves are in need of it. In introducing The Shrewd Manager (16.1–9) immediately following this story, Luke the performer brings the disciples into view again (16.1). This is a reminder of the multiple audiences which are regularly implied, especially in Luke, for particular sayings of Jesus. Jesus speaks with both 'Pharisees' and 'sinners', sometimes in each other's presence (in addition to 15.1–2 see 7.36–50). But all the time a gaggle of disciples is observing at close quarters, and, as we see Jesus turning to them at a point like this, we can also see Luke alerting his hearers to the lessons they can learn from these interactions (see S. I. Wright, 2000a, pp. 219–20; and on the importance of the clues to audience in the Gospels, Thiselton, 1985, pp. 90–1, discussing Baird, 1969).

The Shrewd Manager should be seen as developing the same affirmation of the outcasts' potential as the previous stories. Why shouldn't a man tainted by the economic exigencies of his situation be commended for taking wise and merciful action to make friends as a way out of it? Why shouldn't a disgraceful son have the opportunity to repent, the poor come to the banquet – or, indeed, a Samaritan fulfil the Torah by loving his neighbour? The sayings which follow this story (16.10–13), commending faithfulness in human dealings and single-minded devotion to God, are often held to be a lame addition to the story, an attempt by Luke or his sources to tame the story's rather shocking conclusion in which Jesus tells his disciples to make friends for themselves by means of 'unrighteous mammon' (16.9). However, they may be better seen as a prelude to the next interchange with the Pharisees, who, Luke tells us, were 'lovers of money' and 'heard all this' (16.14). It is the Pharisees, then, who are in danger of unfaithfulness, of trying to serve God and mammon. They are implicitly identified with the 'rich man' of 16.1, the steward's boss. Although modern Western interpreters have regularly pilloried the manager for his immorality and shady dealings, it is the 'rich' for Luke who are more likely to have a negative association than their underlings. In fact, as we shall see more fully in Chapters 7—10, it makes good sense against the social background to see the economic system of which the rich man was a representative and guardian as the real villain of the story (see Herzog, 1994, pp. 233–66). The rich man's commendation of his steward's act of debt remission is like a minor 'conversion'. The disciples who hear the story in Luke's performance, and Luke's own hearers, are directed towards the wise use of money in a corrupt and cut-throat economy.

The Pharisees, Luke tells us, had overheard Jesus' words about faithfulness and not being able to serve God and money (16.10–13) and scoffed at him, since they were 'lovers of money' (16.14). Jesus' response in 16.15–18, which seems at first glance with its comments about the law and about divorce to veer off the topic of riches, serves for Luke to set the context for the following story. He points to the contrast between outward appearance and the heart (16.15) and the continuing validity of the law (16.17), and implicitly contrasts the Pharisees' undermining of the law (by allowing easy divorce, to the economic oppression of women) with God's true will (16.18). This prepares the way for The Rich Man and Lazarus (16.19–31), clearly addressed to a Pharisaic audience again, like The Prodigal Son. Here Jesus invites his hearers to see beyond the outward appearance of luxury to the real destiny of a rich man, and emphasizes that God's will revealed through Moses and the prophets remains binding and a sufficient guide for life (16.31).

This story, like that of The Prodigal Son, performs for Luke's audience Jesus' invitation to the Pharisees to imagine an order of things to which they had become blind. It requires them to entertain the possibility (to put it no stronger) that one who enjoys all the good things of this life may hereafter be deprived of them all, and that, conversely, the destitute may be ultimately rewarded. Although nothing is said about the morality of either the rich man or Lazarus, the context in Luke, the sensitivity to social realities shared by writer, speakers and hearers, and the words about listening to Moses and the prophets all suggest strongly that the story serves Luke's familiar interest of exposing the true character and destiny of people and of social groups (seen, most famously, in Mary's song in 1.46–55, Jesus' Nazareth sermon in 4.16–21, and the Beatitudes and Woes in 6.20–26). But, like The Prodigal Son, it passes no final sentence on Jesus' hearers. It simply warns them by reminding them of the familiar but strangely forgotten realities of God's judgement and his revealed will.

The story also plays on the familiar Pharisaic belief in resurrection. The rich man expresses belief that Lazarus could return (16.27); indeed, when he sees him in Abraham's bosom, it is natural that he should see that he is deserving of resurrection. But this is, it seems, a misguided and twisted notion of resurrection in Jesus' eyes. Instead of living out before death a faith in the God who is able to raise the dead, and thus humbly submitting to his will, the rich man after death pleads for Lazarus' visible resurrection to be used as a sign to convince his brothers. Such a sign is refused by Abraham in the story (16.31), as it was characteristically by Jesus – for example in the very next chapter in Luke (17.20–21).

With Luke 17.1, Jesus' focus returns to the disciples. As always, Jesus' teaching for his followers is not essentially different in content from what he says to crowds or opponents; the will of God is the same for all. It is simply that the emphasis for his disciples is often to warn against complacency; the mere fact of being in Jesus' company is no guarantee that one will obey God's will. Disciples of Jesus must not fall prey to the same danger of hypocrisy, and blindness to their inner condition, that had befallen the Pharisees, and this surely is as true for Luke's hearers/readers as it is for Jesus' contemporaries. Thus the sayings in 17.1–10 warn disciples against being stumbling blocks (17.1–4), underline the need for faith (17.5–6) and urge humility (17.7–10). The healing of ten men with leprosy (17.11–19) is a reminder that sometimes it is 'foreigners' or 'enemies' rather than Israelites who truly give glory to God. Jesus next warns first Pharisees (17.20–21) and then disciples (17.22–24) not to look for 'signs' of the coming kingdom in outward, observable phenomena. In one sense, the kingdom of God is already among them (17.21). In another sense, its ultimate manifestation on the 'day' of the 'Son of Man' will be universal and unmistakable (17.24).

Jesus' warnings to his disciples which continue through 17.25–37 set the scene for the two stories which follow in 18.1–14. The warnings portray the deeply paradoxical nature of the time into which they are entering. The very Son of Man who will one day be revealed in glory must first endure much suffering (17.25). Such will be the hiddenness of God's kingdom that 'the day that the Son of Man is revealed' will be a day of judgement for which many are unprepared (17.26–30). 17.30–32 seems to take literal warnings of Jesus about what to do in a forthcoming national crisis and by placing them in this context, along with the saying about losing one's life in verse 33, make them apply metaphorically to the need for readiness for this ultimate revelation. (Something similar occurs in Luke 12.57–59, where Luke seems to use the saying about agreeing with one's adversary, part of Jesus' literal instructions in Matthew 5.25–26, in the context of urging preparedness for the final great assizes.) The judgement will separate even the closest (Luke 17.34–36) and may fall anywhere (17.37).

Thus we come to The Widow and the Judge (18.2–5), reported in this context by Luke as an encouragement of Jesus to the disciples 'to pray always and not to lose heart' (18.1). The rhetorical force of the story is felt better if we recognize the judge not as a metaphor for God but as a real human judge, gathering in himself the whole atmosphere of injustice within which, in the present, the disciples must watch and wait and persevere. The 'prayer' to which they are urged is therefore not merely a spiritual but an active thing, a working for justice. The story holds out the hope that, even in this unjust world, signs of the kingdom may be seen. How much more, then, will God himself come to vindicate them soon (18.6, 8). But Luke shows Jesus' sober attitude in 18.8. The question is open: will the Son of Man find faith on the earth when he comes? Luke here reprises the challenge to have faith, even as a grain of mustard seed, that Jesus had given in 17.6. In the time of suffering that is to come, to be initiated by the suffering of the Son of Man himself, persevering trust in God, even among disciples of Jesus, is by no means a foregone conclusion.

The Pharisee and the Toll-Collector (18.10–14) is presented by Luke as told to 'some who trusted in themselves that they were righteous and regarded others with contempt' (18.9). Whether these people were disciples of Jesus, Pharisees or another group we are not told, but that simply fits with the impression we have gained that warning against complacency was a consistent note of Jesus' message, whomever he was addressing. The Pharisee in the story, like the rich man in 16.19–31, is an imagined but believable figure, presented as a warning that things might not always be as they seem. What manifests itself as piety may actually be self-exaltation, and self-exaltation leads inexorably, as the proverbial saying in verse 14 says, to humiliation. Conversely, the toll-collector, aware of his sinfulness, will be exalted. The story dramatizes the reversals that Luke celebrates through his Gospel. Characteristically, it is followed straightaway by an account of an action of Jesus, welcoming those without status and power (in this case children), and using them as an example for all (18.15–17).

Luke has one final story of Jesus to perform in his account of the journey to Jerusalem, The Pounds (Luke 19.12–27). Before he gets to it, he relates further incidents and sayings of Jesus which enact the themes of judgement, humility, and reversal of status which have pervaded this travelogue. A rich man's adherence to the commandments is shown as insufficient for entry into the life of God's kingdom, because he is unwilling to recognize God's claim over his riches (18.18–25). The disciples, recognizing the radical character of Jesus' call, are reassured that the wealth of the age to come does indeed await those who are prepared to sacrifice all for it (18.26–30), but immediately reminded again that the Son of Man is about to be cruelly treated (18.31–34). The story of the blind man receiving his sight (18.35–43) gives a foretaste of the kingdom's joy, but the fact that those around Jesus want to ignore him only underlines the fact that the true challenge of the kingdom is not yet truly grasped. The blind man's cry for mercy (18.38–39) echoes that of the toll-collector in the parable (18.13) – the toll-collector's address to 'God' here suggestively replaced by 'Jesus, Son of David'. The blind man is an example of the faith (18.42) which Jesus longs for but perhaps nearly despairs of seeing (17.6; 18.8). The story of Zacchaeus (19.1–10) offers another surprising example of where the blessings of the kingdom, 'salvation' (v. 9), are falling. Zacchaeus displays the generosity from which the rich man in 18.18–25 shrank back; he is a real-life example of the repentance to which, we are invited to imagine, the prayer of the toll-collector in the parable (18.10–14) was the prelude.

It is at this point, Luke says, that Jesus told 'them' (a vague designation for the crowds of disciples and other hangers-on around Jesus?) the parable of The Pounds, 'because he was near Jerusalem, and because they supposed that the kingdom of God was to appear immediately' (19.11). Our question here is how Luke's hearers are meant to think that the parable corrects this misapprehension. Traditionally, the story has been understood as teaching, in a semi-allegorical way, the delay of ultimate judgement, and the need for diligent, obedient service in the meantime. This reading is almost inevitably bound up with the identification of the 'nobleman' of verse 12 as Jesus, who is to go and gain 'royal power for himself and then return'. Some of Luke's hearers may indeed have heard it like this. An alternative reading which I find more persuasive, as truer not only to the setting of Jesus' original performance but also to that of Luke, is of the story as a picture of the dealings of a first-century aristocrat in Palestine with his subjects and servants. (I will deal with this in much more detail in Chapter 9. For a similar approach, see Dowling, 2007; Keesmaat and Walsh, 2011; and literature cited there.) This allows the realism of the story to be preserved, as well as explaining the otherwise uncomfortable juxtaposition between (supposed) self-portraits of Jesus as the Son of Man who will allow himself to be handed over to Gentile torture (18.31–33) and a king who demands that his enemies be slaughtered in his presence (v. 27).[1]

Luke's version of this story is often thought to be a combination of two originally separate ones, that of a throne-claimant and that of entrusting money to servants. But this may be to overlook the specifically political appointments given to the two successful traders on the nobleman's return: they are put in charge of ten and five cities respectively (19.17, 19 – a detail not in Matthew's similar story The Talents). This looks like a credible grant of political power to those with proven economic savvy. The story is united in its focus on the attitude both of the objectors and those entrusted with money to the nobleman, not on the use of the money.

If the story reflects a situation of normal ruthless behaviour by a first-century tyrant, and of the frequent uprisings by one faction or another, how does it serve Luke's purpose in the way he implies in 19.11? It would continue the theme of warning about impending crisis and suffering which came to a head in 17.25–37. In describing this situation of oppression in the story, Jesus is heard as implicitly warning against expectations of imminent political or military liberation that were accompanying his approach to Jerusalem. Anyone who inspired a following like that of Jesus would arouse hopes of a new order. Jesus needed to remind those around him of the way Rome and those who served her were in the habit of treating rebels, and thus defuse any revolutionary fervour which his arrival in the holy city was unintentionally fanning.

This interpretation fits well as the climax of Luke's story of Jesus' journey to Jerusalem, in which he has been continually reversing and upsetting expectations about what the kingdom of God is like, how it can be recognized, who exemplifies it and how it will ultimately appear. The kingdom of God is among his hearers (17.21), but it is not discernible through the standard expected 'signs' (17.20). There will be a day for the Son of Man to be revealed in unmistakable heavenly glory (17:24), but in the meantime he must suffer (17.25; 18.31–34). His followers must be ready to persevere (18.1–8). Those like the Pharisees who considered themselves a spearhead of obedience, preparing the way for the kingdom, should look to the true state of their hearts (16; 18.9-14). The poor, the children, the degraded, the unclean, find themselves the glad recipients and exemplars of the kingdom, both now (18.14a, 15–17, 35–43; 19.1–10) and in the final reckoning (16.19–31; 18.7–8, 14b). The rich, meanwhile, are sent empty away (18.18–25; cf. 1.53). It may seem, as they approach Jerusalem, that Jesus is leading his loyal band into some dastardly act of defiance against the authorities. But he has already taught and demonstrated amply that the kingdom of God's true might is not found in such acts. He has insisted that its final 'appearance' will follow much trauma and will be brought about by God alone. In the meantime, the tale of the ruthless throne-claimant must stand as a warning of the futility of all attempts to force its manifestation through attempting to challenge the imperial aristocracy. If Luke's hearers have already heard of the trauma of the Jewish revolt in 66–70 CE, they will hear sombre echoes of it in the story, and be reassured that Jesus had warned of such folly.

With this story, Luke's hearers are well prepared for the true nature of Jesus' 'triumphal entry' in 19.28–40 (contrasting, not mimicking, that of the throne-claimant!) and for his weeping over the city that will bring its enemies down on itself because it did not recognize the way of peace or the time of God's visitation (19.41–44).

Luke's version of The Rebellious Tenants (20.9–18) is close to Mark's, both in content and in its placement between the question about Jesus' authority (20.1–8) and that about giving tribute to Caesar (20.19–26). Like both Mark and Matthew, Luke records that the Jewish leaders recognized that the parable had been told against them (20.19). One small addition suggests Luke's performative interest: the vineyard owner went into another country 'for a long while' (20.9). On one level, this could simply be a realistic expansion that draws out the situation of an absentee landlord. But it also resonates with the master in Luke 12.41–48 (cf. Matt. 24.45–51) whose delay tempts his servant to maltreat his underlings, a situation used by Jesus as a warning to be ready for judgement. The story of the tenants thus takes on a further eschatological cast, warning Luke's hearers to maintain readiness (and eschew violence) while their 'master' is 'absent'.

On the basis of the stories in Luke's travel narrative, Drury draws a contrast between the parables in Mark and Matthew as being essentially symbolic or allegorical, and those in Luke as being predominantly realistic. He links symbolism and allegory with the apocalyptic tradition and realism with 'the theology of the Deuteronomistic historians and the commonsense wisdom school' (Drury, 1985, p. 141). Luke's realism, he argues, 'is not a merely literary experiment: it is driven and required by Luke's fundamental conviction that theology is realized in the material historical world of people' (p. 141). Undoubtedly, the stories Luke records fit this conviction in the way that Drury describes. But the exposure of biblical scholarship in more recent years to the studies of orality and performance trouble Drury's enticing narrative of a progression from Mark to Luke via Matthew, in which the dominance of allegory and symbol gradually gives way to the dominance of realism. As we have already suggested briefly, and shall attempt to show in more detail over the next four chapters, realism of setting, character and plot, deriving surely from early oral performances, continues to be pervasively visible in Jesus' stories in all three Gospels, notwithstanding the suggestive symbolic touches with which the Evangelists have integrated them into their narratives.

A thread running through Drury's engaging reading of the parables in the Gospels (1985) is that all the Gospels, in various ways, use Jesus' stories to encode a division between Jew and Christian that was hardening in the early Church. A number of the stories were certainly used this way from early times (see e.g. the discussion of anti-Jewish readings of The Rebellious Tenants in Milavec, 1989). Time after time Drury ascribes such simplistic readings to the Evangelists themselves. In the case of a story more easily susceptible to an allegorical understanding, such as The Labourers in the Vineyard, Drury (who doubts our ability to learn much about Jesus' own storytelling from the Gospels) sees Matthew himself as responsible for portraying Jews as the early workers and Christians as the 'latecomers', an interpretation that would persist through church history (Drury, 1985, pp. 92–3). In The Wedding Feast, '[t]he guests who refuse their invitations are Jews. Those who accept are Christians, "bad and good" as Matthew knew them in his imperfect church' (p. 98). In the realistic stories in Luke which have been less readily allegorized, Drury nonetheless sees the same division being reinforced, particularly by the moment of decision which falls in their middle. This, for Drury, expresses Luke's conviction that Jesus is 'the central crisis of sacred history': 'Jesus in his Gospel is not history's end but its turning point, setting it on a new course in which Judaism drops away and the Christian Church goes triumphantly forward' (1985, p. 113, drawing on Conzelmann, 1960 (1953, 1957)).

The Gospels have certainly been used as the basis for such anti-Judaism with unfortunate frequency. But this sounds more like a blunt instrument applied to their textured narratives by Drury than a conclusion drawn from them. On one level, it is too simplistic a reading because of the clear differences of status, standpoint and so on within Judaism that are now universally recognized. Jesus was in no sense 'against Judaism' and it is arbitrary to assume that the Synoptic Gospel writers, who form the main source for this recognition, have forgotten these distinctions or the complex realities of Jesus' own setting, in which 'political' dynamics were equally as important as (what we now call) 'religious' ones. In the words of Horsley's chapter titles, Jesus was 'leading the renewal of Israel against the rulers of Israel' (2012, pp. 111–19). Why should we assume that these wider 'political' dynamics were no longer part of the 'setting' of the Gospel narratives? To be sure, there were developing tensions between the synagogues and the Jesus-followers, but to begin with, these remained intra-Jewish tensions, and were still deeply conditioned by wider circumstances in the empire, as the New Testament letters attest. The Gospel of John certainly stereotypes 'the Jews'. The Synoptic writers, however, preserve the messiness of Jesus' actual situation.

On another level, Drury's reading, while in many ways very sophisticated in its literary sensitivity, overreads Jesus' stories to such an extent that their ambiguities, polyvalence and indirectness get left behind in the rush to see the stereotyped division between Jew and Christian encoded within them. What I have tried to do in the last three chapters is to help us re-enter, in a preliminary way, the narratives of Mark, Matthew and Luke as scripts for performance rather than simply literary texts. This entails recovering the oral dynamics of their dramas, within which the stories remembered as told by Jesus play their part. Such oral performances work not by hard-and-fast allegory, but by echo, innuendo, multiple resonances back and forth, and the often intense identification of audiences with characters in the story (Dewey, 1994). I have tried to show that though these stories *by* Jesus have naturally and inescapably been co-opted by the Evangelists into their stories *of* Jesus, this process has not erased the patterns or textures of Jesus' own storytelling in any of the Gospels. Indeed, in a number of cases these patterns and textures remain quite clear, not least because aspects of the stories seem at first sight to jar with the Evangelist's wider message (e.g. the harshness of the authority figures in The Unforgiving Slave and The Pounds). I have argued that the Evangelists allow us to see something of their own thought processes in connecting their material but also to hear something of Jesus' voice in their performance of his stories. It is now time to look more closely at the individual stories, imagining how they would have been heard by Jesus' own audiences.

Part 3

HEARING THE STORIES WITH THE FIRST LISTENERS

7

Hearing the stories in Galilee

For convenience, I divide up the following chapters on how Jesus' stories might originally have been heard according to the geographical location where they are placed by the Evangelists. This division carries no implication that the stories were first heard, or only heard, in these locations. But it has the advantage of not foreclosing our understanding by imposing a particular theme or rhetorical form on the stories for the purpose of categorization (see above, pp. 1–2). It may also remind us that in any particular scene of Jesus' storytelling there was a physical environment, and many social and cultural phenomena associated with it. They were also told at specific times, and may therefore have resonated with particular episodes or trends in the movement Jesus had started, even if their resonance also goes wider. Thus in this chapter we consider the stories set by the Evangelists in Jesus' Galilean ministry. In Chapters 8 and 9, we discuss the stories set by Luke 'on the way', on the journey of Jesus from Galilee to Jerusalem which forms the centrepiece of Luke's Gospel. In Chapter 10 we will turn to those stories set during Jesus' final days in Jerusalem.

I am not as concerned as Hedrick (2004, p. 91) that we should choose between different versions of a story where they exist. I take it as possible that any of the Gospels may yield clues to the story's original resonance, even though each to some extent imposes their own framework. Where one of the stories has a parallel in the *Gospel of Thomas* (which offers no geographical settings) I have taken that version into account, though in only one case (The Rebellious Tenants) have I found it necessary to give it detailed attention.

As we consider each story, we will see how each performs the double rhetorical function I mentioned in Chapter 3 above.[1] On the one hand, it invites a hearer to enter a world in which possible meaning is opened up, not closed down. On the other hand, it has a framework which is not infinitely malleable but has a definite shape. And we will listen out for the performative dimension, what is being done with these stories, not just what is being said.

We will use the tools of narrative criticism, introduced in Chapter 3, to try to prise open this intriguing moment when Jesus performed a story (recognizing that the same story may well have been performed a number of times). I recognize here that I will be using these tools in a way rather distinct from that in which most narrative critics have used them. First, most narrative criticism has been focused heavily on stories as written textual products: it is, after all, a method of *literary* criticism. I will be using it to imagine the oral dynamics of the stories, but there is no reason why its basic categories of setting, character, point of view and plot should not equally well be employed for this end. As Scott points out, 'at the level of narrative structure there is a relative continuity between oral and written literature' (1989, p. 76). Second, narrative criticism has usually been explicit in bracketing out questions of history (e.g. in what setting did the actual original speaker of these words 'perform' them)? I will be using this approach, however, explicitly to address the historical question of how Jesus would have been heard, and thence, tentatively, the stance of Jesus himself.

The scholarship on these stories is vast and many-sided. To attempt either to synthesize it or to interact with it all would be to overwhelm both author and readers. Since what I am exploring here is a different kind of approach from that which I have seen elsewhere, I have kept my own approach to the foreground. I acknowledge, of course, specific debts where I am aware of them, but entry into the world of parable scholarship is like swimming in a great river: you soon lose track of the precise origin of the great currents which have propelled you to where you are. The corollary, of course, is that these 'hearings' are but a beginning, to be corrected, completed, complemented, at all points – through further evidence, historical and sociological, but also through literary insights.

Three stories are set in Galilee. The Sower occupies an important place in all three Gospel accounts of Jesus' earlier activity. The Wheat and the Weeds follows closely on The Sower in Matthew. The Unforgiving Slave has an unspecified location, but the teaching collected by Matthew in chapter 18, introduced by the vague 'at that time' (v. 1), follows the 'gathering' of Jesus and his disciples in Galilee when he foretells his death (17.22–23) and the incident at Capernaum where Jesus tells Peter to catch a fish from the lake in which he will find a coin to pay the Temple tax (17.24–27).

The Sower (Matt. 13.3–9; Mark 4.3–9; Luke 8.5–8; *Thomas* 9)

Setting

Stories have a setting that may be a combination of geographical, cultural, temporal and religious aspects, and more (Resseguie, 2005, pp. 94–114). This is part of what we mean when we say they invite us into a 'world'. Charles Dickens invited his readers into the world of grimy nineteenth-century London, Emily Brontë hers into that of the wild Yorkshire moors. Into what world did this story of Jesus invite his hearers?

In a word, their own world. All we know about first-century societies points to the fact that the great majority of the population scraped a living together off the land. They were subsistence farmers who survived from one day to the next, and, as we say today, would often be living 'on the edge'. Political pressures, indebtedness to rich landowners, and growing families kept most in poverty. Moreover, the very land they worked was often difficult, not least in hilly Palestine. The area farmed by an individual family would be very small. Seed would be sown on terraced hillsides where it was impossible to avoid some falling on pathways, rocks, or the thorns that were difficult to control.[2] Yet somehow, harvests came, and people (by and large) survived – though not, of course, with anything like today's life expectancy.

Hedrick (2004, p. 75) queries whether the 'seed' parables are amenable to Herzog's economic approach. But Myers gives the lie to that:

> The parable's focus on the majority of the seed, which went fruitless, would be bitterly familiar to the peasant, for whom the grain seed represented his only 'cash flow' – with it he fed his family, paid the rent and tithes, and sowed the next year's crop ... Wealthy landlords always extracted enough of the harvest to ensure that the farmer remained indentured to the land, strangling any prospect he might have to achieve even a modicum of economic security.
>
> (2008 (1988)), p. 176)

So what would be the force of the parable's promise of a harvest? On one level, the story might have seemed trivial, nothing other than an echo of everyday life – hard graft mixed with occasional relief. The yield from the good soil may not have been exceptional (Hedrick, 1994, pp. 172–3; though see Carter, 2001, p. 283, suggesting that it reflects the abundance of a new Eden). But there is more to 'setting' than this. It also encompasses the social memories, traditions, stories and customs evoked by, and thus informing, a particular tale. As Jesus told a story, he was tapping into a whole network of such references which, to various extents, his hearers would have picked up (see Dunn, 2005, p. 48; Horsley, 2008, pp. 89–95).

For Jewish people, the land had considerable spiritual significance. It was God's trust to his people, to tend and care for. Israel's care for her land came to be seen, in the developing tradition, as a mirror of the way humanity had been called to care for the earth: though canonically it was natural to place Genesis 1—3 at the beginning, Israel's calling, instruction and blessing by God preceded the formulation of the stories in those chapters. God's blessing on the land was a sign of his favour and the fact that the people were acting in obedience to him and justice towards each other, while drought, famine, plague and conquest were a sign of his displeasure and their rebellion (Lev. 25.18–24; Deut. 28). This is epitomized in Leviticus 26.14–16: 'If you will not obey me ... you will sow your seed in vain, for your enemies shall eat it.'

Attentive hearers might have picked up other scriptural resonances as well. Allusions to the LXX are particularly prominent in Luke's version of the story but are present in the others too. The 'birds of the air' are not always benign in Scripture. In Pharaoh's baker's dream, they eat out of the basket on his head, but this means they will soon be eating the flesh from his dead body (Gen. 40.16–19). Proverbially, according to various prophets, they eat the dead bodies of those who die in disgrace according to God's judgement (1 Kings 14.11; 16.4; 21.24; Ps. 79.2). 'Thorns' also are both evidence of God's judgement and instruments of it. They grew up in Eden (Gen. 3.18). They would grow up in YHWH's vineyard because of the people's bloodshed and injustice (Isa. 5.6–7). In prophesying the Assyrian invasion, Isaiah had said:

> On that day every place where there used to be a thousand vines, worth a thousand shekels of silver, will become briers and thorns. With bow and arrows one will go there, for all the land will be briers and thorns; and as for all the hills that used to be hoed with a hoe, you will not go there for fear of briers and thorns.   (Isa. 7.23–25)

Hosea pledged that thorn and thistle would grow up on the site of Israel's pagan altars when they had been destroyed (Hos. 10.8).

It is particularly interesting that thorns can also be people, the agents of God's judgement, as it were 'thorns in the side' of Israel (Ezek. 28.24). The godless are like thorns to be thrown away (2 Sam. 23.6). This mirrors the fact that 'seed' was used to refer to the people of God whom he would 'sow' in the land (Jer. 31.27–28; Hos. 2.23). The apocalyptic work *4 Ezra* (incorporated in the book 2 Esdras in the Apocrypha), though later than Jesus, gives one a sense of the kind of identification between seed and people that would have been in the consciousness of people in his time. In response to his anguished address to God about the evil of the world, Ezra receives this response:

> For just as the farmer sows many seeds in the ground and plants a multitude of seedlings, and yet not all that have been sown will come up in due season, and not all that were planted will take root; so also those who have been sown in the world will not all be saved.   (2 Esd. 8.41)

N. T. Wright points to the prophetic use of 'seed' imagery to refer to the returning remnant, the true Israel, especially to the way in which, in Isaiah 55.10–13, the sowing of the word is to result in the return from exile and the renewal of Creation (1996, pp. 232–3). We also note how God's word here is compared to the rain and the snow which water the earth, 'making it bring forth and sprout, giving seed to the sower and bread to the eater' (Isa. 55.10). The prophet uses this everyday evidence of the creative power which provides the means for humans to live (v. 10) as a sign to assure the people that God's word is also able to accomplish his purpose of bringing his people back from exile (vv. 11–12) and giving them a land to inhabit: 'Instead of the thorn shall come up the cypress; instead of the brier shall come up the myrtle' (v. 13). These promises are given to back up the call to 'seek the LORD while he may be found, call upon him while he is near' (v. 6). Hearing this chapter in the background of The Sower enables us to see the materiality as well as spirituality in the implied promise of the story. The story's echo of the prophecy both suggests the power of God to achieve his ends despite human resistance, and also the blessing of land which will epitomize that achievement. Moreover, with the wider thrust of the prophecy in the background, the story would have been heard as inviting not passive fatalism but active repentance.

This identification of 'seed' with 'people' chimes with the Synoptic renderings of the interpretation of The Sower (Mark 4.13–20), as we saw above, p. 64. All three Gospels make an initial identification of the seed with the word (Matt. 13.18; Mark 4.14; Luke 8.11), but their subsequent interpretations of the different seeds focuses on the seeds as hearers (e.g. 'These are the ones sown along the path ... when they hear', Mark 4.15). Given the network of allusion we have suggested, this connection would have been natural for many hearers. This in turn suggests that the interpretation of the parable was not some super-mysterious decoding which none of Jesus' hearers could possibly have achieved by themselves. His rebuke to the disciples (Mark 4.13) indicates that he thought it would not be too difficult. It is not intellectual or artistic complexity which made such a story 'difficult', but the fact that a hearer needed to exercise his or her will to engage properly with it, to gather its echoes so as to enter more deeply into what Jesus was saying.

These echoes of belief and tradition about the land are not to be divorced from the immediate socio-economic setting. This is the mistake of all those who have recognized the realism of Jesus' stories and then gone on to assume that what Jesus was 'really' talking about was some larger, or wider, or other-worldly reality. The land on which Jesus' peasant hearers had to scrape a living was a little portion of precisely the land which God had promised them. George Shillington well summarizes the interconnection between the land in Jesus' present circumstances and the land in their tradition:

> The land on which Jesus lived and told his parables to the people was God's gift to Israel ... And the elect people who occupied the land in trust, the Jewish people, were not to lose their inheritance indefinitely. If a member incurred a debt that caused the person (or family) to lose their portion in the land of promise, the debt was to be forgiven in the year of jubilee and the land returned to the original trustee (Lev. 25). But in the time of Jesus the debt law had fallen into disuse; peasants had lost their plot that sustained life to the elite city dwellers ... In Palestine at the time of Jesus, the land that promised life for the people of God had become for many a sterile place overrun by Roman soldiers and bandits, and used by elite landlords to generate a surplus for their sumptuous city life at the expense of the dispossessed poor of the villages. (Shillington, 1997, pp. 9–10)

This vivid summary stands, in fact, as an excellent introduction to the setting of most or all of Jesus' stories. As for The Sower, Shillington captures its picture exactly:

> [It] creates an image of a sizeable proportion of waste land, and thorns and rocks and thieving birds and scorching sun, with only one portion producing abundantly. A strange and shocking picture of the holy land of promise it is, but one to which many a Jewish peasant could no doubt give his own version.
> (Shillington, 1997, p. 11)

As for the yield from the good soil, it echoes the expectation of apocalyptic blessing in *1 Enoch (Ethiopic Apocalypse)* 10.18–20: Mark (and I would say Jesus) 'is articulating an ideology of the land, and the revolutionary hopes of those who work on it' (Myers, 2008 (1988), p. 177).

But the setting of a story will take a hearer only so far: it invites us further in, to what makes a story a story rather than a mere landscape: the elements of character, point of view and plot.

Character

What strikes a reader about this story today, as compared with most of Jesus' other stories, is the fact that there is only one character, and he is completely anonymous. All Jesus' stories are brief, and do not give opportunity for much explicit character development and portrayal. But this does not mean that even as undefined a person as 'a sower' would have left hearers uninterested or without clues.

The fact that this person is such a generalized 'type' would itself have been significant. Combined with the setting of the story, it would have suggested that he was 'one of them'. In other words, this is a typical scene. It is not something strange or unusual. It beckons its hearers in, and when they have come to the end they are, maybe, left asking: what is my response, as a fellow-'sower', to this situation? Even this brief, undescribed, singular character may become the means of locating hearers in the story's world. They could have felt something of his frustration with the unfruitful seed and his joy at the harvest.

Point of view

The angle from which narrated events are viewed is crucial to the reception of a story. Jesus, as speaker, here reveals himself as one who knows and understands his hearers' situation well. But perhaps what is most striking about The Sower is the very fact that it is a narrative. Jesus does not say, 'You know how it is, the way you always have difficulty getting a good crop because the landscape's so unhelpful.' Jesus places himself in the position of one who can speak of such homely, everyday phenomena not merely as general, ongoing facts, but as a single past event. Such is 'the gathering power' of story, or, indeed, of painting. By drawing a specific scene, however mundane, a whole world of truth may be evoked. Martin Heidegger used the example of how Van Gogh's paintings of the shoes of a peasant woman evoked her entire world (Heidegger, 1971, pp. 33–5, cited in Thiselton, 1980, p. 338).

The story thus carries an implied message about the teller himself: he is one who claims some wisdom, or skill, or authority to portray things thus. Yet the story is not overtly self-referential: it is told in the third person singular ('he'), not the first person ('I').

Plot

The story is so brief that some might think it hardly contains a 'plot' worthy of the name. Yet there is the implied conflict here between the farmer, and the land that seems so resistant to his efforts. Hearers would naturally be waiting for the point at which, at last, he sows in a place where his seed does some good, and a traditional 'law of three' is at work here in the structure: three unsuccessful outcomes followed by one successful. The realistic setting would suggest that the driver of the plot is not carelessness by the sower, nor a practice of sowing before ploughing, as Jeremias thought (1963 (1947), pp. 11–12). Rather, the sower sows wherever he can, and mysteriously, beyond his control, but wonderfully, the seed does find some good soil, within which the process of creation can work its magic. The resolution of the plot, therefore, does not come about through the farmer's own cleverness or observation, but undoubtedly, for a Jewish hearer, from God who alone provides for his people, often in the face of adversity.

The fact that this plot unfolds as something that has happened invites the hearers to link it to their own experience. There would be some, maybe, who recall going for years without a genuinely good harvest. To them, the story with its past-tense definiteness and simple positive plot resolution surely prompts the question: so who is this farmer? And why is his story being presented to us? Given the labour and patience needed for farming, as reflected in the fate of the first three groups of seeds, what is the storyteller getting at by speaking of this great harvest resulting from the fourth?

Such a plot cannot be translated into a different form of rhetoric without loss. Jesus is not simply giving an exhortation ('Cheer up, it'll all come good one day') nor teaching a fact about God ('God will always look after you in the end') nor fomenting revolt ('Do something about the situation!'). The plot draws the hearer into the tension of the situation in a way that those simplistic translations cannot. The loss of seed is real. But so is the possibility of great fruitfulness. That is what the story invites hearers to imagine.

Reflection

The story is suffused with the mood of honest Israelite hope: trust in God, but squaring up to present conditions. It sounds almost like a narrative rendering of a song, Psalm 126: 'May those who sow in tears reap with shouts of joy' (v. 5). In that psalm and, as we have seen, throughout the tradition, sowing and reaping was not just an arbitrary metaphor for prosperity, but rather a fundamental sign of that prosperity.

This mysteriously simple story, in all four versions, would clearly have been open to a range of 'meanings' to its first hearers. Any attempt to define its 'meaning' is to ignore the rhetorical context in which the Gospels set it. It was precisely this openness, presumably, which led the disciples to seek further explanation from Jesus, according to the Synoptics. We should note that even this explanation, although directing the disciples to the importance of response to God's word, still leaves much undecided for a hearer to ponder, and a wide possible range of 'applications'. In what settings has this 'word' been sown, is it being sown, will it be sown? Who is the sower? Who are the people, or kinds of people, who fall into the different categories of hearer?

The original, unexplained story would have invited even more acts of imagination. Fundamentally, hearers might have asked: is there any substance in this at all? What is this teacher getting at? Why is he saying this to us? On what semantic level, if any, are we meant to take this? Even these questions, of course, are a sophisticated modern construct that falls well short of reproducing the likely responses of a crowd of Galilean peasants. For many, one might conjecture, this was their first brush with the new star healer who had become the talk of the countryside. For such, the questions about the story, insofar as any were articulated, would not have concerned *meaning* at all. They would have been much more like 'What's going on here?' A modern comparison might be with a stranger used only to classical art walking into a gallery of late twentieth-century art installations, or a pedestrian suddenly coming across a drama group on a high street. Not just the mental faculties, but the whole person, needs time to get attuned and adjust to the situation. It is not surprising that all the Gospels recall Jesus' command to 'listen'. The point of what he was saying and doing would not be discovered through merely casual attention.

Yet any who did listen would have picked up from this story at least a shape, a mood, a direction. A farmer sowed his seed, and much of it fell in places where it did not come to anything. But there was some which fell on good soil and ended up not only coming to fruition but bearing much seed for future sowing. End of story: but a happy ending. For many, the message would have been as vague as this, at least on first hearing. But what if they continued to think? What if they didn't have opportunity to get near Jesus, like the disciples, to ask him to explain? What if they went off, struck, and pondered the story over future weeks and months? What might they have started to deduce about Jesus' message?

And how then are we to assess the significance of what Jesus is doing here? First, it is clear that such a story was not a form of 'plain speech', despite what has been argued by Jülicher (1910 (1886, 1898, 1899)), Parker (1996) and others. Jesus was not, in any sense, 'explaining' his mission, or God's purpose, or people's responsibility. He was provoking thought, as Dodd (1936 (1935), p. 16) rightly put it. Yet this was not 'thought' about anything one liked. The invitation was to focus on the everyday situation of a Jewish farmer who found that only a proportion of his seed landed on soil where it could bear fruit, but that that proportion did indeed produce a successful crop, full of promise for years to come.

Thus, second, it seems clear that this story was not deliberately designed to befuddle hearers. It is not a piece of arcane fantasy that bears no relation to the hearers' world. On the contrary, we have seen that it dealt with an extremely familiar theme and would have drawn in its hearers to identify with its character. Though it remains thought-provoking and a bit puzzling, its happy ending gives it a positive mood, and would be a reminder of God's providence. Therefore it lends itself to the widely accepted view that the words about the purpose of the parables in Mark 4.11–12, drawing on Isaiah 6.9–10, say more about the divine mystery of revelation and (lack of) response than the deliberate rhetorical strategy of Jesus – whether they be thought to go back to Jesus or to be the work of the Evangelist.

Thirdly, therefore, it seems mistaken to limit the purpose of the story too narrowly, as has happened sometimes when scholars have taken up positions arguing that it definitely teaches an 'imminent' kingdom (Schweitzer, 2000 (1913), p. 325), a 'present' kingdom (Dodd, 1936 (1935), pp. 178–80), a kingdom begun but not completed (Jeremias, 1963 (1947), p. 150), or the 'non-eschatological' kingdom of the Jesus Seminar. It *teaches* none of these. Rather, it invites imagination of the implications of one sowing thus and achieving these familiar results. It asks hearers to recognize the harsh yet hopeful reality of their situation and, through pondering on this simple scene, ask questions about it.

As we have seen, a Jewish hearer who was prompted to ask 'Why is this so?' might readily have ascribed the bountiful harvest on the good soil to God. But what might he or she have thought concerning the seeds falling along the path, on the rocks and among the thorns? These things epitomized the daily struggle. So why were things like that? That basic question was the one consistently asked by Jewish thinkers over the immediately preceding centuries up to the time of Jesus and beyond (see 2 Esd.).

The story gives no answer to such a question. It invites thought and encourages hope. The identification of seeds with people in the parable's application draws out the personal challenge that a careful listener might have received from the story itself, but it does not close down the ongoing signifying power of that story.

The Wheat and the Weeds (Matt. 13.24–30; *Thomas* 57)

Setting

The setting of The Wheat and the Weeds, again, is everyday agricultural life in Palestine, bringing into play the vital importance of sowing seed which will yield the grain on which life depends, life that is a sign of God's blessing. The incident of sabotage is also realistic – whether this was a case of some kind of low-level economic competitiveness or a personal vendetta is left to speculation, but the possibility of personal enmity is universally believable. The master's wisdom in allowing wheat and weeds to grow together is also, surely, something with which Jesus' hearers would have been familiar. There is an economic difference from The Sower, in that this farmer has slaves (who presumably also carried out the initial sowing, v. 24; 'someone who sowed good seed in his field' is likely to be shorthand, keeping the focus on the figure of authority). Once more there is further depth to the setting of the story in the biblical associations of the language of sowing and, especially here, of harvest, familiar to Jewish people as an image of judgement (Joel 3.13).

Character

Here we have not one character but several: the householder, his enemy (vv. 25, 28), his slaves (vv. 27–28) and the reapers (v. 30). (The 'reapers' may have overlapped with the 'slaves'; maybe there were also day-labourers involved at the reaping stage.) All these characters would have been 'types' familiar to the hearers. Much of the land of Palestine had been bought up by wealthy landowners. The poor may sometimes have had little option but to be taken into slavery; at least they were then provided for. They were also entrusted with various responsibilities. If 'reapers' included day-labourers, these too were well-known figures on the Palestinian scene, leading lives of great insecurity (Herzog, 1994, p. 86).

The 'enemy' is presumably another landowner or his slave or agent. Jesus' vignette draws a hearer into a scene in which close partnership between slaves and landowners is portrayed in the dialogue. This is a scene of competitiveness not between rich and poor but between rich and rich. The fortunes of the slaves are bound up with those of the master. The hearers would identify, quite probably, with the slaves, being themselves no strangers to such conflict between big 'houses', and the householder's advice would be seen as prudent.

Point of view

The dialogue in verses 27–30 suggests that Jesus is a narrator who can identify with both masters and slaves. The fact that it is included at all demonstrates a desire to see things from the slaves' point of view. Few if any of his hearers on such occasions would have been likely to come from the nobility, but all had a stake in what the nobility were up to.

Plot

The hostility on which the plot turns here comes not from the terrain itself, as in The Sower, but from a human enemy. The question posed by the opening scene of verses 24–25 is this: will this householder get a crop at all? The next verse (26) gives a note of encouragement: the weeds are growing up, but so is the wheat. The turning point then comes with the dialogue. The slaves' two questions and the master's first answer create an element of suspense (vv. 27–28), with the resolution coming in the master's second answer (vv. 29–30). There is no final scene in which we are told, 'So that's what they did': the story finishes with the master's words about waiting till harvest time to separate wheat and weeds. The law of 'end-stress', by which the way the plot concludes provides the story with its main thrust, means that the story takes on a strong future orientation, as hearers are reminded of the wisdom of waiting for harvest time.

This conclusion to the plot locates the hearers in this time of waiting. Just as the story of the sower drew them into the tension between seed which dies and seed which bears fruit, so this plot draws them into the experience of seeing the useless growing up alongside the useful, and needing to wait until they can be safely separated. Behind this, it reminds them of the reality of petty human vindictiveness which, in this case, is the cause of this particular patch of ground not being as fruitful as it could have been.

Reflection

Like The Sower, this story does not so much 'teach' a truth about (say) the timing of God's kingdom as evoke a scene and prompt imaginative thought. It similarly reflects the daily world of agricultural labour, with the added edge of human enmity inserted. Therefore it, too, would have prompted questions and ideas about why this world was as it was. The ending underlines the hope of harvest that beckons to those who are canny enough to be patient with the frustrations of the present. For those who picked up the scriptural echoes of the 'harvest' picture, there would be the added sense that this scene was actually a microcosm of the wider world, in which the human hostility which aborted some of earth's bounty would not, ultimately, thwart it.

The interpretation of the story recorded by Matthew (13.36–43), like that of The Sower, picks up on this human dimension. As Marshall has shown (1973 (1963), pp. 29–32), this interpretation echoes the end-stress of the story itself on the harvest. Unlike many Christian interpreters, early and late, it does not touch on, or seek to allegorize, the slaves' impulse to root up the weeds too early. Paradoxically, in fact, the 'allegorical' interpretation offered here does not justify the particular allegorical understanding which has often been placed on the parable, of a 'mixed church' or *corpus permixtum* which will not be sorted out till judgement day. Rather, it focuses entirely on the coming judgement as the climax of a dramatic universal conflict of good and evil, of which the everyday scene in a field is seen, in retrospect, to be a single, miniature instantiation. In preserving the essential focus of the story's plot, the interpretation is a natural explanation. Whether it therefore goes back to Jesus is not something that we can discuss here, but it should be seen at least as a clue to the lines of thought of an early reflective listener, rather than obscuring them from view.

One of the main differences between this story and The Sower is the introduction, 'The kingdom of heaven may be compared to' (Matt. 13.24). This is a rather vague introductory phrase, and crucially, what Jülicher called the *tertium comparationis*, or point of comparison, is left unspoken. Thus it is left up to the hearer to make the connection between the kingdom and what goes on in the story (whatever else he is doing, Jesus is clearly not comparing the kingdom simply to the 'man' who sowed good seed in his field). As with The Sower, the explanation (Matt. 13.37–43) does not exhaust either the story's 'meaning' or, more importantly, its rhetorical force.

In the 'ordinariness' of its performance, the story again leaves wide open the questions 'Why? What is Jesus doing here?' Yet, as before, it has a shape which could impress itself on a hearer. Like a miniature portrait, its smallness does not betoken pointlessness or triviality, but great meaningfulness, for once more, like a work of art, it invites us to see something of the universal in the very particular.

The Unforgiving Slave (Matt. 18.23–35)

Setting

Herzog (1994, pp. 131–49) and Schottroff (2006, pp. 196–204) are surely correct that the story offers a snapshot of Palestinian life under foreign rule at its most oppressive. This was a highly indebted society in which the majority of the population lived lives of considerable insecurity, often dependent on the whims and idiosyncrasies of the small ruling class. The exorbitant level of the first slave's debt (ten thousand talents, v. 24) may (or may not) be colourful hyperbole for an individual case, but was grimly true to the reality of the overall economic imbalance. So also was the contrast between this figure and that owed by the second slave to the first, a hundred denarii (v. 28). Yet the latter figure was not an insignificant amount. If a denarius was the usual daily wage, it represented three months' survival. Further realistic touches are seen in the prison to which the first slave sends the second (v. 30) and the torturers to whom the king consigns the first (v. 34).

The religious and cultural scripts which are brought into play here concern the virtues of compassion and mercy. These were seen in Scripture as being at the heart of YHWH's character (see Exod. 34.6–7). The enmity that was seen in The Wheat and the Weeds between two landowners is here played out between two slaves – and ultimately between one of them and the king.

Character

It is the factor of character which constitutes the real stumbling-block for all attempts to read the story in an allegorical fashion, and especially the king as a cipher for God. We may accept that Matthew was not completely off track to say that in the story something is to be compared to the kingdom of heaven (v. 23) but it is surely not the character of the king. Notwithstanding the Jewish ascription of kingship to God, the realism of the story is so overwhelming that a hearer would be forced to ignore most of its details if he or she made that identification.

The king in the story acts according to type, the type very familiar to first-century Jews. He holds vast economic power. He is also ruthless in seeking recompense from one who has had a responsible position in his service, but has now run up far more debt in the process than he has been able to repay. One imagines that the slave was like one of those entrusted with talents in Matthew 25.14–30, who traded enthusiastically – but unlike with them, everything went horribly wrong and he lost his employer a vast sum. (Modern tales of banks collapsing through traders overextending themselves come to mind.) The king is minded to sell him off to the highest bidder – along with his family and the possessions he had presumably accumulated in more favourable times.

The king's act of clemency when the slave begs for mercy would not have been seen as unduly virtuous, though his 'pity' shows he is not totally heartless. No doubt he could well afford to write off the debt, and he only does so when begged by the slave. An act of magnanimity by one in power was an effective way of further increasing dependency. When the news of the slave's harshness towards his fellow-slave reaches the king, his displeasure is understandable. The swift punishment which follows shows that his resources of pity have been quickly exhausted. The portrayal of the king's character is entirely in keeping with what we know of ruthless tyrants of the time. Yet, in a concrete way, he does demonstrate the compassion and mercy which has marked YHWH's dealings with his people and which he calls them to show to others (Lev. 19.18). Note especially the Torah's commands concerning the year of jubilee (Lev. 25.8–55), and all the careful provisions to ensure that the land would be respected as God's, and its inhabitants who fall on hard times well cared for.

The desperate state of both slaves in their indebtedness is apparent. Nothing is said about the character of either, but the first one shows by his treatment of his fellow-slave that he belongs to the same cut-throat world as the king. This is no surprise, for the values and attitudes of those in control of a society are likely to permeate that society. The first slave may be reasserting his power having been shamed by the king (Herzog, 1994, pp. 143–4).

The group of slaves who report the first slave's lack of forgiveness to the king form an interesting 'composite character'. How are we to view their action? On the one hand, their shock at what has happened is natural and understandable. But do they not know what is likely to happen if they report it? Would there not have been another way to persuade the first slave to show mercy to the second? Their involvement of the king in this aftermath of his act of clemency seems to be an act of fear; they know that he is a hard man (cf. Matt. 25.24), and whatever happens to their colleague, their instinct is to stay on the king's side.

Point of view

The brief but vivid snatches of dialogue, and especially that between the group of slaves who report the first slave's ruthlessness and the king, show that Jesus is telling this story 'from below'. He understands and identifies with the slaves and their situation. But there is nothing condemnatory here towards the king any more than there is anything to condone the action of the first slave. The viewpoint is above all that of the sharp observer who directs his hearers' attention to a specific, though in some sense typical, situation.

Plot

This is the most complex plot of the three that we have encountered so far. The opening scene is one of settling accounts between a king and his slaves. The spotlight turns on to one man who 'was brought to him' (note the impression here of the man's passivity and helplessness) (v. 24). The king's decree that he be sold with his family and possessions in order to pay the debt is followed by the man's graphic self-abasement (he 'fell on his knees before him', v. 26) and his master's release of him (v. 27).

The second scene replicates the first with chilling twists. The first slave thinks that it is time he, too, settled accounts. But this is a more hasty, less ordered affair than the king's reckoning. As he goes out, he simply 'comes upon' one of his fellow-slaves – who owed him a mere hundred denarii. Without waiting for any kind of judicial process he seizes him by the throat and demands payment (v. 28). In exactly the same words as the first slave had used to the king, the second slave falls down and pleads, 'Have patience with me, and I will pay you' (v. 29). The first slave, however, refuses and throws him into prison. By shining a light on both the similarities and the differences between the two situations, the storyteller invites ironic comparison between them.

There follows the reporting of this to the king (v. 31), which forms a link into the final scene where the king passes judgement and sentence on the first slave. The king appeals to the intrinsic injustice or unnaturalness of his behaviour: how is it that having been released from so much ('I forgave you all that debt', v. 32) he should refuse to release another? The king's question to the slave, 'Should you not have had mercy on your fellow-slave, as I had mercy on you?' (v. 33) hangs in the air without an answer. The story ends on a dark note; Jesus does not spare his hearers the realistic detail that at this point the king's initial clemency was revoked entirely, as he angrily passed the slave over to those who administered torture on his behalf 'until he would pay his entire debt' (v. 34). The ending of the story at this point rounds it off as a realistic tale and places the focus on the potentially dire consequences of throwing a magnate's brief act of generosity back in his face. It is the kind of incident that Jesus might well have heard of.

Reflection

Listeners' attention would here have been focused on a scene that for some might have been chillingly familiar. Their imagination would have been fired by the plight of the grossly indebted servant. The forgiveness of the king would have been a pleasant surprise. The servant's ruthlessness would have come as an unpleasant shock (though was perhaps rather close to the bone for some). The king's final act of punishment would, in the circumstances, have been no surprise, but none the less sobering for that.

Perhaps the line that would have carried on ringing in their ears most loudly was the king's question: 'Should you not have had mercy on your fellow-slave, as I had mercy on you?' (v. 33), all the more powerful for being dramatized as direct speech. The story appeals to a deep sense of what is proper and just, and provokes horror that it does not happen. But there would surely be for Jesus' contemporaries a striking irony in who it was who was asking this question. This was a ruthless ruler whose character, overall, had little to commend it, yet who was nonetheless capable of enacting the kind of concrete liberation that had always been YHWH's business with his people. We meet such a character again in the judge of Luke 18.1–8. Listeners would have known that one didn't scorn or ignore such a person. On the principle of 'how much more', and without any literal comparison between the king and God, or his torture-chambers and God's holy judgement, one should not scorn the infinite mercy of God. There is a logical line between such a story and Hebrews 12.14–29, and especially verse 25: 'See that you do not refuse the one who is speaking; for if they did not escape when they refused the one who warned them on earth, how much less will we escape if we reject the one who warns from heaven!'

The 'double rhetoric' in this story is revealed particularly in its jarring tension. On the one hand, it is 'open' in that it calls forth repeated questions from the hearer, which are not readily resolved. Why is this king so initially magnanimous? What is the motive of the unforgiving slave? What are we to make of the fact that the king later revokes his forgiveness with such ire? Where does this leave the second slave, who may well have been dependent on the first one who is now thrown into prison? Was he himself released from prison, where we last see him (v. 30)? On the other hand, it is 'closed' in that the tone of warning is impossible to miss. There is a way to respond to the magnanimity of one vastly superior in social terms, and this is not it.

The thrust of the story seems to be to urge hearers to accept the mercy of God wherever and however it was manifested, even in unlikely places. It is perhaps not surprising that this is one implication of one of Jesus' most famous stories, which begins the series he told on the way to Jerusalem.

8

Hearing the stories on the way: 1

In this chapter we eavesdrop on the first hearers' reception of the first five of the ten stories included by Luke in his account of Jesus' journey to Jerusalem, from 9.51 to 19.27. These stories 'on the way' form the centrepiece of the corpus of Jesus' stories. In Chapter 9 we will listen to the remaining five of these stories, and append to them The Labourers in the Vineyard (Matt. 20.1–15), the one story set by Matthew in the period after Jesus had left Galilee for the last time (19.1) and before he reached Jerusalem (21.1).

The Good Samaritan (Luke 10.30–37)

Setting

Given that the hero of the story is a Samaritan, it is plausible to imagine Jesus, near the start of his journey, telling it (first?) in Samaria, where he had not been welcomed in a particular village (Luke 9.51–55). The scene of the story, though, is nearer Jesus' end-point: the Jerusalem–Jericho road, steep and rugged, and a notorious place for being mugged by bandits. Maybe he told it again there. Wherever he was, Galilee and Judea covered a relatively small area, and that road may have been well known to people all over the region, even (by hearsay) to those who had never ventured south from Galilee.

Jesus invites his hearer(s) into an evocative place, and they would not be surprised at what initially happened there. Whether the attackers were 'social bandits', local gangs regarded by some as heroic, or more individualistic robbers, sociological and historical evidence suggests that such occurrences would be a regular feature of life in first-century Palestine (see e.g. Stegemann and Stegemann, 1999 (1995), pp. 173–8). It is a normal element of a society where many are forced to live 'on the edge'. If the mugging was not surprising, nor was the fact that a couple of other travellers passed hastily by, sensing the danger. Culturally and religiously, the setting here is the practical and perennial question of how to act, especially in life's more tricky situations. Israel's Torah and wisdom gave authoritative guidance, but (Pharisaic efforts notwithstanding) that did not remove daily dilemmas. As we shall see below, the main issue is how overriding principles of Torah clash with the purity system and with pieces of inherited wisdom such as that reflected in Sirach 12.1–7, which urges that one should not help a sinner.

Drury (1985, pp. 134–5) suggests that Luke's account of Jesus' story reflects memories of the tale in 2 Chronicles 28.15, in which people from the northern kingdom of Israel, living in Samaria, obey the prophet Oded's instruction to allow Judahites whom they have captured in war to return home: 'they clothed them, gave them sandals, provided them with food and drink, and anointed them; and carrying all the feeble among them on donkeys, they brought them to their kindred at Jericho, the city of palm trees. Then they returned to Samaria.' Whether or not Jesus' hearers would have thought of this, Drury's suggestion is a good illustration of his wider point about the realistic stories in this section of Luke: they continue a tradition embodied in the Hebrew Scriptures, which contain many tales of real life (how 'historical' or 'legendary' is often difficult to judge) that do not 'teach' explicitly but have theological and ethical texture, often rooted in the wisdom tradition (1985, pp. 116, 134).

This background forms part of the setting of Jesus' stories, and Jesus would therefore have been heard as one of the 'storytellers' of old. These, in turn, are not to be sharply distinguished from prophets. Many of these ancient narratives are found in the books of Joshua—Kings in the Hebrew Scriptures, known as the Former Prophets. As Walter Brueggemann argues, this designation is bound to be puzzling for those who think in terms of prophecy as either prediction or social engagement (2004, p. 102). But when we see that this label refers to 'the material itself, not specific prophetic personalities', we can recognize that '[w]hat is prophetic is the capacity to construe all of lived reality – including the history of Israel and the power-relations of the known world of the ancient Near-East – according to the equally palpable reality (in this reading) of the rule of YHWH' (p. 103). The books of the 'Former Prophets', therefore, are theological readings of history on a grand scale, narratives interpreting reality, but they are made up of much shorter episodes which would have constituted part of the oral 'little tradition' familiar to ordinary Galileans and Judeans of Jesus' day. It was precisely that 'little tradition', argues Horsley (2012, pp. 87–94), that preserved the great tales of (for example) prophets such as Elijah and Elisha, recorded in the books of Kings. It was not a surprising step that leaders of popular movements, like Jesus, should have been classed with these figures. In the stories of Jesus, we seem to come much closer to this 'little tradition' than we do in the Former Prophets, where the episodes have already been combined into a grand narrative. The Gospels correspond to that grand narrative, but there is nothing in the Former Prophets that quite corresponds to the rhetorical immediacy with which the Gospels reproduce Jesus' stories. In any case, places such as Samaria, Jericho and Jerusalem reverberated with the tales of the ancestors.

Character

Into the crime scene, sadly familiar to Jesus' hearers, the identity of the characters brings spice. Like most of the characters in Jesus' stories, the priest, Levite and Samaritan are too briefly drawn to be rounded or individualized. They are 'types', identified only by their role (priest and Levite) and ethnicity

(Samaritan). It is Jesus' choice of these 'types' that makes this such a memorable story.[1]

The lawyer with whom Jesus was in dialogue would surely have sympathized with the dilemma of the priest and Levite. Sirach 12.1 had cautioned that one should know the object of one's good deed before doing it; such advice played into the caution shown by the lawyer regarding who his neighbour was. It is disputed if they would be avoiding impurity because of uncertainty whether the man was dead. Bailey (1980, pp. 43–6) argues that the priest was struggling with his conscience, knowing the palaver entailed if he defiled himself with a dead body, while the Levite simply follows the priest's lead. In this he differs from Scott (1989, p. 196), who argues from evidence in the Mishnah and Talmud that 'the Priest and the Levite cannot invoke defilement as a reason not to stop and offer aid'. Casey, in contrast, has strongly emphasized that purity is central to the story (2010, pp. 301–5). The lawyer whom Jesus is directly addressing would surely have picked up this background. The Samaritan observes the Torah but is not bound by the purity laws, so he is free to obey the command of Leviticus 19.18, 'You shall love your neighbour as yourself.' The priest, however, felt himself bound by the law of Leviticus 21.1–4 which forbade priests not to defile themselves with a corpse, except that of a close relative; the Levite followed suit even though that law did not apply to him, thus demonstrating the hold which Pharisaic attempts to spread 'purity' had on people. And, in Casey's words, 'The major command of Lev. 19.18 was elevated by Jesus to the status of a principle which overrode detailed commandments of the Torah whenever there was an apparent clash' (2010, p. 304). This constituted a challenge to the whole purity system as it was in operation at the time.

Any ordinary Jews listening to the story might have indulged in knowing laughter at the behaviour of these leading functionaries. Priests and Levites would be held in low esteem, because beneath their outward cultic role their more important practical function was as agents of Rome. There might also have been secret sympathy with them – for avoidance of danger is a normal instinct.

For any hearer, the priest and Levite would certainly not appear in a heroic light, but nor would their actions be seen as especially villainous. They are caught in the dilemmas of the social system as it was at the time. Moreover, to combine vilification of them with regarding them as standing for 'Jews' or 'Judaism' as a whole, as has happened in some Christian interpretations of the story, is not only morally dangerous but also absurd as a reconstruction of how Jesus or his hearers would have thought of them. They act as many would, but their identification by the role they play in the nation would create a smirk of recognition.

The introduction of the Samaritan would cause the hearers' anticipation to rise. Where is this story going? Would it have flashed through the minds of some hearers that this third man was going to finish off the unfortunate victim and see if the bandits had left any loot for others? Be that as it may, the negative estimate of Samaritans, their sworn enemies, by Jewish hearers is soon fundamentally challenged. Where the priest had seen, and simply 'passed by on the other side' (v. 31), and the Levite had 'come to the place', seen, and passed by on the other side (v. 32), the Samaritan's behaviour is described in a series of no fewer than twelve verbs: 'He came ... he saw ... he was moved with pity ... he went ... he poured ... he bandaged ... he put him on his animal ... he brought him to an inn ... he took care of him ... he took out two denarii ... he gave them to the innkeeper ... he said "Take care of him"' (vv. 33–35).[2] This detailed concentration on the figure of the Samaritan portrays the nature of love for one's neighbour more eloquently than any abstract statement of principle could possibly do.

Note particularly the difference between the Samaritan and his two predecessors in their initial approach to the wounded man. The priest and Levite spotted the man before they reached him, it seems, and so had time to take the decision to keep their distance (vv. 31–32). The Samaritan, however, came right upon the man before he saw him (v. 33). That is the moment of truth: would the Samaritan check the body for more spoils, or beat a hasty path over or up the road, or what? Jesus puts his finger on the key: the sight of the man moves the Samaritan with pity (v. 33) and everything else flows from that. Instead of escaping the scene as far and as fast as possible, the Samaritan enters into it as deeply as possible, tending the man's wounds, taking time to bring him to a place where he could be cared for, making costly provision for his welfare, and promising to return and continue to serve his needs (vv. 34–35). As so often in Jesus' stories, it is a brief snatch of direct speech from a character's mouth through which the significance of what is going on comes fully to life (v. 35). The Samaritan's commitment to ongoing care contrasts with the fleeting flash of pity displayed by the king in The Unforgiving Slave.

One envisages a hearer responding to the character of the Samaritan in two simultaneous ways, in tension with each other. On the one hand, he or she is predisposed against this person; whoever might be expected as a 'foil' to the priest and Levite, it is not a Samaritan! On the other hand, a narrative of tender, persistent love unfolds in this person's actions, each step marking a further effort of the narrator to appeal to the hearer's sense of all that is truly admirable and human. The response of the lawyer to Jesus' closing question encapsulates this tension exactly. He cannot fail to recognize who the neighbour is, but he cannot bring himself to name him (v. 37).

It is also interesting that the Samaritan is clearly a man of some means (note the oil, the wine, the animal, the promise of indefinite financial support). This underlines incidentally the fact that wealth itself was not a negative indicator of character for Jesus (though for Margaret Thatcher to use the story as a justification for the capitalist system was very far-fetched).[3]

As for the wounded man, he remains completely passive throughout, a victim, like Lazarus in Luke 16.19–31.

Point of view

The narrator places himself firmly within the socio-cultural world of first-century Palestine. But, within this, his voice is independent, and his perspective fresh. He does not present the events of the story as a validation of one party, group, nation or kind of person over against others: it is behaviour with which he is concerned. It is the tradition which has called the Samaritan 'good', not Jesus: as a narrator he 'shows' but does not 'tell'. The robbers' victim is simply 'a man' (v. 30) – and although scholars may be right that Jesus and his hearers would have assumed that the man was Jewish, this, like much else, is left ambiguous. The conflict between ordinary members of the community, the attackers and the attacked, echoes a motif found elsewhere in Jesus' stories (e.g. The Wheat and the Weeds and The Unforgiving Slave, discussed in Chapter 7 above, pp. 97–103). The fact that neither robbers nor victim are identified keeps the focus on the Samaritan's actions. Some Jewish hearers may indeed have found themselves adopting the perspective of 'the victim in the ditch' (cf. Funk, 1982, p. 34) and thence being led to ask themselves how willing they were to receive help from an enemy. But the story itself seems to come from, and invite, a viewpoint that reorders the familiar world of violence and ethnic conflict more deeply. Both the anonymity of the victim and the use of a Samaritan as an exemplary character make this a story about 'everyman', though in a way that grates sharply against any narrow form of Jewish (or any other) nationalism. Whoever is the victim and whoever has the power to help, this is what love looks like: this is what being a neighbour means.

Plot

The 'law of three' operates here, in which the actions of the third character, the Samaritan, form the climax of the plot. The priest and Levite offer a contrasting foil, but are not to be sharply differentiated from each other, any more than the unfruitful soils in The Sower are to be sharply differentiated. The introduction of the Samaritan as the third and main character would seem, as has often been noted, like a category mistake (e.g. Scott, 1989, p. 198). 'Priest, Levite and ordinary faithful Jew' would have made more sense than 'priest, Levite and Samaritan'. This jarring surprise creates tension, as the hearers wait to hear the ultimate fate of the victim and how the Samaritan will act.

The resolution of the plot comes not through some miracle, or divine gift (as in The Sower), but through human deeds of compassion. We should also note the stress given to the story by its ending. The point to which it leads is not the final state of the victim. That is irrelevant to its purpose. The narrative finishes with the Samaritan's promise to repay the innkeeper whatever he has spent on the patient. The focus is on the Samaritan's ongoing care. That is the image which lingers in a hearer's mind.

Reflection

It is hard to seek to hear again a story as familiar as this through the ears of those around Jesus. An attempt to do so, however, convinces me of two things. First, the allegorical and Christological understanding of the story so common through much of Church history, in which the Samaritan stands for Christ coming to rescue fallen humanity, certainly does not represent the lines on which Jesus' first listeners' minds would have travelled. It does, however, remain a beautiful and poetic later 'hearing' of the story, with an integral link to its first telling, in that the Samaritan's behaviour was clearly imagined and commended by the storyteller. The tale comes from one who knew what painstaking love looked like. The allegorical reading only becomes deeply unattractive when it leads to the generalizing of priest and Levite as representatives of Judaism: but this may happen as readily with those who eschew allegory.[4] As we have seen, this is implausible as an original response to these first two characters. It also misses the category-difference between them and the third. Jesus is precisely *not* drawing a contrast between Jews and Samaritans, but rather turning the tables on his own hearers by first lulling them with uncomplimentary but believable portraits of their own leaders, with which they would have sympathized, and then using as his hero someone from a tribe they would have deeply mistrusted. The very fact that Jesus appeals so eloquently through the Samaritan's conduct to his Jewish hearers, represented in the text by Luke's lawyer, shows his belief that they too have the capacity to show such compassion.

Second, the simple moralistic understanding, so common still in popular discourse, in which the 'goodness' of the Samaritan is all that matters, not his ethnicity (nor the role played by his foils, the priest and Levite), also falls far short of genuine entry into this vivid communication. The setting, the characters, the point of view and the plot's unfolding are all, as always, integral to the story's warp and woof, and to fail to re-enter the scene is to miss its jarring challenge and urgent invitation. This is not only, in the explicit words of Jesus Luke records, 'Go and do likewise', but also – as and when the message sank in – 'reorder your mental world so that you see how universally such compassion is possible'.

The Rich Fool (Luke 12.16–21; *Thomas* 63)

Setting

With this story we are in less dramatic territory, back in the everyday world of growing crops, of the potential for accumulating wealth, on the one hand, and the reality of poverty, on the other. The latter is an unspoken truth in the story itself, though it is hinted at in the question from the crowd which prompts it (12.13). Younger sons might easily end up very dependent on the generosity of the elder to whom the greater part of the inheritance fell. Hearers of Jesus' story would have been aware both of Jewish teaching on the duty of the rich to care for the poor (e.g. Sirach 3.30—4.10) and of the wider cultural values of wealth being used for the community and of 'limited goods', which implies a negative evaluation of hoarding (Scott, 1989, p. 137). They would also have been all too familiar with the expansionist activities of the aristocracy. Sirach had given stern warnings to the rich against complacency, reminding them of their inevitable death (11.14–28), in a way that closely prefigures Jesus' story.

Character

Given this setting, the rich man in this short story would have cut a familiar figure. We should not imagine that when Jesus introduced him, listeners were neutrally or positively disposed towards such a person. This was the very kind of individual responsible for eating up more and more of what had once been land shared out among the population, and thus driving further into the impossible distance the vision of a promised inheritance for all Israel that had been kept alive since ancient times.

At the same time, there was a tradition of seeing wealth as the blessing of God: for those who believed, like Jews, that the earth and all it contained belonged to God (Ps. 24.1), this was only natural. So any negative audience response to this person would not have been on account of his wealth per se, but rather on account of the normal way the wealthy behaved. Further, if we take seriously the Lukan setting as a plausible context for the tale, a natural urge by those who felt oppressed by their social situation would be to aspire to at least a measure of the wealth currently enjoyed by their oppressors. Thus the attitudes of this rich man would not have been an object of merely spectator interest to the crowds who heard Jesus or the individuals whose dispute prompted him to tell this story. They would have brought into play those fundamental feelings, tensions and perhaps inarticulate questions which made up the staple experience of first-century Jews who were both heirs to promises of land and blessing and subject to the oppression of the rich and domination by foreigners.

The character of the rich man is portrayed not by 'telling' but by 'showing', through the internal monologue to which the narrator makes the hearers privy (vv. 17–18). This allows a vivid glimpse into his pattern of thinking. It might also have almost seduced a hearer, for that pattern seems so eminently reasonable. If there is too much grain to store in the current barns, pull them down and build bigger ones! Then (says he to his soul) you will be able to sit back, relax and live luxuriously off your accumulated wealth! Hedrick (2004, p. 96) seems a touch literalistic when he suggests that the farmer would have been thought foolish for not being prepared and for planning to pull down his existing barns at the very moment when they were needed; Jesus is summarizing the man's response to the situation rather than giving a detailed sequential unfolding of events.

If some hearers had indeed been seduced into thinking this a reasonable and sensible course of action, they would have been shaken by God's response to the man's thoughts: 'You fool!' (v. 20). Through invoking the direct perspective of God, the narrator now offers a decisive verdict on the man's character. 'Fool' is a double-edged accusation. On the one hand, the 'fool' in Israelite thinking is one who denies God's existence (Ps. 14.1). A hearer might thus evaluate the man as one whose preoccupation with his own future comfort has driven out all thanksgiving to God, whose bounty has given him this abundance, as well as the concern for others which God commands. On the other hand, folly is the opposite of wisdom and prudence, fundamental attitudes commended in Scripture because they are not only right but also good sense: they lead to true life (Prov. 2.1—3.35). So the folly of this man lay also in the lack of good sense which led him to ignore both his own mortality and the fact that the wealth in which he had sought security could only ever be 'his' on a temporary basis. He had lived in an illusion. He may have been rich, but that is shown to be an unreliable indicator of wisdom.

The story is unusual in having only one human character. This itself underlines his self-absorption. It is only God who can puncture it.

Point of view

Jesus as narrator here adopts something of the 'omniscient' stance of many of the narratives in the Old Testament. He shows us the inner workings of the man's mind, and thus reveals himself as a man of insight (Sellew, 1992). Moreover, he invites his hearers to listen to God's own verdict. Thus he leads them into this situation about which they might have mixed emotions of both resentment and envy, and offers, indirectly through the mouth of the character of God, an authoritative perspective on it.

Plot

In an engaging story, the nature and actions of the characters, in both predictable and surprising ways, are frequently the main drivers of the plot. In this case, a verdict on character forms the very climax of the plot. Indeed, this is a 'revelation' plot rather than a 'resolution' one. The question eventually answered is not 'What will happen to this man?'; his fate, like everyone else's, will be death, though perhaps an earlier death than he might have expected. (There is no time lapse before God's warning in v. 20, but this is just as likely because the issue of timing was of no interest to the storyteller as because it happened immediately after the man's own musings.) Rather, the question answered is 'How should one evaluate such an attitude?' The story's answer is plain: it is folly.

Once more we notice how significant the ending of a story of Jesus can be. The key emphasis here is not on the fact of the man's death, still less on what might happen to him afterwards. It is on God's words of judgement on his life. Again it is a snatch of direct speech in the form of a question which hangs in the air for hearers to ponder: 'And the things you have prepared, whose will they be?' (v. 20).

Reflection

This story focuses Jesus' hearers' thinking on the attitudes which lie behind familiar behaviour. As we have seen, the rich man and his thinking could have provoked mixed responses. On the one hand, this was clearly one of the élite who made life so hard for the majority of the population. On the other hand, here was a man whom God seemed to have blessed, and wasn't this the sensible course to follow for such a one? Wasn't this a state to which to aspire?

God's verdict on the rich man as Jesus presents it is nothing new in the line of Israelite teaching. The rich, like everyone else, are but as the beasts which perish (see Ps. 49, esp. vv. 10, 12 and 20). The freshness of the parable lies in the narrative invitation to imagine it.

The Barren Fig Tree (Luke 13.6–9)

Setting

A fig tree planted in a vineyard would not have been an unusual sight: 'they were used for trellising grapevines, as well as for bearing figs' (Hedrick, 2004, p. 86). The main emphasis of the setting of this story is the fact that this fig tree was found, after three years, to be unfruitful. The issue of how many years one was supposed to refrain from eating from a newly planted tree is probably a red herring; the whole logic of the plot is that the tree's lack of fruit raised the question of whether it still merited the space it was taking up. It is an everyday agricultural scene.

Character

The man, like many others in Jesus' stories, is anonymous, but we know at least that he had a gardener (v. 7). This certainly places him above the normal run of peasant farmers, perhaps in the same league as the father of the prodigal son who had hired servants (Luke 15.17). The little dialogue that takes place with the gardener in verses 7–9 is reminiscent of that in Matthew 13.24–30 between the householder and his slaves concerning the weeds growing among his wheat. It is an image of human beings sharing a basic common interest, contrasting with those pictures we find elsewhere in Jesus' stories of stark separation between those whose fundamentally shared needs should bring them together (e.g. Luke 15.11–32; 16.19–31). The impulse of each man is a natural one; on the one hand, to save the space and put the soil to more productive use; on the other, to give the fig tree another year, in the hope that the effort expended on it thus far would not go to waste.

There would perhaps have been nothing surprising in either standpoint, though Hedrick dissents (2004, pp. 86–7). He thinks that the owner is overreacting by planning to fell the tree: if it was performing a useful function in trellising the grapevines, why cut it down – when, in any case, it would still take up room in the ground, unless completely uprooted? And has not the vintner been failing in his duty if only now he thinks of manuring the tree?

Hedrick's questions are legitimate and illustrate the necessary filling in of gaps by a hearer. At the same time, as Hedrick would acknowledge, these are only possibilities, and perhaps again his imagination is working somewhat literalistically. In any case, neither character in the story is developed at all. A vivid touch is the words of the owner that tell us (as the narrator has not) that he has been looking for fruit on the tree for the last three years (v. 7).

Point of view

The dialogue between owner and gardener, though brief, is dramatized. Jesus imagines an employee (or perhaps slave) who is confident enough to challenge his master's decision. This is not a storytelling point of view which takes the side of one social group over another, but one which recognizes a shared interest in good use of land. The fact that it is the gardener in the story who has the last word suggests the storyteller's own perspective on things: the tree should be manured and given a final year to see if it will bear fruit.

Plot

In such a short story the plot structure is naturally minimal, but it is there nonetheless: an opening disappointment and tension leads to debate about how the situation is to be resolved. Though no resolution is explicitly reached in the story, the end-stress on the gardener's view invites a hearer to linger over his appeal.

Reflection

A story which suggests no evaluation of character or even resolution of plot naturally invites an allegorical interpretation, and in this case interpreters have not been slow to identify the barren fig tree with Israel. Support for such a reading is found in the incident in Mark 11.12–14, 20–21, in which Jesus curses an actual fig tree, and Mark, by interleaving the account with Jesus' prophetic action in the Temple, interprets the cursing as a sign of judgement upon Israel, or at least her ruling establishment.

A problem with any allegorical hearing of the story, however, is the dialogue between the characters. If God is seen as the owner who has the right to decide to destroy the fig tree, who then is this gardener advising him what to do? No doubt a Christological meaning has been read back into this, but it is difficult to imagine original hearers discerning this (to say nothing of the theologically misleading picture it could lead to – but that is another story). Rather than hearing the story as an allegory – a literary form entailing a series of fixed correspondences between literal terms and figurative meanings – it is better to hear it, like The Sower and The Wheat and the Weeds, as tapping into the deep-rooted link between the fortunes of Israel's land and the blessing of her God. Each of these three stories is a story of hopeful possibility despite setbacks: hope that somewhere there is good soil; hope that, if care is taken, there will be a harvest of wheat despite the weeds; hope that, given one more year, the fig tree may bear fruit. In the last two cases, a clear warning accompanies this note of hope. Eventually, the weeds will be burned; and here, the gardener concedes that if the fig tree remains unfruitful after another year then the owner can cut it down (Luke 13.9). In his reflection on the fortunes and possibilities of the land, I have little doubt that Jesus was reflecting on the fortunes and possibilities of the nation.

But we must respect the narrative rhetoric as it has come down to us. This is very understated. Even to call the story of the barren fig tree a 'warning of judgement' or 'a promise of a last chance' for Israel is too strong. As always with Jesus' stories, this is neither a direct promise nor a direct warning. It is an invitation to imagine. It leads up to a glimpse of hope, but within a mood of urgency.

The Great Banquet (Luke 14.16–24; *Thomas* 64)

Setting

The story of the great banquet unfolds against the backdrop of the social customs of Palestine under the aegis of the Roman Empire. Throwing a feast such as this was a way of displaying status and reinforcing social distinctions (Green, 1997, p. 555). Sending out servants both for the initial invitation and for the last-minute summons was established practice. The refusal of the final summons by those who, presumably, had initially accepted the invitation was an affront to the host's honour, hence his anger (v. 21). Equally, to bring in (by force if necessary) the 'poor, the crippled, the blind, and the lame' (v. 21) – and then anyone at all (presumably vagabonds) from the 'roads and lanes' (v. 23) – was an act designed as much to shame the initial invitees as it was to benefit the new ones. The host's closing words proclaim as much: 'For I tell you, none of those who were invited will taste my dinner' (v. 24).

In Israelite tradition, the banquet was an element of eschatological vision (Isa. 25.6–9). It would be 'for all peoples' (v. 6), and was bound up with the destruction of death itself (v. 8). There is also an allusion to an eschatological banquet in the Dead Sea Scrolls, at which the 'Chief Priest' and 'Messiah' take the leading places, and from which all the unclean, including those with physical blemishes, are excluded (1QSa 2.11–22, discussed by Bailey, 1980, pp. 90–1).

Character

The host would be a well-known type, an overweening landlord who could be generous on occasions, but as much for his own ends as those of others. He has a slave at his beck and call. There is no indication that hearers would regard this man as different from any others of his type. He is ready to take offence (v. 21) and wants to spite those who have declined his invitation (v. 24). The first invitees, presumably knowing the kind of person he is, are bold and offensive in their refusals, but might also win hearers' sympathy for their chutzpah. The later guests, tellingly, are neither differentiated nor individualized at all. They have little say in whether they come in or not. This no doubt reflects the attitude of the wealthy class to the majority: they are not poor individuals but 'the poor' en masse. Perhaps as strikingly as in any other of Jesus' stories, attention to character here overturns the familiar understanding of the parable as portraying a gracious God under the figure of the host.

Point of view

The portrayal of the first invitees and their excuses suggests Jesus is poking fun at the host. Here ordinary people, Jesus' hearers, are being asked to imagine a challenge to the system of honour and shame, and specifically to a lordly man who is the very embodiment of it. The system is seen as being undermined from within, in a comic fashion. It is a 'carnivalesque' scene, as described originally by Mikhail Bakhtin: 'everyday social hierarchies are turned upside down and mocked by normally suppressed voices of the culture' (Resseguie, 2005, p. 75).

There is nothing to suggest that this storyteller is in sympathy with the host. Rather, the story comes from a wry observer of customs, drawing a sequence of events on which his hearers, too, would look on with weary familiarity, lightened by the challenge to the lord's imperiousness given by the first invitees.

Plot

After a brief introduction to the story (14.16b), attention homes in on the moment when the dinner is ready and the slave is sent out to bring in the guests (14.17). With typical narrative skill, the excuses then made by 'all alike' (14.18) are exemplified by three specific cases (14.18–20), the use of direct speech making the excuses particularly vivid.

The basic conflict of the plot has now been set up, and the hearers wait to see how the host will respond once the slave has reported the excuses (14.21a). The host is angry at being shamed, but determined to have the last laugh. In order to shame in turn those who have refused his invitation, he sends the slave to go and bring in the social outcasts: 'the poor, the crippled, the blind, and the lame' (v. 21b). In the scheme of the plot, and the mindset of the host, there can be no question of an empty table. Interestingly, the slave's response is 'what you ordered has been done' (v. 22). Is there a suggestion here that this was something which had happened before, and the slave knew the master's wish before he had expressed it? Or is this a case of the foreshortening of the narrative, in which the narrator does not trouble to spell out that the slave went out and did his master's bidding, but hastens to the climax of the story? Either way, the energy of the host in seeking a full house is then seen in the fact that he sends the slave out a second time, on this occasion to 'compel' people to come in, to underline his authority and honour.

The ending of the story, characteristically, is not the mundane factual conclusion of events ('So that's what happened'), but rather a pregnant utterance: 'For I tell you, none of those who were invited will taste my dinner' (v. 24). The storyteller's focus is not on the execution of the man's wishes, though that of course is assumed, but on the pronouncement whereby he reclaims control of events. The first guests' refusal of his summons is turned into his own decisive rejection of them.

The story is thus one of how the poor, disabled, outcasts and beggars get fed as a by-product of a wealthy man's desire to reassert his honour. There is little hint of any compassion in the man's action – though, as often, it is possible to hear the story differently. Thus Green writes of the man's 'transformation' – 'He initiates a new community grounded in gracious and uncalculating hospitality' (1997, p. 562). I remain a little sceptical of the idea of 'transformation', as what is portrayed in the story is simply an individual instance, rather than a continuing pattern of hospitality (i.e. he is more similar to the king in The Unforgiving Slave than the Samaritan in The Good Samaritan). The exercise of force expected of the wealthy continues to be played out in the command to 'compel' the vagabonds to come in.

Reflection

Luke's setting of this story at a meal in a Pharisee's house (14.1) is suggestive, as is the preceding warning to Jesus' dinner-companions about seeking the place of honour at feasts (14.7–11) and encouragement to show hospitality to those who could never repay them (14.12–14). For this places the story in the context of the honour–shame culture which pervaded the Roman world and to which, in Jesus' eyes, his more well-off fellow-Jews, such as some of the Pharisees, were all too prone to try to conform.

The story of The Great Banquet, against this backcloth, does two things. First, it pricks the bubble of the honour–shame system by pointing to how easily it implodes. When those who regard themselves as social equals fall out, it is fundamentally threatened. Second, it shows how the logical consequence of such an implosion is the breaking down of all social barriers. The doors are flung open to all and sundry.

Interpreters have regularly overlooked these crucial social dynamics. Partly this is because they have taken the comment of a guest in verse 15 that precedes the story, 'Blessed is anyone who will eat bread in the kingdom of God', as indicating a turn by both Luke and Jesus from the mundane and the moral (teaching about social humility) to the supramundane and the spiritual (teaching about God's invitation to the 'heavenly banquet'). But this is surely to misunderstand both Luke and Jesus. Luke's readers and Jesus' hearers should be in no doubt by now that, for Jesus, the feast of the kingdom has already begun, here and now. 'Blessed is anyone who will eat bread in the kingdom of God' is a comment by one who sees God's kingdom as a purely future reality, without regard for its present implications. Jesus' story of the banquet, far from affirming that perspective (still less offering a coded account of salvation history), vividly pictures the present arrival of the kingdom – the banquet for which Isaiah's vision inspired hope – through the implosion of the old order.

The story thus invites self-questioning by Jesus' fellow dinner-guests and their like – continuous with Jesus' challenge to the lawyers and Pharisees in 14.1–5, when he heals a man with dropsy on the Sabbath. It shows how the system of honour which they find so alluring might itself crack open so that the poor and the crippled may flood in and eat bread. Effectively, the story asks a question, comparable to Jesus' questions in verse 3 ('Is it lawful to cure people on the sabbath, or not?') and verse 5 ('If one of you has a child or an ox that has fallen into a well, will you not immediately pull it out on a sabbath day?'). The question is this: 'If the social conventions are so fragile that they can crack apart so easily, is it not time to set a feast for the poor and outcast willingly, rather than merely to preserve one's honour?'

In the unique style of which narrative is capable – not 'teaching', not 'promising', not 'judging' – the story acts as wry prophetic comment on the society Jesus experienced. In so doing, of course, it will imply teaching, promise and judgement, but such things belong to subsequent reflection on what has been heard, not to the performance of the story.

This hearing of the story commends itself not least because there is something in the narrator's point of view and drawing of character which resonates closely with some of his other stories, in which, as here, signs of the kingdom are seen despite the fact that those in power have clearly not undergone a fundamental conversion of heart. For instance, the time of jubilee is briefly seen in The Unforgiving Slave, though the following events show that the king has lost none of his innate harshness; and justice is done for a needy widow in The Widow and the Judge, though the judge neither fears God nor has any respect for human beings.

It is worth underlining too just how much more justice this does to the story than the old allegorical reading which saw it as a picture of the refusal of God's invitation by 'the Jews' (a swingeing stereotype indeed) and his offer of salvation to 'the Gentiles'; and even to the more restrained modern readings which continue to see the excuse-making guests as symbolic of the Pharisees who are rejecting Jesus' offer of God's 'kingdom' (a reality often understood in modernity in overspiritualized terms). Both these approaches assume that hearers would ignore the familiar social scripts that the story brings into play. Both assume that a man giving a banquet in a story would lose all contemporary social associations and be straightaway understood by Jesus' hearers as a cipher for God. Both devalue the material situation and experience of 'the poor, the crippled, the blind and the lame' by taking them as, in some sense, the willing respondents to an invitation to come into God's kingdom (notwithstanding the fact that the second group, at least, are to be 'compelled' to come in). Both detach the story from the context in which Luke sets it, in which the practical manner in which one relates to one's fellow-human beings now is no mere metaphor for more ethereal realities, but is of the essence of Jesus' challenging actions and words. And the old allegorical reading, in particular, validates an anti-Jewish 'replacement' theology which is foreign to the rest of Jesus' teaching.

The story portrays an incident in which the collapse of the current social order opens the way, despite the host's fierce defence of his honour, for the hungry to be fed. It has nothing to do with anyone's repentance, but a great deal to do with the inexorable and earthly coming of God's kingdom. To those with ears to hear, it would have given a lot to think about, leading to the ultimate question: will I be a willing participant in this event (exactly as Jesus exhorts his hearers in 14.1–14), or, like the host, contribute to it despite myself, clinging to the old order?

That Luke understood the story along these radical lines is further suggested by the immediately following pericope, in which Jesus underlines to those following him just how costly it will be to be a genuine disciple, to learn his way (14.25–33). It entails not just casual (still less enforced) generosity, but giving up all one's possessions (v. 33), all those outward expressions of status and security which maintained the identity and power of the élites under whose spell some leading Jews had fallen. For the people of God not to take this radical path would be as counter-intuitive as salt losing its saltiness, if people will but think it through (14.34–35).

The Prodigal Son (Luke 15.11–32)

Setting

In Luke's narrative, the theme of table fellowship is quickly resumed. After the sayings about the cost of discipleship and the danger of salt losing its saltiness (14.25–35), Jesus is found at table again (15.2), but this time with 'sinners', rather than Pharisees. He is, in other words, willingly enacting the new social order to which he had been pointing during the meal in 14.1–24. The Pharisees and scribes remain resistant to it.

The two short parables of The Lost Sheep and The Lost Coin in 15.3–10 appeal to the hearers' sense of what is natural and humane. The logic is exactly the same as that in 14.5: 'If one of you has a child or an ox that has fallen into a well, will you not immediately pull it out on a sabbath day?' If you have lost a sheep, do you just abandon it to its fate? If you have lost a precious coin, do you just resign yourself to the fact? Well, then, can you not apply the same logic to people who are 'lost' in a more comprehensive sense than these? Do you not see their condition as something to be remedied rather than just accepted? Do you not want to recover the outcasts and restore the wholeness of the body of God's people?

It is at this point that Luke records Jesus as launching into one of his longest stories, The Prodigal Son. The realism of the setting must once more be emphasized. From start to finish, this is a story about something that might have happened in Jesus' own environment. And although the rhetoric of story is different from the rhetoric of question and logical inference which Jesus has used in the parables of the lost sheep and lost coin, the ultimate force is similar, for the story, like the shorter parables, portrays a this-worldly scene from which hearers are invited to make wider application to their this-worldly behaviour – in the light, of course, of the traditions of Torah which have shaped, and are meant to continue shaping, Israel's life.

The cultural background which enables us to imagine this scene in three dimensions has been well studied (see esp. Bailey, 1976, pp. 158–206). The younger son's request for his share of the property is a grave insult to the father, and his subsequent departure for a foreign country and behaviour there is an abandonment of the family and of the mores of Judaism for unclean territory and employment. It is shocking, but believable. Hearers may have detected in this action a desire to secure the future, knowing the soft-heartedness of his father and suspecting that things might get harder when his brother, to whom the greater part of the inheritance would fall, became head of the family. In a setting of pressure on land and the possibility of scarcity, younger siblings even in families that could employ servants (v. 19) were not necessarily secure (cf. the situation of the questioner in Luke 12.13, to whom Jesus tells the story of The Rich Fool). The father's apparently silent acquiescence in his request is remarkable. It runs directly counter to the advice of cautious Sirach (30.20–24), and his welcome of his returning son confirms that for him, reconciliation and family unity overrides all considerations of honour and shame. This is further underlined by the way he throws dignity to the winds and runs to meet his son, perhaps dangerously running the gauntlet of suspicious villagers in the process (Bailey, 1976, pp. 181–2). Meanwhile, the elder son's response to events is more conventional. Jesus' hearers would recognize his reactions as being normal and expected. His brother had broken sacred bonds and this was not to be taken lightly. The compassion and forgiveness shown by the father in the story, meanwhile, imitate the compassion of God which his children were called to imitate (Exod. 34.6–7; Lev. 19.18).

Character

The enduring power of this story lies partly in the fact that its characters are recognizable figures to whom people across all cultures can easily relate. Without denying this, we should also note that they belong to a social grouping with whom Jesus' intended listeners, the Pharisees and scribes, would particularly identify. The fact that there is an inheritance to divide, hired hands around, a ring to bestow and a fatted calf to kill certainly communicates a degree of wealth. It is probable that those being directly addressed would have imagined a family much like their own, in which honour and wealth were important to maintain (cf. Luke 14.7; 16.14). With such an identification in place from the moment Jesus mentioned monetary inheritance (15.12), hearers would be the more open to think about the behaviour Jesus describes.

This story is a beautiful instance of character being 'shown' rather than 'told'. It is the actions of the characters, and their words, whether voiced internally (vv. 17–19) or aloud (vv. 21–24, 27, 29–32), through which their qualities are revealed. Only twice does the narrator offer a direct statement about their attitudes: the father was filled with compassion (v. 20), and the older brother became angry (v. 28). These statements have all the more force for being isolated cases in the narrative. It is worth tracing in some detail how Jesus' hearers might have responded to the actions of the characters and the perspectives offered through their words.

There is no doubt that the Pharisees would have been highly disapproving of the son's shameful request and they, at least, would have had no sympathy with him.[5] After this jolt to the ears, they would have wondered how the father was going to react. The fact that he simply acceded to the request might have been interpreted variously. This man seemed to be 'one of them'. Was this a sign that he had already 'sold out' on the deeply held social values which held communities together? Was he careless of the family's honour and future? Was he simply weak? Or was there another possibility? At this stage in the story, they would not have been sure.

The son's quick departure for 'a distant country', and his squandering of the money in dissolute living (v. 13), would have hardened Pharisaic hearts towards him further. The tale of the son's decline in fortunes (vv. 14–16) would have been reassuring: he was getting what he deserved. Might opinions have started to change with the son's voicing of his thoughts and plans? Would Jesus' listeners have been moved with pity at this point? Or might there have been some who just looked forward to the humiliation the lad would receive when he returned home as a hired servant?

The real shock of the story, its invitation to its hearers to take a stance, comes with the graphic portrait of the father's actions in verse 20. The father is the one with whom Jesus' interlocutors identify, and identify profoundly. But what is he up to now? While his son was still 'far off', his father saw him (does this mean he had regularly been on the lookout for him?) and 'was filled with compassion' (the narrator thus opening a window on the kind of human emotion which an honour–shame system could easily keep concealed). He then ran, and put his arms round him, and kissed him. How did the grumblers of verse 2 respond to that?

There is still an opportunity for the son to be properly shamed; the father might yet see sense! But no; the prepared speech about being a hired servant is interrupted by the father, who commands that his son be given all the signs of restored dignity and honour – the robe, the ring, the sandals – that the fatted calf be killed and a celebratory feast be held (vv. 21–24). At this point, the whole reality of the social situation in which Jesus and his hearers are actually embroiled is brought before the hearers' eyes. Here, in the story, is a feast at which a father is welcoming with widespread arms a wastrel son who has brought shame on his house. Here, in the flesh, is Jesus sharing a table with toll-collectors and 'sinners'. Imagine the thought process: is there not something in the behaviour which is deeply natural, logical, humane? Is this not, in fact, the way things should be?

It is a moment in the story which would have caused a previously sceptical hearer of Jesus who had been softened to any degree through elements in the narrative thus far to take a deep breath. But it is not, of course, the end. The older brother, who has thus far not been seen at all, makes his appearance. In the portrayal of him outside in the field, and then hearing music and dancing as he approaches the house (v. 25), Jesus' audience are invited to see themselves, eavesdropping on the kingdom celebrations that are taking place. His anger on hearing what has happened mirrors the grumbling that Jesus has observed around him (v. 2). He then speaks directly to his father (vv. 29–31), and, as so often, direct speech throws a character's attitude into relief. His words are surely such as to arouse sympathy among hearers. He has worked like a slave for years, he has always been an obedient son, yet he has received no special treats from his father (v. 29): so where is the justice (he implies) in killing the fatted calf for this returning good-for-nothing?

It is a mistake to hear this in absolute or abstract terms as the protest (for instance) of 'justice' against 'love'. The genius of story is to portray human reactions in all their 'gut' honesty, without having to categorize them thus. The key is that this is an understandable response which can only be countermanded if there are other factors to override it. Jesus reflects back to the Pharisees just the kind of thoughts which they have entertained in response to his own praxis of welcome. As hearers they are led up to the climax of the story by a storyteller who knows how they tick and can express, with painful yet respectful accuracy, the attitude they strike.

The father's response to his older son (vv. 31–32) offers just those overriding factors which are necessary to countermand this attitude. The father, let us remember, is the character with whom, at the beginning of the story, they would have identified closely. So they must now listen closely to his verdict on the situation. And that verdict has two elements. First, he will not let his older son get away with the slight on his own generosity. The son has fundamentally misunderstood his privileges as a son, in being in his father's company and having the freedom of his possessions (v. 31). By implication, whatever he had asked for, he would have received. Second, he has misconstrued the significance of his brother's return (v. 32). For an Israelite family, such a return was nothing less than a resurrection. It was the 'finding' of something (someone) infinitely precious who had been lost. The father has already declared this to his slaves (v. 24). The older son, in other words, has been blind to the generosity of the father which he could have been enjoying all these years, and that is why he is angered and puzzled by the welcome extended to his disgraced brother. His father's response invites him to see things differently. Through that response, the storyteller invites his hearers to see things differently too.

Point of view

The skill of storytelling we have seen in this portrayal of characters by Jesus is to quite an extent the skill of creating situations which were easily recognizable by hearers, and persons who act in ways to which hearers would make a predicted response, whether closely identifying with a character, feeling antipathy towards them, or moving between the two. Jesus tells the story, in other words, from the point of view of one who is genuinely appealing to his hearers. He is not a distant narrator but one who entices an audience into emotional involvement.

Moreover, the structure of the story indicates clearly where Jesus wants to lead the Pharisees. As narrator, he neither condemns nor condones anyone in the story directly. But the portrayal of the father as vulnerable to deep compassion, and allowing natural human love to overrule considerations of honour and shame, opens a window on his own perspective.

Plot

There is skilful symmetry in the plot of this story, with the tales of the two sons mirroring each other. The younger requests his share of the inheritance (v. 12); the older had free access to his all the time, without realizing it (v. 31). The younger went off and squandered his inheritance in wild living (v. 13); the older worked dutifully for his father (v. 29). The father 'goes out' to meet them both (vv. 20, 28). While we discover the character of the younger son straightaway, it is not until the elder's speech towards the end of the story that he shows his colours. In the middle, there is the dramatic moment of the younger son's return, and the celebration that follows.

The effect of the plot is to place the two sons on a level. Both need, and are in fact recipients of, the father's love. Right up until his return, the younger son doubts it, thinking he has forfeited his family status for good – doubts only dispelled, one imagines, by the tangible signs mentioned in verses 22–23. The older son has still not realized it in his speech in verses 29–30. The question left for the hearers is whether the symmetry of the plot will be completed by his responding positively to his father's pleading, and coming to join the party.

Again we should note the power of end-stress and of the direct speech of a character, through which the narrator places weight on an aspect of the story. The father's statement in verses 31–32 hangs in the air with gentle chiding and provocation for the hearers.

By all these means, the plot foregrounds the perspective of the father. As we saw, his initial acquiescence in his son's request probably disturbed a hearer with its uncertain significance. The resolution of this uncertainty comes in two stages. First, when the younger son returns, having made his initial affront far worse, the father is revealed (to his son and to the hearers) as a man of great compassion. Second, when he goes out and pleads with his older son, his compassion is revealed as extending to him too, and entailing the desire that his family should be united. It is the father's words, finally, with which the story ends, given added weight by the fact that this is the second time he has spoken them.

Reflection

Traditionally, this story has been seen as making its appeal on the basis of the character of God, reflected in the figure of the father. Our exploration suggests that it works its magic in a more subtle way. By invoking a scene from the contemporary world, depicting characters and leading hearers through a chain of events, it appeals to the hearers' sense that, surely, primordial family love must override the demands of codes of honour. Such love and compassion are indeed rooted in the revelation of God's own character in the Scriptures, as noted above. For any hearers who had completely suppressed that sense, maybe it awakened it, or maybe it fell on deaf ears. But it is not hard to imagine Jesus telling such a story in the setting which Luke gives it: a 'parable', in the etymological sense, 'laid alongside' his own habits and practices as a means of enabling others to see them in a different light. Instead of dishonouring Israel through his actions he was working to restore its unity, and appealing to others to join him in this task.

9

Hearing the stories on the way: 2

The Shrewd Manager (Luke 16.1–9)

Setting

The story of the shrewd manager,[1] more than any other of Jesus' stories, depends on some grasp of setting not only for full appreciation but also if it is to make any sense to a twenty-first-century reader at all. The precise nature of the manager's transaction with his master's debtors has been much disputed, and how one understands the background of this will to some extent affect how one conceives the story's possible effect on the first hearers. Other readable summaries of how events might be imagined as unfolding are given in Herzog, 1994, pp. 239–58; S. I. Wright, 2000a, pp. 224–30; Bailey, 2008, pp. 334–41.

The main co-ordinates of the social matrix are reasonably clear. The manager belongs to the 'retainer' class, those in the service of the élites. Though this provided a degree of wealth and status not attainable by the majority, it remained an insecure existence. The need to keep on the right side of both one's superior and his clients called for treading a careful path. At the same time, it would be possible to supplement one's income by charging tenants, merchants or others more than required, with or without the boss's connivance – much as the collection of taxes and tolls was subcontracted by the Roman authorities to individuals who could make a business out of it. For an enterprising spirit, it was a role that could offer tangible rewards.

The insecurity of the position is seen in the manager's self-questioning after the master has dismissed him for what we might call embezzlement – exceeding, somehow, the normally expected extent of profiteering from his role, effectively depriving his master of income that might have been his. (The master, no doubt, is more concerned about his own losses than the exploitation of his clients.) As a 'white-collar worker' for, perhaps, many years, the manager is not strong enough for manual labour, and begging is socially shameful (v. 3). He therefore resolves to make himself attractive to his master's debtors as a potential employee (v. 4: they may have been the master's social equals and thus in a position to take on a manager). He seeks to ingratiate himself with them by reducing the level of their debts before they find out about his dismissal (vv. 6–7: note the 'quickly' in v. 6, cf. Bailey, 1976, pp. 98–9). It may be that this reduction is to the manager's own disadvantage (reducing or eliminating his planned 'cut'), or it may be the cancellation of an illicit interest rate charged by the master – or it may simply be a piece of shrewd dealing. As for the debtors, they are happy to be able to maintain both 'public propriety' in their dealings with the rich man, and the 'private awareness' which enables a quick transaction under the counter with the manager (on this cultural distinction see Bailey, 2008, p. 339, citing the Arabic Christian commentary by Ibn al-Tayib).

Being dogmatic about the precise nature of such a transaction in a story of Jesus when the story does not make it explicit is unwise; the storyteller may, after all, have left it deliberately ambiguous. Equally, to fail to recognize that the story does tap into the realities of economic life in the first century is to de-historicize it implausibly, and to fail to engage with how its first hearers may have responded to it. In the background, undoubtedly, are the teachings of Torah concerning justice, and especially the commands not to deprive the poor of their just due, perhaps explicitly including the prohibition of lending money at interest (see e.g. Lev. 25.8–58, esp. vv. 35–38).

The master's commendation of the manager for his shrewd action (v. 8a) is explained far more easily through imagining the social setting than it is in traditional readings which see the master as a God-figure. When he heard what his retainer had done, instead of taking further punitive action he praised him. Did he recognize a kindred spirit, and give a nod and a wink to another canny businessman? Had he already discovered a new-found popularity among his clients, who assumed that the reduction of debt had been carried out on his orders – a status which he was loath to relinquish by reversing the reduction? (Bailey, 1976, p. 102). Is the implication of his commendation that the manager was actually reinstated? Again, we cannot be sure what Jesus may have envisaged or how his hearers may have taken this. Perhaps in this and other cases what we have is a very pared-down version of a story in which originally much more detail was offered. The key point is that if this is a story (presumably fictional, but not necessarily so) earthed in the ways society worked, its conclusion is quite believable. Human beings act inconsistently and out of self-interest much of the time, and it should be no surprise that a master who starts by dismissing a servant should end up, for his own reasons, praising him.

Character

The question of character is again crucial to our appreciation of this story. The problems the tale has posed for interpreters have to a great extent revolved around the character of the master and manager and what hearers are meant to conclude from the fact that, at the end, the former praised the latter.

Once released from treating the master as a cipher for God, we are then free to take seriously not only his retainer's character but also his own. As a rich man he would almost inevitably have been regarded as one of the oppressors. Hearers will assume that he is a 'child of this age' just like his manager (v. 8b). But the final favourable judgement of Jesus on the manager's wisdom (v. 8b, if this is taken as Jesus' own reflection on the story) is also a favourable judgement on the master who praised him.

There is ambiguity at the start of the story, because all we are told is that the manager is accused of squandering the rich man's property (v. 1), not that the accusations are correct: maybe the accusers had a grudge against him for some reason. It is not in fact until the end of the story that the narrator calls him 'the unrighteous manager' (v. 8). The exhortation in verse 9 echoes this phrase, in the words translated by the NRSV 'dishonest wealth'. The most natural way to take verse 9 is as an encouragement to use wealth which has been gained dishonestly for good ends, not to continue in dishonesty. This suggests that the manager is called 'unrighteous' because that is how he is at the beginning of the story, not that the solution he found to his problem was unrighteous. Whether the initial accusations against him were true, or whether he was simply part of a category of people (like the toll-collectors) for whom 'unrighteousness' was an inescapable part of their role, that is where he started, but it is not the way he finished.

No particular judgement on him is implied by the unfolding sequence of events itself. Hearers might well not be especially sympathetic to his plight, just as they were mostly not sympathetic to the tax- and toll-farmers. Nor, however, would they have been on the side of his master. 'A rich man' (v. 1) was not a figure with whom ordinary hearers such as the disciples (the immediate recipients of this story, according to Luke) would identify. Though it was natural to arraign his manager (v. 2), it sounds like the rough-and-ready justice, without thorough investigation, to which people were all too accustomed.

With the manager's internal dialogue (vv. 3–5) listeners are invited more deeply into his world. At this point both his human predicament and his resourceful response might have warmed the audience towards him. There is a close parallel here with the preceding story, The Prodigal Son, in which the younger son also has an internal dialogue in his extremity, leading to determined resolution (15.17–19). In both cases the storyteller plays on a hearer's compassion for one who is 'down'. And when the master's commendation of the manager comes it is not for his dishonesty but for his shrewdness (v. 8). The label 'dishonest' may be the narrator's assessment of the truth of the opening accusations in verse 1, or it may reflect a more general (Pharisaic?) evaluation of the dubious and unclean nature of an occupation entailing such close collaboration with a Gentile élite. Whatever the case, despite this label, the story gradually leads a hearer to sympathize with him as one who finds himself in a tight spot and takes prudent action to escape from it.

Through its proximity to The Prodigal Son, and through the link word 'squandered' (15.13; 16.1), Luke invites us to see the manager in a similar light to the prodigal. Neither character is idealized; indeed, both start out as disreputable. But, by the ends of their respective stories, both are seen to have taken wise action to escape from their plight. It is significant, too, that the wise action taken by the manager is a forgiving action. Just as hearers witness a crumbling of social hierarchy in the story of the great banquet, so they glimpse a hint of jubilee emerging in the exigencies of the cut-throat world of the management of great estates.

Point of view

The story is told from the point of view of one who knows the ways of the world and wants listeners to observe them to their own benefit. Specifically, through (perhaps) surprising the listeners with the master's commendation of the manager, the storyteller emerges as one who can see good in actions which, from another perspective, look shady or self-serving. Hearers are invited to see that the cancellation of debt, on however limited a scale and with whatever motives, cannot be a bad thing – leading as it does to an improvement in relationships all round.

Scholars have often discussed where 'the parable proper' ends – in particular, whether verse 8b is to be taken as part of the story or is a comment external to it. An awareness of 'point of view' makes such discussions largely redundant. Luke almost certainly regards the saying in verse 9, beginning 'And I tell you', as a saying of Jesus, since Luke never uses such an 'I' to refer to himself as author except in his Prologues (Luke 1.3; Acts 1.1). That means that verse 8b, too, is most naturally read as Jesus the storyteller's observation on the story, an overt clue to 'point of view'. It is then seen as no accident that the manager is both shrewd and a 'child of this age'. It is precisely that paradoxical conjunction to which Jesus wants to draw attention. The 'children of light' to whom the 'children of this age' are contrasted may be an ironic reference to how some more pious Jews (such as those at Qumran (1QM1) or perhaps the Pharisees thought of themselves). It may also, or instead, be a term to describe the children of the new age whom Jesus is calling, but who are slow to catch on to their vocation, that is, the disciples. Once more, therefore, we can detect behind the story the eye of an independent observer, seeking to woo those around him to a new evaluation of character and behaviour.

Plot

The plot of this story, like that of The Prodigal Son, contains an element of character development. Through the pressure of impending dismissal, and prudent thinking, the manager reaches a better place than where he was before (and so, maybe, does his superior). To label the story 'the dishonest manager' is therefore unhelpful, as are any hearings of this and other stories which regard them in static terms. That is to overlook a fundamental feature of plots – they entail the changing of situations and, often, people.

It is a reasonable assumption that the puzzles in the plot of this story that confront a modern reader would not have puzzled Jesus' hearers. The plot's logic can be explained by attention to the setting in Jesus' social world, as explored above, though certain details admit of different possible solutions.

But it is also worth highlighting the gaps or leaps in the action, which occur in the story in the form in which it has reached us. These point by contrast to the elements which are emphasized and which are therefore to be taken as most important for early hearers.

As we saw above, the opening scene seems to move from accusation to sentence without trial (vv. 1–2). Although the master asks for an 'accounting' (v. 2), this is more in the nature of a full report of the manager's misdeeds before his departure, for the master seems already to have decided the outcome: 'you cannot be my manager any longer' (v. 2). It is possible, though, that the latter statement is to be heard more as a threat than an actual dismissal, with an implied 'if these accusations turn out to be true' unspoken. Whatever the case, the emphasis is on the judgement of the manager and the urgent need for him to take self-preserving action. Thus the plot moves straightaway, without any recorded answer by the manager to the master, to the manager's internal musings about what to do (vv. 3–4), and from there straight to his execution of his plan (vv. 5–7). The assumption must be, as Bailey recognizes (1976, pp. 98–9), that there is time for him to do this (1) before he is physically evicted from his position, (2) before the master can stop him and (3) before the debtors find out that his authority as manager is under threat of being removed – although nothing of this has been stated. Finally, we are told nothing of the debtors' responses to the manager's action, but the story moves straight to its climax, the master's praise. This is followed by the narrator's affirmation of that praise in verse 8b. Jesus, as if to counteract any doubt on the issue, widens out the commendation into a general contrast between the respective wisdom of the 'children of this age' and the 'children of light'.

All this clearly indicates where the weight of the story lay as it was remembered: on the decisive action of the manager and its commendation as shrewd by his master. This does not reduce the story to 'one point'. It does, however, illuminate its stress, which lies not on the actual outcome for the manager (as it would in a 'resolution' plot) but on the evaluation of his decision-making (thus making this a 'revelation' plot). By seeing 'wisdom' in this, Jesus also sees wisdom in the master who commends it – who is, like the manager, a 'child of this age'. The story thus hangs in the hearers' consciousness as a vignette of common sense from the everyday world, in which self-interest and the release of debts are seen to coalesce.

Reflection

Like Jesus' other stories, that of the shrewd manager starts with a quite specific context but transcends it. Through focusing on a single chain of events, it invites a fresh perspective on the world more widely. Especially, the narrator's comment in verse 8b draws attention to the story's suggestion of the truth that 'children of light' (whoever they are, or think they are) can learn a thing or two from the 'children of this age'.

The sayings that Luke has collected in 16.9–13 sit more comfortably with the story than has often been assumed. Verse 9 clarifies that Jesus' commendation of the manager's action does not imply any overvaluation of material security. On the contrary, the 'dishonest wealth' will one day 'fail'. The important thing about the manager's train of thought was the making of 'friends'. Such friendship, Jesus implies, will last. This is one of those eternal realities that can begin right now among those who are, to all outward appearances, 'children of this age', and who will be welcomed into 'the eternal homes', literally 'the tents of the age to come'.[2] The faithfulness with 'dishonest wealth' which Jesus urges in verses 10–12 is not presented as a contrast to the manager's initial supposed 'squandering' but rather as a description of how he acted under threat of dismissal. The wealth that he and his master regularly gained was certainly, to an extent, dishonest. But his action of remitting part of the debts was a reversal of this, a faithful use of that which had been unjustly gained – similar to that of Zacchaeus in Luke 19.8. Verse 13 then has a much more immediate reference to the story than is possible if the 'rich man' is read as God. The manager has, in fact, decided to serve God in preference to his wealthy master, through action which is just and merciful.

Laid beside these sayings, the situation of Jesus' mainly poor hearers, that of his Pharisaic opponents, and the immediately preceding story The Prodigal Son, The Shrewd Manager puts lots of questions out in various directions. Are people to be judged by their social position, or their action? By what they have been in the past, or by what they are and might be now? How might it be possible for other individuals who find themselves for many reasons on the wrong side of Torah, or a disgrace in a system of honour, to find a good way out and forward? How should one spot the signs of God's kingdom, his coming new age, in the midst of this present one (cf. Luke 17.20–21)? What constitutes wisdom in the midst of a cut-throat world and economy? Where, indeed, is wisdom to be found? And if it can be stumbled on by a self-interested manager and his master like this, what potential might be realized through people seeking it deeply, wholeheartedly and with insight into what constitutes it?

The Rich Man and Lazarus (Luke 16.19–31)

Setting

The contemporary realities of wealth and poverty are immediately invoked as Jesus embarks on the story of the rich man and Lazarus. The contrast between the two is stark: the first dressed in all the marks of luxury, and displaying his wealth in self-indulgent daily feasts (v. 19), the second a poor man who could not satisfy himself with the rich man's leftovers, whose body was covered with sores and licked by dogs (vv. 20–21). The vivid details of the rich man's 'purple and fine linen' and the dogs licking Lazarus' sores are what narrative critics call 'props', filling out the setting with colour (Resseguie, 2005, pp. 105–8). All the evidence points to the fact that this was not an unrealistically exaggerated contrast. The story does not, of course, imply that all the rich were so extravagant (or so careless of the poor), or that all the poor were in as parlous a state as this beggar. By the use of these opposite examples, however, Jesus epitomizes the social problems of his time and place, and invites reflection not only on the fate of individuals but also on economic realities generally (cf. Bauckham, 1991).

The contrast is made the more poignant by the fact that Lazarus lay at the rich man's gate. This proximity is Lazarus' particular tragedy, and the rich man's particular judgement. It is a contrast continued beyond death itself, since the rich man is afforded the fine burial expected for such a one. Lazarus, by implication, is left without any burial at all (16.22).

The post-mortem scene reflects standard pictures of the afterlife. So the 'setting' of Jesus' story continues to be the 'world' of his contemporary hearers, their world of belief as well as their social environment. It is clearly a particularly Jewish 'take' on the afterlife, with Abraham taking pride of place as the father of the nation. It is also significant that he was regarded as legendary in his hospitality, no doubt in view of his entertainment of YHWH's messengers (Gen. 18.1–8). The Jewishness of the story assumes even more significance when we get to verse 29 and Abraham responds to the rich man that his brothers should listen to Moses and the prophets, who had enjoined care for the poor (see, classically, Deut. 15.7–11; Amos 2.6–8). Up until this point, it is not clear whether the rich man is Jewish or Gentile, whereas Lazarus' Jewishness is assumed from the start: his name is a Rabbinic form of Hebrew *Eliezer*, meaning 'God helps'.

Character

How the characters in the story would be 'heard' is vital. The point has often been made that the rich man does nothing evil while the poor man does nothing good. This is true on the level of the narrator's explicit comment, though it runs the risk of underplaying the social evaluations that a hearer would give to the scenario without any need for such comment. At the same time, this 'inaction' is important to note, for the narrator's concern is surely more with the character of current society than that of any individuals within it (cf. again Bauckham, 1991). It is the whole state of affairs which is being held up to scrutiny.

Furthermore, the rich man's inaction itself speaks volumes. He could, one imagines, at least have ensured that Lazarus had a roof over his head and enough to eat. He is not being asked to care for the poor on the other side of the world, which, of course, is not yet a 'global village', nor even on the other side of town, but for a specific poor man who lies at his own gate. Later, when we discover that the rich man is from a Jewish family, we read back into this inaction a neglect of Moses and the prophets (v. 29). Bailey notes that even though he can see Lazarus in Abraham's bosom, he doesn't speak to him: he 'never talks to untouchables' (2008, p. 387).

The lack of any character portrayal for Lazarus highlights his role as a victim, utterly dependent on the generosity of others. It deflects thought away from any idea that Lazarus is a moral example in his life. The rich man is undoubtedly a negative figure, while Lazarus in his passivity points entirely to the need for help from beyond. Some, however, might see significance in his silence after death (cf. Bailey, 2008, p. 389): certainly there is no hint of gloating or vindictiveness against the rich man.

Point of view

The narrator adopts the oblique stance of one who observes his surroundings, knows the traditions of his people, and creates a fiction to focus on a possible course of events. It is the viewpoint of one who claims insight into unseen reality. We have seen this before in the internal speeches made by characters in Jesus' stories (12.17–19; 15.17–19; 16.3–4). Now the narrator envisages a whole tableau beyond death, and in particular a dialogue between Abraham and the rich man.

The point that Jesus is not here teaching about the nature or geography of the afterlife, but adopting a standard view, is clarified by attention to the narrative-critical category 'point of view'. Jesus stands not in a place of new insight with respect to the fact of ultimate judgement and separation between the righteous and the wicked. He uses the mythological imagery available to him. He does, however, stand in a place of new insight into the kind of people to be classed in the category 'wicked'. The one who cried 'Blessed are you who are poor' and 'Woe to you who are rich' (Luke 6.20, 24) dramatizes in this story the complete reversal of the overeasy reading of circumstances which labelled the rich 'blessed', not the poor. He does so not as a statement but as a narrative fiction.

Plot

We have already noted a striking feature of this plot: before their respective deaths, the characters take no action – beyond the daily business of survival, which they undertake in grossly opposing ways: the rich man eating and dressing far more lavishly than necessary, the poor man barely keeping body and soul together. In their inaction the rich man is culpable and the poor man pitiful.

It is after death that the plot gets under way. Hearers learn first of the poor man's destination (v. 22), which comes as immediate relief after the picture of his suffering. To learn then that the rich man is in Hades, suffering torments, would be a jolt. For those who themselves have felt the impact of such people's callous neglect, the jolt might not be unwelcome. For those whom Luke names as Jesus' interlocutors at this point, '[th]e Pharisees, who were lovers of money' (16.14), it would be much more uncomfortable.

Listeners would perhaps envisage that for the rich man to be able to see Abraham with Lazarus at his side would only increase the torture (v. 23b). Yet it might also suggest that there is still hope for the rich man. His pleading to Abraham in verse 24 may have aroused sympathy, just as the musings of the lost son (15.17–19) and the dismissed steward (16.3–4) may have done. But Abraham's response (16.25–26) indicates that this plot is going to take, in Via's terms (1967) a 'tragic' direction rather than a 'comic' one. There is poetic justice in the reversal they are now experiencing – the one who received the 'good things' is now in agony, the one who received 'evil things' is now comforted. And, crucially, a great gulf is now fixed between them: a graphic image of the limit set by death on the time within which humans need to discover the way of obedience to their judge, the time of testing which they are allowed. The 'way out' which the lost son and the dismissed manager found in time has been found by this rich man, but too late.

Hearers might have expected this to be the end of the matter. But the desperation of the rich man (and perhaps also a shred of compassion?) shows itself in his plea to send Lazarus to his brothers, in order to warn them (v. 28). Will the horror of the situation be somehow compensated, though partially, if those still alive can be scared by the appearance of a dead man into conformity with the will of God? Abraham's response is, on one level, encouraging. 'They have Moses and the prophets; they should listen to them' (v. 29). They have, in other words, the guidance they need to live responsibly before God. The rich man is not convinced: 'if someone goes to them from the dead, they will repent' (v. 30). Abraham's final, laconic answer echoes the rebuke that Jesus gives to those who seek 'signs' (Luke 17.20–21): 'If they do not listen to Moses and the prophets, neither will they be convinced even if someone rises from the dead' (16.31).

Some scholars have treated the dialogue in verses 27–31 as an addition to the original story. It is certainly conceivable that on different occasions Jesus extended or abbreviated stories, or that other material has been added by Luke or others to an original story. But these later verses can plausibly be read as the climax of the plot of a single story. What they do is to bring the focus of the story back to the world of the living, where it started. This is entirely in keeping with the rest of Jesus' stories, where the focus is on the world of the living throughout. Again the law of end-stress is vital. On the evidence of his recorded words overall, Jesus was more likely to direct attention to the challenge that lies before humans in life than to the nature of their experience after death.

Reflection

Taken together, these comments build up to a reading of the story as drawing on both a familiar aspect of the social scene and familiar beliefs about the afterlife to suggest a shockingly unfamiliar scenario: a rich man facing the pain of irreversible negative judgement. As a story, its rhetoric does not hector or indict individuals directly. Nor does it 'teach' in a direct fashion. Nevertheless, it addressed a deeply uncomfortable question mark to Jesus' contemporaries. It partakes of a similar prophetic character to Mary's song in Luke 1.46–55, the Beatitudes and Woes in Luke 6.20–26, and a number of Jesus' other stories. The banquet is thrown open to all in the midst of an oppressive order (14.16–24). But where it is not, surely it will be, once that order's claims on human life have crumbled (16.19–31).

The Widow and the Judge (Luke 18.2–5)

Setting

This short story is vaguely set 'in a certain city' (v. 2). 'City', of course, denotes in the ancient world a much smaller conurbation than today. Perhaps the key thing about this 'city' is that it was a community large enough to have someone appointed to deal with disputes. It could be a city anywhere, but the probable Jewishness of the judge is suggested by the phrase 'who neither feared God nor had respect for people'. For a Jew such as Jesus, such attributes would be so normal in a Gentile judge as not to be worth mentioning. What gives the story its opening interest is presumably the fact that this judge was a Jew, from a culture steeped in Scriptures which enjoined the fear of God and respect for people as foundational to life (e.g. Prov. 1.7–19). In Jewish terms, then, the 'city' may simply have been a community large enough to have a synagogue. Socially, the vulnerable position of widows in ancient society was proverbial, and the Torah commanded Israelites to look after them, because God cares for them (Exod. 22.22; Deut. 10.18). In this case the widow's 'opponent' was no doubt someone whose avarice or scheming was likely to deprive her of her livelihood.

Words from Sirach 35.14–18 may have echoed in Jesus' hearers' memories as they heard Jesus' story, especially verses 16–17: 'He [God] will not show partiality to the poor; but he will listen to the prayer of one who is wronged. He will not ignore the supplication of the orphan, or the widow when she pours out her complaint.' This makes our reading of the judge's character interestingly ambiguous, as we shall see.

Character

The character of the judge as it would have been perceived has been disputed, with Hedrick arguing that his having 'no respect for people' should be taken in a positive sense as meaning that he showed no bias or partiality, as in the instruction of Sirach 35.16, and especially Leviticus 19.15: 'You shall not render an unjust judgement; you shall not be partial to the poor or defer to the great' (Hedrick, 1994, p. 196). In that case, however, the judge would seem to have a split character, for presumably if he did not fear God he would not have regard for the precepts of Torah – or would he? Hedrick argues that 'not fearing God' would have meant, at the period, not following all the detailed practices of the Torah, and so would not have been heard as negatively as we might assume (p. 195). This would allow for some basic sense of right and wrong in observing Torah principles, and showing deference to no one is, after all, just the attitude any society wants in a good judge.

Perhaps it is better, though, to see him as one of those genuinely ambivalent characters so familiar from Jesus' stories, stuck on the horns of a dilemma. Has he imitated one element of Sirach's picture of the just God – showing no partiality – while ignoring another – attending to a widow's complaint? This is seen in his continued refusal of the widow in verse 4a, since the widow has been asking for justice, not favouritism, and to fail to do such justice is to fail in obedience to Torah. The judge's internal musing in verse 4 (a familiar feature, by now) shows that he has not changed his character even when he decides to give in to the widow. He is simply fed up with her – or possibly, depending on the translation of the Greek *hupōpiazē*, afraid of being beaten up by her. The narrator's observation in verse 6, 'Listen to what the unjust judge says', confirms what the story itself implies about his character: he is blind to a vital element of justice. I suspect, *pace* Hedrick, that this one-sided view of what justice entails is because he indeed does not 'fear the Lord' in any sense.

With the introduction of 'a widow' (v. 3), an audience was likely to envisage a pitiful figure, perhaps even totally passive, like Lazarus in Luke 16.19–20. They could not have been more wrong. Persistence, the quality she has become famous for, is repeatedly stressed in verses 3–5. She 'kept coming' to him (imperfect tense, v. 3a). 'For a while' the judge refused her (v. 4a). She 'keeps bothering' him (v. 5a), while her 'continual coming' (literally 'coming to the end') threatens to wear him out, or perhaps end in fisticuffs (v. 5b). She is no pitiful pleader for mercy, but a dogged fighter for justice.

Point of view

This feisty little scene is observed with wit. One can see the storyteller enjoying poking fun at the judge. He gets his come-uppance at the hands of a poor but dogged woman. It is the sort of event of which Jesus might have heard. Whether or not he had, his hearers will have been entertained and provoked by it, as comedy or carnivalesque. A spirit of hope also lies behind it. Are godless and careless organs of justice not, perhaps, as immoveable as they usually seem? This note of hope is explicitly enhanced by the narrator's comments following the story (vv. 6–8a), though qualified by the musing of verse 8b about whether the Son of Man will find faith on earth.

Plot

The plot of the story draws explicit attention to the fact that the character of the judge does not change, since its resolution, emphasized by the direct speech of the judge and its position at the end, makes this clear in the judge's own words: 'Though I have no fear of God and no respect for anyone, yet because this widow keeps bothering me, I will grant her justice, so that she may not wear me out by continually coming' (v. 5). In other words, the plot highlights the potential of sheer persistence to win victory despite human intransigence.

Whose story, though, is this? The judge's or the widow's? Walther Bindemann (1995) has proposed that because of close structural similarities between this story and The Shrewd Manager, it is to be seen as the judge's. The manager's master is pushed by events into reversing his initial negative treatment of his retainer; the judge is forced into retreating from his disregard for the widow. Both stories puncture the pomposity of figures with authority, in a 'comic' way levelling out the social landscape.

The similarity is suggestive. However, this is surely to be seen as the widow's story. The conflict to be resolved is the suit brought against her by her opponent, and it is then intensified by the judge's lack of action. The climax of the story is the judge's determination that justice be done, notwithstanding his unchanged character. Interestingly, the storyteller does not explicitly say that justice has gone in the widow's favour, though surely that is to be assumed. And the chief agent of that resolution is the sheer persistence of the widow.

Reflection

In its short compass, the story of the widow and the judge brings into striking focus the pattern we have seen in several other stories. Justice is done, notwithstanding the motives and characters of those who have it in their power – whether the king in Matthew 18.23–35, the host in Luke 14.16–24 or the master and his retainer in Luke 16.1–8. An unlikely hero emerges in the figure of the widow, like the figure of the retainer in Luke 16.1–8. An audience is invited to envisage signs of God's kingdom appearing under the very noses of the authorities who oppose it.

The Pharisee and the Toll-Collector (Luke 18.10–13)

Setting

The next short story in Luke's journey narrative follows immediately after The Widow and the Judge, and Jesus' reflections on it. The setting is unambiguously Jewish: the Jerusalem Temple – the place where Jesus himself is heading. This was the focus not only of Jewish faith but also of Jewish national identity. First built under King Solomon, destroyed by Nebuchadnezzar of Babylon, rebuilt after the exile and recently renovated in magnificent fashion by King Herod the Great, this was not only a place of regular pilgrimage for Jews but also – if Josephus' *Jewish War* is to be believed (*Bel.* v. 21, 564) – the destination of worshippers and offerings from the Gentile world. It was the place where, through the regular offering of sacrifices, atonement was made for sins and the unclean restored to the life of the community (cf. Luke 17.14). It is possible that it was the sight of smoke rising from a sacrifice that inspired the toll-collector's prayer, 'make atonement for me, a sinner' (Bailey, 1980, p. 154). Here, in Jewish belief, was the place where God lived (Pss. 46; 48), the God whose praise reached to the ends of the earth (Ps. 48.10). What might occur in this place was therefore going to be of great interest to any Jewish hearer. For Jesus' contemporaries, however, it was not only a focus for faith, but compromised by being the centre of an oppressive system in which tithing for the Temple added to the burden of taxation by the Romans (Herzog, 2005, pp. 164–5). The Pharisees were enforcers of this system.

Bailey (2008, pp. 350–3) has identified close thematic similarities between this story and Isaiah 66.1–6. Perhaps those listening to Jesus would have picked up some of these: God's assertions that his real home is heaven and earth (v. 1); that he looks to the humble and contrite (v. 2); that animal sacrifices are not a necessary sign of true devotion (vv. 3–4); and that those who 'tremble at his word' will be vindicated, and their enemies put to shame (vv. 5–6).

Character

The two characters are familiar from Jesus' world: the Pharisee, guardian of Jewish tradition and advocate of intensified Torah-observance, closely associated with the ruling priestly hierarchy; the toll-collector, employee of the Roman rulers, unclean in many Jewish eyes, and probably ready to exploit his neighbours. As is well known, the outcome of the story would have contradicted the expectations of most Jews, for it is the toll-collector who returns to his house 'justified', 'vindicated', rather than the Pharisee. He is the one who has been shown to be in the right. In Herzog's words, 'the toll collector repents of his role in an oppressive system, the Pharisee does not' (2005, p. 165). (The language of vindication and justice closely echoes that used in The Widow and the Judge, and Jesus' comment in v. 8.)

As is also regularly pointed out, however, it is important for us who know the end of the story not to pass judgement on the Pharisee too soon. It is likely that this was a very realistic picture. Many of Jesus' hearers, on visiting the Temple, would have seen pious Jews praying like this, 'by himself' (v. 11), aloof from others from whom they might contract uncleanness. The Pharisee's prayer simply voices what his posture already declares: that he is thankful to be a good Torah-abiding Jew, not like so many others. His practice exceeds the demands of the law (fasting twice a week; giving a tenth of all his income, not just the prescribed commodities of grain, wine and oil, v. 11) (Bailey, 1980, p. 152). This was outstanding piety as most people would recognize it, genuine and well intentioned, even though, in Jesus' view, its practitioners had serious blind spots.

The toll-collector, by contrast, stands 'far off', presumably not only from the Pharisee but also from the inner sanctuary of the Temple. Not even adopting the usual upward-looking attitude of prayer, he beats his breast as a sign of mourning and beseeches God to show mercy to him as a sinner.

It is only the narrator's comment, with his characteristically penetrating insight (cf. Sellew, 1992), which tells us the outcome (v. 14a). No visible change has occurred in either man as they leave the Temple precincts for their homes. Nothing is said about any experience they might or might not have had of God or his holiness or his mercy. One is just seen to be in the right rather than the other. The narrator sees the tale as exemplifying the thrust of old wisdom: 'all who exalt themselves will be humbled, but all who humble themselves will be exalted' (v. 14b; cf. 1 Sam. 2.3–8; Sirach 10.13–15). This proverb points a hearer to a quality of behaviour that lies deeper than outward appearance and invites the conclusion that, when it comes to character, things are not always what they seem. There is also a hint of the danger of identifying piety with one element of obedience to the neglect of others. The Pharisee, maybe, was genuinely grateful for his privileges as a Jew, and genuinely desirous of pleasing God through the enthusiastic observance of various precepts. But the wisdom of humility and self-knowledge was missing.

Point of view

Behind the story lies again the eye of a keen observer. The perspective is independent but not neutral. In that sense, it is similar to that of the so-called 'omniscient narrator' of much Old Testament narrative. Hearers are invited to weigh up two contrasting stances, to peer beneath the surface of a common event and see reality beyond appearance. Having listened in to the prayer of the Pharisee in which he lumps the toll-collector together with various types of lawbreaker, hearers are also invited by the ending of the story to question the easy evaluations which one group may make of another.

Plot

The two worshippers, Pharisee and toll-collector, go 'up' to the Temple (v. 10) and then 'down' to their homes (v. 14). The plot is enclosed between these points. Whereas at these beginning- and end-points the physical movements of the two characters are the same, their characters move in opposite directions in a hearer's estimation, as it were in a cross-shape. The Pharisee starts high but is brought low; the toll-collector starts low but is brought high.

This is a 'revelation' plot similar to those of The Rich Fool (Luke 12.16–21) and The Rich Man and Lazarus (Luke 16.19–31). Its goal is not the resolution of a crisis or conflict (although the 'crisis' of the toll-collector's sinfulness is indeed resolved) but the revelation of a truth. The revelation of that truth is in tension with expectations and thus invites hearers to reframe the way in which they see people.

Reflection

The form of narrative means that this story cannot be construed as a judgement by Jesus on all Pharisees, whether as a group or individuals; nor, of course, is it a validation of all toll-collectors and their like. It invites its hearers to contemplate a possibility – that when it comes to familiar 'types' from their society, stereotypes can be deeply misleading. Specifically it prompts the audience to realign their faculty of judgement so that rightness is calibrated according to the deepest, widest wisdom instead of particular outward manifestations.

The Pounds (Luke 19.12–27)

Setting

The situation envisaged in this story is of a kind known from Josephus. The opening is non-specific – 'A nobleman went to a distant country to get royal power for himself and then return' (v. 12). But Jesus' hearers would immediately have thought of occurrences such as the accession of Archelaus, son of Herod the Great, when Herod died in 4 BCE. Most interpreters of the story, however, treat this as little more than realistic colouring for an essentially spiritual or eschatological message about the return of Christ: for example, Bailey (2008, p. 398) writes of the Archelaus story as 'background'. Elizabeth Dowling (2007) has taken it with much more seriousness, leading, I think, to a much more credible hearing of the story as originally told.

It is worth recounting Josephus' story in detail. For convenience I will follow the version in his *Jewish War*, though it is also found in his *Antiquities*, 17.219–22, 299–318, 339–44.

Herod's final will bestowed powers over his kingdom on three of his sons (Jos., *Bel.* I, 670). Philip was granted Trachonitis and the surrounding area, Antipas was to be tetrarch of Galilee, while Archelaus was to be king. However, Caesar himself (Augustus) was acknowledged as Herod's ultimate executor. Therefore, Josephus writes, 'Archelaus was to take Herod's ring to Caesar, with the state documents under seal.' Indeed, Archelaus refused the crown from the enthusiastic populace of Jericho until he had been to Rome for the confirmation of his succession (*Bel.* II, 7). Before he set off, however, he had to deal with a clamour for punishment of some of those responsible for what was seen as sacrilegious behaviour sanctioned by his late father. Unable to quieten them by persuasion, he did so by violence, killing around three thousand even as they were sacrificing in the Temple (*Bel.* II, 7–13).

Leaving Philip in temporary charge, Archelaus set off for Rome. He was accompanied by various other members of Herod's family, 'who professed the intention of supporting his claim to the throne, but whose real purpose was to denounce him for his lawless actions in the Temple' (*Bel.* II, 15). This was just the first of several protests against Archelaus' claim. Sabinus, the procurator of Syria, arrived in Jerusalem to sort out Herod's estate (*Bel.* II, 26). Antipas, Archelaus' brother, laid claim to the kingdom on the basis of an earlier will of Herod, and was supported by Sabinus, who sent letters of denunciation of Archelaus and praise of Antipas to Caesar via the family members

accompanying Archelaus (*Bel.* II, 26). There were widespread disturbances throughout Palestine (*Bel.* II, 46–86). In Rome, another group of Jews had been permitted to come to plead for 'racial autonomy' (Herod having been an Idumaean not a Judean), preferring direct rule from Rome via its officials in Syria to the reign of the Herod family. They listed Herod's tyrannies before Caesar, citing Archelaus' slaughter of citizens in the Temple as a sign that he would surely rule in the same manner as had his father (*Bel.* II, 86).

After hearing from both Archelaus' accusers and his advocate Nicolaus, Caesar Augustus' verdict was a significant adjustment to Herod's last will. Archelaus was to receive half the kingdom, but only the title 'ethnarch'; he was not to be called 'king' until he had shown himself worthy of it. His brother Philip was now to be a tetrarch as well as Antipas. In effect, Herod's kingdom was divided into three. Archelaus was to rule Idumea, Judea and Samaria; Antipas, Perea and Galilee; and Philip, Batanea, Trachonitis and Auranatis. Other members of Herod's family were granted property, and some Greek cities were removed from his kingdom and added to the Roman province of Syria (*Bel.* II, 93–100).

Archelaus' return to his territory was not the end of his troubles or those of his subjects. Josephus tells us that he 'treated not only Jews but even Samaritans so brutally that both peoples sent embassies to accuse him before Caesar, so that in the ninth year of his rule he was banished to Vienne in Gaul, and his property transferred to Caesar's treasury' (*Bel.* II, 111). His territory was brought under direct Roman rule. In the time of the first Roman procurator, Coponius, 'a Galilean named Judas tried to stir the natives to revolt, saying that they would be cowards if they submitted to paying taxes to the Romans, and after serving God alone accepted human masters' (*Bel.* II, 118).

All this proves highly illuminating not merely as background for the story of the pounds but also as a way into its entire mood and logic. That a person such as Archelaus should have wanted to make sure his money was working for him in his absence (v. 13) is eminently believable, as is the total amount entrusted: ten pounds – two and a half years' wages for a labourer, but a readily disposable amount for Herod's son. (There is an inconsistency between the ten slaves at the beginning of the story and the three who come forward later, verses 16–18. Presumably hearers are meant to take this as the storyteller focusing on the percentage profit gained, rather than the quantity of the original sum: the first slave made a profit of 1000 per cent, the second of 500 per cent, the third of nothing, and the reduction to three must be something to do with the economy of the storytelling, focusing on key distinctions and not enumerating unnecessary details: cf. Bultmann, 1963 (1921), p. 190.) The note that 'the citizens of his country hated him and sent a delegation after him, saying "We do not want this man to reign over us"' (v. 14), closely echoes Josephus' account of the embassy permitted to come to Caesar to plead for 'racial autonomy' but also reflects, in summary form, the several different strands of opposition to Archelaus' rule that Josephus describes. In verse 15, the high-born man returns 'having received the

basileian'. The NRSV's translation of *basileia* as 'royal power' rather than 'kingdom' in verses 12 and 15 suggests that the translators recognize the allusion to Archelaus, who was indeed given some of the powers of royalty but without the title of king.

The story continues in a thoroughly realistic way. Of course the newly affirmed princeling would want an account from the slaves whom he had left to trade with his property (v. 15). It is not surprising that he should reward success in this venture not simply with continued employment but with political power over cities (vv. 16–19). Nor is it at all out of character that he should give the third slave short shrift for just burying the money (vv. 20–23). Not only did this show a lack of courage and common sense; it showed also a foolish lack of logic with regard to the owner's character. If the slave knew his master to be a hard man and if he found himself unable or unwilling to trade, why did he not at least put the money on deposit at a bank (v. 23)?

The punishment of the third slave is simply to take away his pound and give it to the one who has shown himself most adept in trade (v. 24). This is, again, thoroughly credible, and a normal pattern still, *mutatis mutandis*, in finance and trade: those unwilling to take any risks are bound to lose out – the principle enunciated by the nobleman in verse 26. It is a much milder punishment than that meted out to the 'wicked slave' in the similar story in Matthew 25.14–30. The nobleman in this story in Luke has bigger fish to fry: he will execute vengeance on those who had protested against his rule by having them slaughtered before him (v. 27).

Josephus' account of Archelaus' brief and brutal rule demonstrates this story of Jesus to be perfectly realistic. One does not need to suppose that Jesus and his hearers knew all the details as Josephus chronicles them. It is clear that the kind of thing which happened in the story Jesus tells is exactly the kind of thing which *did* happen, and it would be the stuff of common conversation. Archelaus' deposition took place in 6 CE, within the lifetime of Jesus and his hearers, a mere two and a half decades or so before Jesus will have told this story. Moreover, such an episode epitomized a wider pattern of the period. Client kings only held their kingdom by the will of Caesar; but their subjects by no means always just accepted Caesar's man. Josephus' account of Herod the Great's own rise to power amply demonstrates this (*Bel.* I, 285–363). In the previous century, the Seleucid ruler Alexander, son of Antiochus Epiphanes, had upheld the right of the Jewish high priest Jonathan against accusers from among his own compatriots (1 Macc. 10.59–66).

Character

Crucial to the story is the way the character of the 'nobleman' is perceived. As with some other stories, this question tends to be obscured entirely by the frequent opening assumption of contemporary readers that the nobleman is a cipher for Christ who is going away and then returning. The question returns

to haunt such an assumption, however, with the slave's troubling words about him being a harsh man (v. 22) and his summary execution of the rebels (v. 27).

Far more plausible, in my view, is the 'realistic' reading already outlined. In such a setting, the person who immediately springs to mind at the opening statement about the nobleman's departure (v. 12) is Archelaus, whose harsh character was well known. Everything that then follows confirms this. This man is one of the élite of the élite. He has ample money to trade with, and subordinates to whom to entrust it (v. 13). He is hated by citizens of his country (v. 14), and for good reason. He is known as a harsh and grasping man, taking what he did not deposit, and reaping where he did not sow (v. 21), and agrees with this description (v. 22). He has no patience with the slave who has failed (v. 24). The concern of the bystanders in verse 25 ('Lord, he has ten pounds!') offers a nice foil to spotlight his ruthlessness. His response to them in verse 26 is his motto: in effect, 'the weak will go to the wall'.

Moreover, the slaughtering of his enemies (v. 27) is entirely in character for Archelaus, and for many other rulers in the ancient world (not to mention the modern one). Here Dowling's research is fascinating and decisive (2007, pp. 83–4). The word used for 'slaughter', *katasphazō*, is found only here in the NT, but eleven times in the LXX, eight of which occur in 2 Maccabees with reference to the brutal slaughter of subjects by Antiochus and his henchmen.

What, though, of the slaves? Are the first two heroic and the third an anti-example, or vice versa? Or are they all simply victims of a system, the first two 'playing' the system effectively and the last tragically misjudging it? Traditional interpretations about using one's 'talents' till 'the master returns' treat the first two slaves as wise and the final one as foolish. Dowling, by contrast, advocates that in the original story, it is the third one who would have been seen as heroically standing up to the cut-throat economic system, while the first two demonstrate by their exorbitant profits that they have been oppressing the people like their master (2007, pp. 85–93). The third slave does, at least, protect what he has been given, an honourable thing to do in a peasant culture (p. 91).

On the analogy of the other stories of Jesus we have studied, it is likely that all the slaves are perceived as being in a morally ambiguous position. The contrast is not between 'good' and 'bad' (whichever way round one labels them) but between 'canny' and 'imprudent'. The third one has his responsibility removed, while the first two are given much greater responsibility, but that does not mean that hearers evaluate the first two more highly than the third, or sympathize with them more, or vice versa. Some might have thought the third slave an underdog hero; others might have thought him a fool. In this, as in other cases, it is important to move beyond the notion that Jesus' stories offered simple moral examples and choices. Many of them display the hard realities of their social world in their ambiguity with little if any explicit moral evaluation.

Point of view

One of the main clues for traditional readings of the story is the nobleman's words in verse 22, 'You wicked slave'. But the reason for this is that traditional readings have paid scant attention to the basic issue of 'point of view'. These words come from the mouth of the nobleman who, as we have already seen, is assumed to be a ruthless potentate: they express his point of view, not the narrator's. Jesus' audience, the great majority of whom would have felt more in tune with the position of slaves than that of their masters, would have no reason to accept that point of view as valid or true in an absolute sense. They may well have thought the third slave foolish in his inaction, but they are unlikely to have seen him as wicked.

The narrator's viewpoint remains remarkably concealed in this story, which is told without further comment. If the link with Archelaus is accepted, and at least some awareness of this piece of recent history among the hearers is assumed, the tale comes simply as a fresh rehearsing of a sadly familiar event, or kind of event, from the perspective of the now-familiar restrained observer. It is a reminder of the ruthlessness of imperial power and what can happen to those who, in however small a way, stand up to it.

Plot

The main question about plot which has regularly emerged from scholarship on this story is whether it was originally one plot or two. It is certainly unusual in its structure among Jesus' stories, in having two distinct plot elements intertwined – the trading and the rebellion. Given the flexibility of stories it is perfectly conceivable that this is indeed a combination of two, and/or that Jesus sometimes told these tales separately, sometimes together. But the conclusion from our examination of 'setting' is surely that the story makes very good sense as one connected plot. The character and actions of the nobleman remain consistent all through. The instructions to his slaves to trade and his cruel treatment of his opponents are simply different aspects of his persona as a first-century ruler hungry to maintain power. The use of the 'law of three' in the story of the slaves is a simple way of building up contrast between the way of success (the first two slaves) and the way of failure (the third).

In an attempt to soften the story's ending, Bailey comments that we do not hear of the nobleman's command to slaughter his enemies being carried out; in his view, it therefore has an open ending, like The Prodigal Son (2008, p. 406). But this is implausible. The story ends where it does because, as so often, the direct speech of a character in the drama forms the climax of a vivid performance. We do not need to hear that, or how, the command was carried out, just as we do not need to hear what happened to the wounded man after the Samaritan left him at the inn. The Samaritan's final words to the innkeeper encapsulate his character (Luke 10.35); the nobleman's final words to his slaves encapsulate his. The outcome of the plot of The Pounds, in both its strands, is the outcome of such a man's character within the social world of the period.

In that sense it is not surprising. It is tragic nonetheless. So what would hearers have made of it?

Reflection

If the above comments are true to the texture and workings of the story, we are left asking about its purpose and implications. The narrator has given us few clues to his own point of view in the story itself. So how might our attempt to hear it through the ears of Jesus' fellow-travellers relate to the way in which it has normally been understood?

Interpreters have often taken their cue from Luke's introduction to the story in verse 11: 'he went on to tell a parable, because he was near Jerusalem, and because they supposed that the kingdom of God was to appear immediately'. I believe this is an important clue, but that it has been misunderstood. It has been taken as Luke's way of saying, 'This parable is about "the delay of the *parousia*"; here Jesus was warning his hearers that his arrival in Jerusalem was not his enthronement, and that they would need to submit to him as king and exercise the responsibility entrusted to them wisely for some time before the king returned in his power.' Such an understanding places the main focus of the parable on the theme of the nobleman's departure and return. (It may also be boosted by the erroneous assumption that 'parable' always implies that the story's elements are to be taken metaphorically, even allegorically: an obvious example where this is not the case is Luke 14.7, where the 'parable' that follows is a quite straightforward piece of advice about table etiquette.) The treatment of the three slaves then becomes a lesson in the importance of right use of what has been entrusted to the disciples – a theologically awkward lesson, it has to be said, if the treatment of the third slave (v. 26) is supposed to represent how God, or Christ, treats lazy or inadequate disciples. The treatment of the rebels becomes a picture of the final judgement of those who have resisted Christ's rule.

I think this is a misreading on two levels. First, it ignores the realistic setting and characterization which would have drawn the hearers into a scene familiar from their own recent past. Second, it places too much emphasis on the departure-and-return motif in the plot. That motif sets events in train, inasmuch as it creates the need for the man to maintain his control and economic clout during his absence through entrusting money to his slaves for trade, and the opportunity for rebellion. But it is hardly the focus or the climax of the plot. It just reflects the necessity in that political order for vassal rulers to have their power confirmed from the centre of empire – which happened in this case to be a long way away.

It is much more likely, in my view, that Luke accurately portrays Jesus as issuing an implied warning against a heightened atmosphere of expectation that could easily lead to enthusiastic patriots taking matters into their own hands in a violent way. While, for some, the expectation of an imminently appearing kingdom led only to waiting, watching and praying, undoubtedly there were those who throughout this period followed the logic: 'God's kingdom is coming – so let's rebel against the human rulers.' The notion that God's rule is to be exercised through human beings was, after all, woven into the Scriptures (see particularly Gen. 1.26–28; Exod. 19.6). But this storyteller was well aware of what had happened, more than once, in recent history as a result of misguided application of this truth. We recall that after recounting the deposition of Archelaus, Josephus mentions Judas the Galilean (also mentioned in Acts 5.37) who tried to stir up revolt against the Romans so that they could continue serving God alone (*Bel.* II, 124): in Acts 5.37, the Pharisee Gamaliel observes that Judas 'perished, and all who followed him were scattered' – as part of his argument that the council should do nothing about the Jesus-followers, because they would just fizzle out if their movement was not from God.

Such a hearing of the story places the emphasis on its end-stress, the slaughtering of the rebels. The storyteller is heard with his sad, wry tone recalling how attempts to establish God's kingdom have ended up in the past. He, for one, will not be taking that path – though ironically it will not make any difference to his fate. His followers should be warned that his arrival in Jerusalem does not herald a political claim or triumph, lest they erupt into revolution that is doomed to failure.[3]

The Labourers in the Vineyard (Matt. 20.1–15)

Setting

The context for this story is the practice of hiring day-labourers to augment the normal workforce and bring in the grape harvest before the fruit rotted on the vines. Being a day-labourer offered a very insecure living and understandably was a resort of the desperate, perhaps members of large families whose smallholding could no longer support them, particularly when rents and taxes were high. A denarius was the accepted daily wage.

As an agricultural story this plays off the theme of the land as entrusted to Israel, explored above in Chapter 7. Immediately the presence of a landowner and a vineyard would have evoked the current situation in which this land was gradually falling into fewer hands:

> The owners of great estates increased their holdings through foreclosures on loans, leading to hostile takeovers of peasant farms. When possible, the land was converted into vineyards so it could produce a product with a higher return than the mixed grains grown by subsistence peasant farmers. (Herzog, 1994, p. 85)

The activity of the landowner is believable. He needs extra hired hands at this time of year, and the more he can get, the better. His going into the market-place at intervals throughout the day shows him being proactive in this, as he keeps discovering he can do with more manpower. Some have thought it surprising (and therefore an indication of a metaphorical meaning) that the landowner should go himself, rather than send servants or slaves (he has, after all, got a manager, v. 8). Herzog sees this as a cartoon-like feature of the story: as part of Jesus' strategy to 'codify systems of oppression in order to unveil them and make them visible to those victimized by them', he 'designs a confrontation between two social groups who might never have encountered each other, the elites and the expendables' (1994, p. 87). More mundanely, perhaps this landowner is on the same sort of economic level as the father of the prodigal son: well-off enough to have staff and an inheritance, but living close by, not an 'absentee landlord', and hands-on enough to be very involved in the business.

As for the labourers, the fact that some were willing to stay all day in the market-place waiting for someone to hire them is an index of their need for employment, however short-term.

Character

What sort of a person is this landowner? Audiences would not be likely to have high expectations of the behaviour of such a person, but perhaps this one would surprise them. His 'equal pay' policy is not something decided on a whim, but seems to be settled in his mind from early in the day, if not before. There is a clue in the words he speaks to those hired at nine o'clock: 'I will pay you whatever is right' (v. 4). Are we to imagine these words accompanied by a nod and a wink? He is not saying outright to these men that they will get a denarius like those who have been working since early dawn, but nor is he being specific about a lesser amount.

The fact that he does indeed give each of the workers a full day's pay may be seen as an act of justice. Bailey calls him 'the compassionate employer' (2008, p. 355). A denarius was the standard rate on which they could expect to survive. Yet perhaps Herzog is right that there is no reason to imagine this landowner as a model of altruistic compassion (1994, pp. 84–7). His 'equal pay' policy is good for those who have had less opportunity to work, but it is also a blatant display of power, demonstrating his absolute authority over his hired men. Apart from the first-hired, no wage is named at the time of hiring. The fact that he calls the last-hired to be paid first, so that the longest-working have to look on while all get the same amount (vv. 8–10), can be seen as a deliberate attempt to remind all the workers of his clout. (In contrast, Bailey sees the fact that the master takes the last-hired into the vineyard even for a short time as showing that he does not want to humiliate them by just giving them the money: 2008, p. 359).

The beginning of the landowner's address to one of the grumblers, 'Friend', as also the fact that he just addresses one of them, shows perhaps a rough camaraderie (cf. modern English-speaking 'mate'?). Certainly, he has kept his agreement with them, something not to be taken for granted: 'I am doing you no wrong: did you not agree with me for the usual daily wage?' (v. 13). But the bottom line is, as he puts it himself: 'Am I not allowed to do what I choose with what belongs to me?' (v. 15). As Herzog points out, in Israelite culture this is a blasphemous statement (1994, p. 94). He seems, in other words, similar in character to other powerful figures in Jesus' stories. His action does genuine good for its objects, but that does not make him into an ideal in the eyes of Jesus' hearers. Herzog puts it in this way: 'Far from being generous, then, the householder is taking advantage of an unemployed work force to meet his harvesting needs by offering them work without a wage agreement' (1994, p. 86).

As for the workers, they will be perceived by hearers primarily in terms of their need rather than their character (as with Lazarus in Luke 16.19–31). Most of them do nothing more in the story than work and receive wages. It is only those who have worked the longest whose character the hearer is invited to assess in moral terms. How would their complaint come over to a listener: 'These last worked only one hour, and you have made them equal to us who have borne the burden of the day and the scorching heat' (v. 12)? As with any interesting story, different hearers would surely have responded differently. Some would have identified with the sentiment absolutely in its protest against what seems unfair. Some, however – the more desperate, perhaps – empathizing with the relief and delight of the workers hired later, may have wanted the grumblers to shut up in case the landowner changed his mind.

The complaining labourers do, at least, stand up to authority and for this many would have admired them. Within a system where, however crudely calculated, payment was in proportion to labour expended, they voice a protest that will resonate deeply and instinctively with many. He has 'done them no wrong' by the terms of their contract, but does that mean he has done true justice? The words of the landowner, however, prompt an alternative perspective. He has kept to his agreement with those he has hired. 'Are you envious because I am generous?' This is a subtle story where evaluation of character hangs in the balance.

Point of view

The main question about the point of view of this story is the same as that we addressed to the story of The Pounds. Is the point of view of the landowner, expressed in the questions in verse 15, the point of view of the narrator? What clues do we have as to how the storyteller wants us to evaluate these events and these people?

The narrator gives us a finely balanced, realistic perspective. Neither the landowner nor the labourers emerge as unambiguous characters. It is significant that the landowner's final words are in the form of two questions, rather than a statement (v. 15), and less harshly phrased than the nobleman's questions to the 'lazy' slave in Luke 19.22–23 (preceded as they are by the words 'I will judge you by your own words, you wicked slave!'). This opens up the plot for examination. Hearers are not compelled to a verdict. From the landowner's perspective, they are asked to consider whether the first workers are being wrongly envious. But if their sympathies are not with the landowner to begin with, they may be reluctant to see things from that perspective.

In its context in Matthew, the story is related to what precedes and follows by the saying in 19.30 and 20.16 (see Chapter 5, p. 73). As a conclusion to the story, 'So the last will be first and the first will be last' (20.16) may or may not be taken as the comment of Jesus as narrator upon it. But even if it is, it simply picks up a motif from the story about the last and first (v. 8) to generalize the story as an instance, from the real world, of the kind of upheaval in social hierarchy which the kingdom of God entails, the upheaval in which Jesus and his disciples are caught up. It is a kingdom that is coming – maybe in part through the agency of those with power, maybe in part despite them. In this new order those to whom 'the system' has denied honest labour are provided for. The proverbial saying of 19.30 and 20.16 makes no comment on the virtue or morality of either the landowner or the grumbling workers. It laconically highlights their interaction as an example of that reversal, prophetic and proverbial in its inevitability.

Plot

Where do the tension and weight of this story lie, and whose story is it?

The opening of the story lacks tension. Though the need for extra day-labourers at harvest time was not in question, there is no mention of the landowner being desperate for more workers after the first batch, which would give some sense of expectation to his repeated excursions to the market-place, as if it were a race against time to gather the grapes. Indeed, he seems repeatedly not to realize how many he will need, since at five o'clock he asks those standing around why they had been there idle 'all day' (v. 6). But questions are, for this very reason, aroused about this man and what he is up to, creating suspense. If his visits to the market-place are not driven by urgent necessity, are they driven by altruism or some other motive?

The pivot of the plot comes in verse 8 when the owner calls the manager to pay the workers, 'beginning from the last and then going to the first'. Having followed the sequence through the day from 'first hired' to 'last hired', hearers now observe the line coming to receive their wages in reverse order, the 'last hired' coming first. The pattern of the plot (as well as the landowner's words in v. 8) therefore expresses the truth of verse 16. But the fact that this is the centre of the plot strongly suggests its main emphasis. This is not a story, fundamentally, about a landowner getting the workers he needs, nor about labourers getting the wages they need (whether or not they deserve them). It is a story about a landowner determining to act in a way which teaches his workers a lesson.

As so often, it is the direct speech coming towards the end of the story on which the stress falls. Thus the landowner's answer to the grumblers' representative in verses 13–15, and in particular his questions in verse 15, are the ultimate disclosure in this 'revelation' plot. We discover the way that he has been thinking all along. As we have seen, the narrator does not directly endorse this response. But through the design of a plot in which this answer is the culmination, the narrator wants its questions to continue troubling his listeners.

Reflection

This realistic reading of the story, in which the narrator is seen presenting a canny landowner who plans to teach his day-labourers a lesson through the granting of equal pay for different hours, is far more plausible as a reconstruction of its original dynamics than any of the traditional allegorical (or semi-allegorical) understandings. The details of the story are seen to make sense as part of the whole. Taken without the comment in verse 16, the story engages hearers with the tale of a vineyard-owner who, from whatever motives, decides not only to pay his workers the same amount but also to make it clear to all that he is doing so. The moral evaluation of this is left ambiguous. Is this an act of injustice (contravening true justice, despite the keeping of an agreement)? Or is it, by contrast, an act of true justice (providing for the needs of all, despite contravening the 'natural' expectation of wages measured according to hours worked)?

We have noted an emphasis in other stories on the hopeful fact of fundamental justice being done, notwithstanding ambiguous or simple self-seeking motives in its agents. This seems to be the case again here. Rather than needing to make an assessment of the landowner's character, Jesus' listeners are asked to note, and imagine, the hungry being fed, and the reversal this entails. It is a comment to disciples (see the context in 19.27–30) on the huge upheavals in the social and traditional order now taking place, in which they themselves, and Jesus himself supremely, are caught up. It is a prophetic story, with that unique twist of rhetoric that narrative gives to prophecy: fierce denunciation and passionate promise mutate into wry observation. A proverbial saying carries just the right mood for a summary comment: 'So the last will be first, and the first will be last.'[4]

10

Hearing the stories in Jerusalem

Four stories of Jesus are set by the Evangelists during Jesus' last week in Jerusalem. The first, The Rebellious Tenants, has been one of the most hotly debated of all Jesus' stories. Its prominent position in all the Synoptic Gospels suggests its importance in the shared memory of Jesus' final conflict with the Jerusalem authorities, but has not led to consensus about its interpretation. The second, The Wedding Feast, is Matthew's 'equivalent' of The Great Banquet in Luke, but has a much harsher edge and emphasis, and is thus placed appropriately within this scene of climactic tension. The final two, The Ten Virgins and The Talents, form part of Jesus' 'eschatological discourse' in Matthew. While Matthew thus uses them as expressions of Jesus' warning to his disciples to be prepared for the 'birth pangs' of the Messiah (24.8), the 'coming of the Son of Man' (24.37), they also reflect the mood evoked by Jesus' own imminent suffering, that of a time of fateful decision.

A fifth parable, The Two Sons (Matt. 21.28–31), also set in this final week, has some features of a story, such as past-tense recitation and a plot-pattern of reversal, but is too brief to admit of a full narrative analysis. With its full application in verses 31–32 to the situation of those responding positively or negatively to John the Baptist's ministry, it functions as a provocative similitude, inviting the chief priests and elders to indict themselves for their rejection of John's call, much as Nathan's parable of the ewe-lamb invited David to indict himself for his stealing of Uriah's wife (2 Sam. 12.1–7). As presented to us by Matthew, its thrust is much more direct than the full-length stories, essentially focusing more statically on the simple contrast between the two sons rather than on the development of events and character through time.

The Rebellious Tenants (Matt. 21.33–41; Mark 12.1–9; Luke 20.9–16; *Thomas* 65)

Setting

The story of the rebellious tenants has come down to us in four versions, in the three Synoptic Gospels and the *Gospel of Thomas*. Modern interpreters almost invariably have taken the story in its Synoptic form as an allegory of the plan of salvation, in which the father represents God, the tenants Israel (or its rulers), the messengers the prophets, and the son Jesus. The uncompromising verdict of the father on the murderous tenants is then taken as representing the judgement of God on Israel, or at least its rulers, together with the bequeathing of the vineyard to 'others', that is, Gentiles.

The view of Jülicher that this story, at least in the (supposedly) allegorical shape in which we have it, is the work of Mark (or one of his hypothetical predecessors) rather than Jesus has been influential. From C. H. Dodd (1936 (1935), pp. 124–32) onwards, however, a number of scholars have seen a realistic, non-allegorical story lying underneath the present Synoptic versions (see the summary in Kloppenborg, 2006, pp. 106–21). The situation presented in the story has been seen as representing, in some way, a plausible occurrence in first-century Palestine. The similarity of the version of the story in *Thomas* to the non-allegorical reconstruction of it made by Dodd, before the full Coptic *Thomas* was discovered, seemed to confirm that there was indeed a realistic story of Jesus underneath what seemed to be allegorical overlay (Scott, 2007a, p. 27) – on the basis that it is thought much more probable that an allegory should be developed out of a simple story than vice versa. Particularly convincing was the noting by Martin Hengel (1968) of evidence from the Zenon papyri of goings-on in the third century BCE similar to those reported in Jesus' narrative. These attest the existence of large vineyards in the region controlled and exploited by the Hellenistic rulers of the time, whose agents sometimes encountered opposition from the tenants (for details see Kloppenborg, 2006, pp. 119–20).

Many of those who recognize the basic realism of the scene continue to identify the 'meaning' of the story in more or less allegorical terms, however, as pointing to the death of Jesus at the hands of the Jerusalem leaders (e.g. Snodgrass, 1983). I suggest that we must stay longer with the story itself and the dynamics of original audition than such a reading does. It is useful at this point to recall that there are only two stories of Jesus in the Gospels that are given point-by-point explanations, The Sower and The Wheat and the Weeds. Those who hear The Rebellious Tenants as implying a point-by-point allegory may be influenced by the fact that Jesus is reported as explaining these earlier stories in such a way. However, the Evangelists report no point-by-point explanation of The Rebellious Tenants. The fact that the story resonates with the wider Gospel narrative in various ways does not mean that it cannot still be heard, primarily, as a realistic story.

Another major reason for seeing it as 'allegory' in the Synoptic Evangelists' hands is the development of the opening description of the vineyard on the basis of Isaiah 5.1–2. Matthew (21.33) and Mark (12.1) do indeed expand the bare description in *Thomas* ('A good man had a vineyard'), and use a number of words that are the same or similar as those used in Isaiah's 'love-song of the vineyard'. 'Put a fence around it' (*phragmon periethēken*), and 'built a watchtower' (*ōkodomēsen purgon*) employ the same words as Isaiah 5.2 LXX. 'Dug a winepress' (*ōruxen . . . lēnon*, Matthew, and *ōruxen hypolēnion*, Mark) employs the same word for 'dig' as Isaiah 5.2 and a different, though related word for 'wine press' (*prolēnion*). It is not surprising that the performance of

Matthew and Mark should have deliberately evoked this traditional symbol of Israel as vineyard, explicitly named as such in Isaiah 5.7: 'For the vineyard of the LORD of hosts is the house of Israel, and the people of Judah are his pleasant planting.' But this is not so much 'allegory' as deeply rooted 'metonymic referencing'. Horsley explains this well:

> Communication through a performance or recitation, therefore, depends ... on extratextual factors as meaning is evoked *metonymically* from the tradition with which the hearers are familiar. In contrast to the originality of conferred meaning in modern literary texts, traditional oral performance cannot depart from, because it depends on, traditional references of symbols, phrases and formulas. Each performance causes what is immanent to come to life in the present: it recreates the networks of inherent meaning.   (Horsley, 2008, p. 66)

Horsley uses the example of how hearing a recording of Martin Luther King's 'I have a dream' speech evokes for him 'a whole movement, a whole period of my life and the life of American society' (2008, p. 67). This evocation is metonymic because King's speech is not a mere cipher for those things; it was actually part of them.

By echoing the vineyard-song in Isaiah, Jesus' story awakens consciousness of physical land as the symbol of all God's entrustments to Israel, to which the specific vineyard in Jesus' narrative related as part to whole. As we saw in discussing The Sower, what happened to the land was a barometer of what was happening to the people, so the echoes go wider still. An 'echo' is very different from the use of an image which simply represents an alternative reality, as in allegory (e.g. Christian's burden representing sin in Bunyan's *Pilgrim's Progress*). When a speaker echoes a text or well-known trope, it lingers in the mind and calls into being a range of associations in the imagination, setting a whole interpretative horizon for the speaker's words. Thus the allusion to Isaiah does not destroy the realism of the story, but simply evokes the world of meaning within which Jesus and his hearers would understand the travails and fate of their land.

A foundational symbol, however, such as the 'vineyard' standing for Israel, could be exploited in different ways, and the 'song' in Isaiah leads to a different set of imagery from that found in Jesus' story. In Isaiah, the problem is found in the vineyard itself, which yields wild grapes or 'thorns' (*akanthas*, Isa. 5.2, 4, cf. The Sower). In the Gospels, the problem is the tenants and their greed. In reality, of course, the problem in Isaiah turns out to be the 'tenants' as well ('he expected justice, but saw bloodshed; righteousness, but heard a cry!', v. 7b). Herzog rightly locates the link between Mark 12 and Isaiah 5 not in an identification of the vineyard-owner with God, but in their highlighting of 'the acquisitive greed of the ruling class' (1994, p. 104). Vineyard-owners like the one in Jesus' story are just like those denounced by Isaiah as adding 'house to house ... field to field, until there is room for no one but you' (Isa. 5.8). Thus Matthew and Mark have developed the vineyard symbol in a different way from Isaiah, but have presented Jesus as having the same kind of prophetic target as Isaiah's prophecy. It is also notable that Luke has omitted their expansion of the opening of the story. Matthew and Mark have themselves omitted various details from Isaiah 5.1–2 LXX: the fertile hill on which it is situated, the trench dug around it (the Masoretic Text (MT) also includes 'cleared it of stones'), and the choice vine ('vines' MT) planted within it.[1] The Evangelists' performance thus deploys the rhetoric of allusion rather than that of allegory.

Other important reasons why the Synoptic Gospels have been understood as 'allegorizing' an originally realistic story of Jesus are found in their account of the aftermath of the narration. Jesus quotes Psalm 118.22–23 (Matt. 21.42; Mark 12.10–11; Luke 20.17). This saying about the rejected and then privileged stone was certainly applied early on to Jesus himself (see e.g. 1 Pet. 2.7, 8), but at this point in the Gospel narratives one envisages it having a less specific resonance. Like the Psalm itself, it proclaims in more general terms the truth that God reverses human verdicts. Even if Snodgrass is right that there is a play on the Aramaic words for 'stone' and 'son' (1983, pp. 80–118), there is no need to draw the conclusion that this play would have had a messianic meaning for either Jesus or his hearers.

Then Matthew records Jesus' pronouncement 'Therefore I tell you, the kingdom of God will be taken away from you and given to a nation producing the fruits of it' (21.43). This echoes the verdict of the hearers themselves on what will happen to the murderous tenants (21.41) and turns it round on those same hearers (compare the conclusion of Nathan's parable of the ewe-lamb, 2 Samuel 12.7; and Jesus' final words to the lawyer in Luke 10.37). The saying is not so much 'allegorical' as once more tapping into the old symbolic network of land and fruitfulness.

Matthew (21.44) and Luke (20.18) then cite another saying of Jesus quoting Isaiah 8.14–15, about the stone crushing the one that falls on it, or on whom it falls. This too can be heard as a simple prophecy of judgement, of decision time, although a reference to Jesus himself as the 'stone' from the point of view of Matthew and Luke would be natural. Then all three Synoptic Gospels record how the Jewish leaders perceived that Jesus was somehow speaking against them (Matt. 21.45; Mark 12.12; Luke 20.19). As I have argued above, this comment should not be taken as implying that the leaders understood the story as a full-blown allegory. All that is required is that they hear it as a warning of judgement against the 'tenants' of the 'vineyard', and a threat that their responsibility for it will end brutally in response to rebellion, and be transferred to others.

Scott's assertion that these various features show that the Synoptics have made of this story 'a thoroughgoing allegory of salvation history' (2007a, p. 28) is thus much overstated. In the Synoptics as much as in *Thomas*, the story can be heard as a 'thoroughgoing realistic story'. The planting of a vineyard was a normal occurrence, but only one the very wealthy could afford, because of the five years required for the crop to mature and the investment in labour to tend the vines in the meantime (Herzog, 1994, pp. 104–5). It was a project of capitalism rather than one of subsistence. The details about the planting in Matthew and Mark (following Isaiah), omitted in Luke and *Thomas*, add realistic colour to the scene: the fence and the watchtower for protection (for hostile attempts on agricultural production, recall The Wheat and The Weeds), and the press for the grapes on the same site. The man's departure 'for another country' suggests his importance and wealth, though he is not necessarily as high born as the nobleman in Luke 19.11–27 (he is not going 'to receive royal power') or as wealthy as the owner of the talents in Matthew 25.14–30. Luke's touch that he is to be away 'for a long while' has been taken as hinting at the delay of the *parousia* but is not at all unrealistic: it may simply reflect the fact that the owner knew that it would be several years before the first grapes appeared. Herzog suggests that the language does not imply that the landowner has gone to a foreign country: 'He was probably meant to be Jewish, so that his absentee home can be understood to be a city either in Galilee or, more reasonably, in Judea, perhaps even Jerusalem' (1994, p. 104).

The owner's sending of a slave ('slaves' in Matthew) to get his due proportion of the fruit is the expected next step. The tenants would have been granted a certain proportion in payment for their services and would probably have planted vegetables between the rows of vines in the years before the latter came to fruition (Herzog, 1994, p. 103), but the main purpose of the venture was of course the profit for the owner. The violent rejection of this first slave/slaves, and subsequent ones, by the tenants has invited much speculation about what they could hope to gain. Were they really so foolish as to imagine that they would get away with this? The story invites us to consider that at least they thought that it would be worth the risk. To think of this action as unrealistic folly is to underestimate the despair of those who saw their very livelihood threatened by the expropriation of their land by powerful élites. If resistance could arise even to a throne claimant such as Archelaus (cf. Luke 19.11–27), how much more might the tenants of a more local aristocrat take a risk on his absence and seek to grab property for themselves?

Thomas is the only version which explicitly states that the slave sent first, who was beaten and not killed, returned to tell his master. This surely is assumed in the other versions – that, following each sending, either the return of a bloodied and bruised slave, or the ominous non-return of any, prompted the owner to send others. If this sounds a risk on the owner's part, it simply reflects his determination to have what is rightfully his. The implication that he considered his slaves' lives expendable is not unrealistic. The sending of his son in an ultimate attempt to claim what is his seems, from one angle, like a risk too far. But the son in this culture carries the father's authority. Short of coming himself, this was the most persuasive ambassador he could have sent. The word 'beloved' in Mark and Luke, a pointer to identification with Christ in an allegorical reading, in a realistic reading accentuates the risk the father is taking; it is a natural climax to this stage of the plot (cf. Dodd, 1936 (1935)), p. 130).

The tenants' logic in thinking that by killing the son the inheritance will be theirs (explicit in all the Synoptics, but not *Thomas*) was explained on the basis of a Mishnaic law by Jeremias (1963 (1947), pp. 75–6), but Kloppenborg has rightly questioned the applicability of this law at Jesus' time (2006, pp. 112–13). Desperate and determined people who have had a run of success do not necessarily pause to ponder the niceties of legal custom. Surely they think they can claim the inheritance by sheer violent seizure. Perhaps they consider that the owner has been absent for so long and has shown himself thus far reluctant to return, and that therefore there is a good chance, particularly now that he knows their mood, that they will get away with it.

When the tenants threw the son out of the vineyard, whether this was after they killed him (Mark 12.8) or before (Matt. 21.39; Luke 20.15), this is hardly an unrealistic element, whatever wider echoes it may have, especially in Matthew and Luke, of the crucifixion of Jesus. It is a triumphant and symbolic rejection of the owner and claiming of what, the tenants believe, is now theirs. Nor is the vengeance then exacted by the owner (not mentioned by *Thomas*) in the slightest degree surprising. In any period, a landlord is likely to evict such tenants, and the rough justice of the first-century Roman Empire might well entail a 'miserable death' (Matt. 21.41).

Thus far, this appears a tragic but simple story exemplifying the truth that violent resistance to powerful figures operating under the Roman hegemony will end only in misery and death. In the closing question of Mark 12.9a ('What will the owner of the vineyard do?'), 'the parable codifies the futility of violence' (Herzog, 1994, p. 113). The exploration of the characters in the story, however, adds another dimension.

Character

The question of character in The Rebellious Tenants is a case in point of the importance of paying attention to the Evangelists' notices concerning a story's audience(s) if we are to appreciate its force as a performative act. Different audiences will understand and respond in different ways (cf. Thiselton, 1985, pp. 90–2). For the Synoptic Gospels, there are different 'layers' of audience for this story (cf. Luke 15.1—16.1).

All three locate the story in the Temple. Mark says Jesus was 'walking' there (11.27), Matthew that he was 'teaching' (a typical Matthean emphasis, 21.23), and Luke that he was 'teaching the people' (20.1) – and specifically that he told 'the people' this parable (20.9). Luke in both these instances uses the word *laos* that he often uses for the crowd who are sympathetic to Jesus: cf. especially Luke 6.17; 7.29; 18.43; 19.48; 21.38; 23.27. In this public space, where a lot of ordinary folk are around, Jesus is approached by the 'chief priests' and 'elders' (Matt. 21.23; Mark 11.27; Luke 20.1: Mark and Luke also include 'scribes'). First they ask him by what authority he does what he does, and Jesus replies with a counter-question about the baptism of John. Then (in Matthew only) he uses the short analogy The Two Sons (Matt. 21.28–32) to raise the question of where, among the population around him, true obedience is to be found. Then comes the story The Rebellious Tenants. Here the Temple hierarchy is in the foreground after the immediately preceding incident, but the wider setting (according at least to Matthew and especially Luke) is the people as a whole. It is the authorities' response to the story which all three writers note (Matt. 21.45–46; Mark 12.12; Luke 20.19) – Matthew now including the Pharisees, keen presumably to include them in Jesus' implied indictment. But 'the people' are again in the (perhaps immediate) background. It is because they feared the crowd(s) (Matt. 21.46; Mark 12.12), or the 'people' (*laos* again, Luke), that the leaders are prevented from arresting Jesus at that point.

The direction of a hearer's understanding of this story depends to a great extent on his or her initial, and ongoing, evaluation of the character of the man introduced in its first sentence. Bailey takes an exalted view (without reference to the different audiences, and undoubtedly influenced by the traditional identification of the man with God). The owner is the wronged party who goes to great lengths to win over his rebellious subjects. In his sending of his son, Bailey speaks of his 'vulnerability' (2008, p. 419), writing that the man hopes the violent tenants will sense his 'indescribable nobility' (2008, p. 418). For Bailey this story should be called 'The parable of the noble vineyard owner and his son' (2008, p. 410).

Herzog offers a much more convincing view of how the people at large would have responded to this introduction. They would have been disposed against him from the start:

> [T]he creation of a vineyard would, on economic grounds alone, have disturbed the hearers of the parable. Because land in Galilee was largely accounted for and intensely cultivated, 'a man' could acquire the land required to build a vineyard only by taking it from someone else.   (Herzog, 1994, p. 102)

In the absence of other indicators, one should assume that the 'man' of the parable's opening is to be classed among the wealthy and exploitative. The planting of a vineyard, leasing it to the tenants, and sending a slave to collect the revenue would all be standard elements of such a person's strategy. For the ordinary Jewish crowds, such a person was an oppressor. The Jewish leaders, however, picking up exactly the same social signals about the vineyard-planter's position, would have seen him as 'one of them'. The chief priests were members of the wealthy Jewish aristocracy, and Pharisees (Matt. 21.45) would often be their advisers, though 'they were sometimes torn between their loyalty to the tradition and loyalty to the temple hierarchy who were client-rulers for the Romans' (Horsley, 2012, p. 132).

How then might the different audiences have responded to the vineyard-owner's behaviour once the first slave (slaves in Matthew) has/have been rejected? The people may have regarded the sending of others, however many exactly there were and on however many occasions, as a sign that he is careless of their lives. *Thomas*' version of the story suggests a 'softer' hearing, such as might have sounded more attractive to the Jewish leaders, predisposed in the man's favour, when he is recorded as commenting, 'Perhaps he [i.e. the slave] did not know them [i.e. the tenants]', or 'Perhaps they [i.e. the tenants] did not recognize him [i.e. the slave]'. In other words, we might put it, the man in *Thomas* thinks 'there must be some mistake': he does not see behind their treatment of this first slave the reality of the tenants' rapaciousness. So what of his sending of a third embassy (Mark 12.5a; Luke 20.12) or still more (Mark 12.5b)? Again, though both groups of hearers might agree in attributing this to perseverance, foolishness or frustration, the leaders would have been likely to take the man's side, while the people would have seen this as further evidence of callous disregard of his own slaves' lives.

When, finally, the man thinks that they will respect his son (as in all four versions), it might seem like sheer naïveté – perhaps blended with arrogance: he cannot conceive that his authority would be flouted so blatantly. Perhaps, though, both audiences would have recognized a legal requirement whereby the man had no alternative but to come in person, or send a representative vested with his authority, if he was to claim redress (Snodgrass, 1983, p. 37). Here, in any case, the sympathies of the two audiences might have started to converge as they see the tragedy coming. The adjective 'beloved' (Mark 12.6; Luke 20.13), especially, starts to draw in hearers who might, up to this point, have regarded the protagonist with cold aloofness. The sending of the slaves to violence and death might have struck the crowds as callous folly. The sending of a beloved son changes the mood, from their point of view, considerably. Indeed, the fact that they will have sympathized with the first ambassadors, the maltreated slaves, means surely that their emotional guard is down when they hear of the murder of the son.

At this point we turn to the different responses of the audiences to the tenants' actions. For the Jewish leaders, the tenants' brutality surely epitomized precisely the kind of violent, revolutionary undercurrent of feeling that terrified them most as protectors of the current order. But the crowds, too, though not identifying with the owner, would not thereby automatically have approved of the tenants' actions. God's indictment against his 'vineyard' Israel had been for the people's bloodshed (Isa. 5.7), and, if that prophetic song found an echo at all in their minds, they will have been troubled to hear of such violence, even though they might sympathize with the tenants in their desire for freedom and land, and a small minority might have thought the tenants' response fully justified.

Hearers in both camps might thus have experienced something genuinely tragic in the classical sense about these characters, the situations in which they find themselves and the outcome of the story. The Jewish leaders have identified with the landowner, greeted with some horror the extraordinary risk he has taken in sending his son, and undoubtedly recognized justice in the tenants' punishment, but are left wondering whether this can really compensate for the son's death. The people have been instinctively on the side of both the slaves and the tenants, an uncomfortable position to be in.

They have been shocked at the owner's risks with his subordinates' lives but also troubled by the tenants' extreme measures, and especially by the murder of the beloved son. They are not surprised by the tenants' punishment; this does not endear them to the landowner but it does leave them wondering whether the tenants' strategy was worth it. Both audiences, then, see risks taken which have horribly misfired, and are brought together in a shared bad taste in the mouth, a sense of the futility of an entire system founded on and generating violence.

Point of view

The element of tragedy in this story on both sides indicates a narrator who is able to see a situation in the round, and the effects of a particular social order on those living within it. As usual, hints of an explicit point of view on particular characters or events are minimal. *Thomas* alone calls the owner a 'good' man, which tallies with the more sympathetic portrait in *Thomas* that we have already noted. *Thomas* also omits the punishment of the tenants, thus leaving the landowner as a more starkly tragic victim than in the Synoptics.

Jesus portrays both a landowner driven unintentionally to sacrifice his son in the cause of maintaining his authority and tenants driven by foolish desperation to end up sacrificing themselves in the cause of gaining ownership of the land. The fact that Jesus concludes the story, in Mark (12.9a) and Luke (20.15b), with a question – 'What then will the owner of the vineyard do?' – and then proceeds immediately to answer it – 'He will come and destroy those tenants, and give the vineyard to others' (Mark 12.9b; Luke 20.16) – only underlines the shared understanding between speaker and hearers of the inevitable outworking of such events: it offers no moral judgement. In Matthew, indeed, this is a rare recorded moment of audience participation in a story of Jesus: the audience themselves answer the question (21.40, 41: cf. Jesus' question to the lawyer in Luke 10.36). All the Synoptic versions imply a narrator who wants to emphasize the inexorable outworking of events and audiences who comprehend this full well.

Plot

John Kloppenborg has surveyed in great detail different options for construing the plot of this story (2006, pp. 121–48) and, of necessity, what I offer here is a briefer account of how it works.

If we are attentive to the social setting of the story, we appreciate that conflict is implied at the very beginning, before it becomes overt. The planting of a vineyard was not a neutral or altruistic act. It evoked tensions at the heart of Palestinian life in the first century.

From this basis, one trajectory through the plot follows the attempts of the tenants to resolve this simmering conflict by raising it to the level of full-blown violent rebellion, leading ultimately to the revelation of the folly and futility of this route. But with the treatment of the master's first slave(s), another trajectory opens up, following the persistent attempts of the master to claim his rightful dues. This, eventually, he does, but only at the cost of a beloved son, as well as a number of slaves dead or wounded. The death of the son is at the intersection of these two trajectories. It is the decision point beyond which the defeat of the tenants' course of action is inevitable and the master will surely reclaim his property by force. Neither trajectory seems to have greater weight than the other.

Attention to the plot structure puts a question mark against attempts to see in the sending of the slaves and the son an allegorical account of God's sending of the prophets and Jesus. Each of the versions is different at this point, and this variety can best be explained as a range of storytelling techniques, reflecting the style of the Gospel 'performers', rather than a desire to turn a simple story into an allegory. We can see this if we set them out thus:

Thomas 65.4–11: two sendings: first one slave, then another: first beaten (nearly killed), second beaten
Mark 12.2–5: many sendings of individual slaves: first beaten, second beaten over the head and insulted, third killed, subsequent ones either beaten or killed
Matthew 21.34–36: two sendings of several slaves, more the second time than the first: variously beaten, killed and stoned both times
Luke 20.10–12: three sendings of individual slaves: first beaten, second beaten and insulted, third wounded

Thomas' version is the simplest. Two slaves come in succession, are beaten, and then followed by the son, who is killed. Mark's version exhibits his prolix tendency to include redundant details in individual pericopae. The third servant is the first to be killed, but any sense of economic build-up to a climax is then broken by the addition 'And so it was with many others; some they beat, and others they killed' (12.5). Matthew's is typically shorter, with just two sendings as in *Thomas*, and it is characteristic of his performances that more than one slave comes the first time (compare Matthew's 'doubling', for example of the demoniacs in 8.28–34, the blind men in 20.29–34 and the animals in 21.1–11). This seems to be a way of creating emphasis. The precise number is not important: 'beat one, killed another, stoned another' (21.35) gives a representative example of the way they were treated, not limiting their number to three. There is no build-up at all through the servants to the son; Matthew's is the only version where a servant is killed on the first sending, and the only difference in his second sending is that more are sent. Luke, artistic storyteller that he is, has each of the three servants treated progressively worse, but saves the climax of murder for the son. *Thomas* and Matthew use the 'law of three' with the third sending being that of the son; Luke uses the 'law of three' with three sendings of servants, the son coming on the fourth occasion (cf. the pattern of The Sower).

All this makes it difficult to see any pattern of progressive 'allegorizing'. If *Thomas* is taken as representing an early version, Mark certainly makes it untidier, rather than putting it into a neater schema. Matthew and Luke tidy Mark in different ways, but apparently for the sake of narrative neatness, in their different styles, rather than for allegorical purposes. If one wanted to create an allegory of salvation, one might more readily do so in the spare manner of *Thomas*, minimizing unnecessary detail, than in the more elaborate manner of Matthew, Luke or especially Mark, with their realistic but redundant and variously organized touches. (*Thomas*, of course, which lacks an overall narrative, is ironically the one version least likely to be accused of 'allegorizing' tendencies by modern scholarship.)

The plot, then, like other elements of the story, is realistic. It makes sense as a story in its own terms without the need for an allegorical reading, although elements of it certainly resonate with the wider story both of the Gospels and of Scripture as a whole. Through the law of end-stress, its emphasis is uncompromising. *Thomas*, with its lack of emphasis on the outworking of history, omits this ending, but it is clear in the others. Rebellion is bound to lead to punishment and to the loss of the very land for which the rebels have fought.

Reflection

For various reasons, this story has called for a long treatment. It is one of only two common to all three Synoptics, and a part of its interest and complexity lies in the fact that it exists not only in these three different versions but also in *Thomas*. In the Synoptic accounts, it occupies a crucial place in the narrative of Jesus' final week. And it has traditionally been seen as focusing on the person and fate of Jesus himself, to an extent that no other of his stories has been.

I have proposed a realistic reading in which the unfolding events constitute a plausible snapshot of life as it had been in the recent past, was still and would continue to be for the Jewish nation under Roman rule. No character, including those of the father and son, need be taken in an allegorical sense for the story to 'work', and to work in a challenging and effective way on the hearers, though as we shall suggest shortly, this is one story where, from one angle, God does indeed appear. It is time now to draw together the various narrative threads we have traced in order to try to encapsulate that working.

Jesus' primary hearers, the senior Jewish leaders, are drawn into a story in which they naturally sympathize with the figure of authority, the vineyard-owner. They are deeply fearful of types such as the tenants, and they listen aghast as the owner's attempts to gain his rightful dues meet with increasingly violent, disastrous consequences. They accept completely the justice of the final verdict: that the authority figure should destroy the tenants and entrust the vineyard to others who will be dutiful.

At some point, however, the echoes of Isaiah and elsewhere start to do their work. No story about a vineyard can lack resonance with a Jewish hearer, any more than can a story about a sower, seeds, soils and fruit. A piece of the land stands by synecdoche for the whole of the land. A single vineyard stands for the LORD's whole vineyard. And at the end of the story, when the logical conclusion is drawn – that the owner will destroy the tenants and give the vineyard to others – one hears the realization start to dawn: in fact, we are the unreliable tenants. We are the ones who have been complicit in violence, whether or not we admit it. We are the ones on whom judgement must come at the hands of the very people we have been serving, the Roman authorities. In this sense, the owner reminds them of the God who alone owns the land, as well as the Romans who are the current undisputed human masters.

The leaders realize that they are on the wrong side, just as Jesus has recently indicated that, as guardians of the Temple, they are no better than social bandits (Mark 11.15–17: see Herzog, 2005, pp. 165–70). In Matthew, Jesus spells it out for them (21.43). In Mark and Luke, he does not need to. In all three versions, they realized that he was speaking 'about them' (Matt. 21.45) or 'against them' (Mark 12.12; Luke 20.19). However, we should not take this conclusion to mean that the ordinary people who are listening in are 'off the hook'. They, too, experience in the story both the tragedy and futility of violence.

This self-implication in violence to which Jesus seems to be leading his hearers, and especially the leaders, may indeed awaken consciousness of the history of violence against the prophets, culminating in the killing of God's Son, as the allegorical reading has understood the story. It fits with the direct denunciation of the scribes and Pharisees for acting in character with their ancestors who murdered the prophets, placed by Matthew in 23.29–36, and of Jerusalem itself as 'the city that kills the prophets and stones those who are sent to it' (23.37).[2] But through the realism of the story it is not limited to that. The allusion to the song of the vineyard in Isaiah 5, especially clear in Matthew and Mark, evokes, as we saw, the indictment of YHWH against his people – an indictment of violence in a quite broad sense (Isa. 5.7). It is deeply ironic that having seen that the story has been aimed at them, the Jewish leaders go on to urge the Roman authorities (successfully) to commit a very ugly act of violence just a few days later.

The Jewish leaders are not required, by the story, to identify themselves with the tenants in all details. As we have seen, they are more likely to feel some identification with the owner to begin with, but by the end are forced into a position of asking whether, as guardians of the vineyard, they themselves are guilty of that of which the tenants are guilty, and therefore liable to a similar judgement. This is a similar pattern to that of The Prodigal Son, in which the Pharisees are likely to identify initially with the father, and share his shock and sorrow at his younger son's behaviour, but end up being invited to see themselves as the older brother resisting his father's compassion.

A realistic reading of the story forecloses the culpably anti-Jewish interpretations which have marred Christian history (see Milavec, 1989). Interestingly, Matthew's version, which indicts the Jewish leaders most explicitly, in fact makes this clearest. By emphasizing twice that the vineyard will be given to other tenants or a 'nation' who will return its fruits as they should (21.41, 43), he underlines the fact that the owner is interested in justice rather than ethnicity (cf. Carter, 2001, p. 429). The realism of the story requires that hearers envisage, first, just a specific vineyard being let out to more responsible tenants and, then, generalizing from 'part to whole' on the basis of the Israel-as-vineyard motif, any who are wicked and violent in the land being ejected from stewardship of it in favour of any who are trustworthy. Both Jews and Gentiles might come into either grouping, though it is specific Jewish leaders who are now warned lest they find themselves in the wrong one. Herzog regards the 'rejected stone' as the 'people of the land' to whom will be restored their rightful enjoyment of God's bounty (2005, p. 203).

What was it in particular which made the Jewish leaders recognize that through this story Jesus was speaking about them and against them, such that they wanted to do away with him? Most of all, perhaps, as we saw in Chapter 4, the slantwise implication that the land would be snatched from their tenancy. Jeremiah's experience as recorded in the OT epitomizes the unpopularity of a prophet who foretells disaster for his own people. The Slavonic version of Josephus' *Jewish War* helps us to imagine the mindset. It records that within the sacred precincts of the Temple had been an inscription in Greek, Latin and Jewish (*sic*) 'declaring that Jesus, the king who never reigned, was crucified by the Jews because he foretold the end of the city and the utter destruction of the Temple' (*Bel.* V, 199; see Williamson's edition of Josephus (1959), p. 400). An announcement that the sacred city and sanctuary at the heart of the nation would be destroyed was bound to implicate the current guardians of that place. Jesus was not holding his hearers directly responsible for an event which would take place 40 years on, but the violent mood and action of the story pointed to a pattern of violence which was, indeed, to escalate in the coming years and would lead only to disaster for his people and their land. Interestingly, a Jewish scholar, Frank Stern, does not hear a veiled prediction of Jesus' own death at the hands of the Jewish leaders in this story, but rather an indictment of the people as a whole:

> The leaders alone were not responsible for the son's death – any more than they were responsible for John's death or the death of the prophets. The people had strayed and become as rebellious and destructive as wild grapes. Therefore, the entire vineyard needed to be destroyed – Jerusalem, the Temple, its priests, the elders of the city, the merchants, bakers, cheese makers, potters, builders, and masons. In short, Jesus condemned everyone who disobeyed God and refused to repent.
> (Stern, 2006, p. 118)

As a kind of 'prophecy', Jesus' story is very indirect. It invites the hearers to make identifications and 'go figure' for themselves. In this sense, it is thoroughly in line with all his other stories, coherently realistic, yet 'mysterious' in the sense that they are past-tense narrations rather than direct accusations, promises, warnings or encouragements. What they perform is a profound and piercing prompt that goes deeper than any of these. It is completely plausible, in line with his general tactics through his ministry, that an explicit prediction of the Temple's destruction should have been given to the disciples alone, as the Evangelists record (Matt. 24.2; Mark 13.2; Luke 21.6). It is not surprising that if Jesus used such indirect rhetoric as this story for a more public audience, it was difficult for the authorities to find testimonies against him that agreed (Mark 14.55–59). Equally, it is not surprising that they were provoked deeply in a way that determined them to get him out of the way by some means or other.

Despite its dark, foreboding tone, The Rebellious Tenants still carries an appeal. Jesus points to inevitability in the way that violent revolt will be treated. He does not, however, imply that such revolt is itself inevitable. In this way, the story acts as an indirect plea, just as most of his others do, including – for example – The Sower and The Prodigal Son. Even at this point, a change of heart was possible. The Gospels narrate with deep irony that the leaders proceed to act with the very violence against which the story implicitly warns.

The Wedding Feast (Matt. 22.2–13)

Setting

Despite its similarity in content to The Great Banquet (Luke 14.16–24), a quick glance at the texts of the two stories side by side in the Greek shows only a very small commonality in wording. In addition, the Matthean story includes two significant elements completely absent from the Lukan: the violence of the invited guests and of the host in response, and the host's treatment of the man without a wedding garment. In a short story, such additions make a considerable difference to its weight and balance. It is therefore important to treat it separately from the Lukan version, recognizing that Jesus may well have told several variants of the same story on different occasions.

The story in Matthew is set higher up the social ladder than that in Luke: the banquet is given by a king. Further, it is not any banquet but a wedding feast (22.2). Such occasions were opportunities for lavish display, hinted at in the story by the mention of 'oxen and fat calves' (v. 4). Through ostentatious generosity, a potentate might seek to win or cement the loyalty of his subjects and underline the folly of resisting his power (cf. Schottroff, 2006, pp. 39–40, and references there, including to the banquet laid on by Herod Antipas for 'his courtiers and officers and for the leaders of Galilee', Mark 6.21). This situation readily explains the fact that when the king sends his slaves out a second time, some guests not only refused the invitation but also killed its bearers (v. 5). No one in the story thinks this is a lovely, innocent treat laid on by a delightful rich benefactor for those who have little. The king's response to those who have thus scorned his invitation is, entirely realistically, swift and brutal (v. 7).

As in The Great Banquet, the king's replacement of the initially invited guests with others from the streets (v. 8) is surely a face-saving act to uphold his honour. The fact that 'both bad and good' (*ponērous te kai agathous*) are brought in (v. 10) sounds like a Matthean touch (cf. the parable The Net, Matt. 13.47–50, although note that in 13.49 a different word is used for good/righteous, *dikaiōn*). It mirrors the fact that the original invitees were not 'worthy' (v. 9). The difference here from the Lukan story corresponds to the difference between the Matthean and Lukan versions of the Beatitudes, the former adding a moral touch to what, in the latter, are unambiguous promises to a social group ('Blessed are the poor in spirit', Matt. 5.3, rather than just 'Blessed are you poor', Luke 6.20). But this moral flavour does not detract from the realism of the Matthean story. It merely emphasizes that in order to save his honour the king was impelled to have at his table not (as we might say) the 'great and the good' whom he had first asked but a ragbag collection of all and sundry.

That this is far from sheer benevolence on the king's part is shown in the final episode of the story in verses 11–14. Even the gathering in of the general populace in verses 9–10 is now seen not to have been unconditional. The wearing of a wedding robe was expected and the absence of one was in this case taken as an insult on a par with the first guests' violent rejection of the summons. How the man's lack of a wedding garment is to be explained depends on how one conceives of the custom here. Schottroff mentions two possibilities attested in Rabbinic sources (2006, p. 40): either the king provided such a garment or the guests were given time to prepare. If the host at such a royal feast normally provided one himself (at least for any who could not afford one?) then the man in Jesus' story had either wilfully refused one, or missed the person handing them out in the crowds who jostled into the feast. If it was to be expected that each person brought his or her own, then it seems that the man was unlucky to be spotted by the king (or represents several people), because it is very likely he would not be the only person in the crowd not to have possessed one. Perhaps he (and others?) assumed that, as they were being urged to attend, they could come just as they were, with impunity; or perhaps they were just ignorant of the expectation. All this has a close bearing on the issue of character, which we shall address shortly.

How realistic is the king's final sentence of punishment in verse 13? In consigning the man to a place of torture, entirely so. As Schottroff notes, 'the place of pain and darkness is an image of the dungeons of the palaces, where horrible punishments were inflicted. Emperors carried out dreadful punishments even on their own sons' (2006, p. 41). The language of 'outer darkness' and 'weeping and gnashing of teeth' may give Matthew's overlay of apocalyptic terrors on to words the king in a realistic story is more likely to have used. But there is no reason to think that Jesus himself would not have seen or imagined apocalyptic terror coming to the heart of the real world.

Character

The king's behaviour confirms what any crowd, including the Jewish leaders who appear to be among those still addressed here (cf. Matt. 21.45–46), would have assumed about his character. He is a ruthless ruler determined to keep his subjects' loyalty, by displays of generosity if possible but by force if necessary. When the guests refuse the first time (v. 2), he presumably thinks (like the vineyard-owner in the previous story) 'they cannot be serious' and sends other slaves. This time he has no patience, but responds in rage to the refusal of his invitation and sends a military expedition to destroy those who have murdered his slaves, as well as their city (22.7). The instruction to his slaves to gather new guests is somewhat less forceful than the equivalent in Luke's story – there is no mention of 'compelling' in verse 9 – but there is little doubt that this is an 'invitation' they are expected to accept. His treatment of the man without a wedding garment, so problematic for allegorical readings, is perfectly consistent as part of his character portrayal in a 'realistic' hearing. It highlights the absurd, neurotic quality of one whose honour must be upheld in every particular. Whether the storyteller means us to imagine this one unfortunate man as an example of what happened to many, or as an isolated case, it makes little difference to a hearer's evaluation of the king's character.

The behaviour of the first guests in verses 5–6 is reminiscent of that of the tenants in the preceding story. As in that story, the Jewish leaders may have reacted first in horror, succeeded by the painful realization that they too are not guiltless of violent intentions and actions. While other hearers may, at least tacitly, have sympathized with it as expressing frustration at dominance by the ruling powers, all would have known that such violence was contrary to the law of God, and the victims are, after all, slaves not masters. The guests take a risk that may express desperation or foolhardiness, and is soon proved to have been utter folly. Note that the statement 'those invited were not worthy' (v. 8) is an evaluation from the king's lips, not the narrator's; hearers would have had a more nuanced response. The subsequent guests are character-wise a great mixture, 'good and bad': their role in the story is simply to be recipients of the king's display of hospitality.

The man without a wedding garment may have been regarded as ignorant, careless, miscalculating, defiant or purely unlucky, depending on the precise nature of the custom and how it was implemented. Perhaps the ambiguity was present to some extent in the original story too. His speechlessness (v. 12b) may point to this being a totally unexpected response from the king, thus emphasizing to the hearer his innocence and the king's unreasonableness. At the end the man is just a victim of arbitrary power.

Point of view

The narrator performs this story as a tale of something that happened (in reality or realistic fiction), with only slight hints of what point of view he himself takes on it. We are probably to hear a wry wit in the shaming of the king, soon to be overridden by the dark ending in which the king cruelly shames the man without the wedding garment. Within the story itself, the description of the new guests as 'both good and bad' shows probably a desire to depict a contrast between the initial invitees, assumed to be upright characters in a socially acceptable sense, and the mixture he must now invite to save his honour and fill his house. The apocalyptic perspective given by the language of verse 13 implies a narrator who sees in such an occurrence the judgement of God. The story is introduced by the familiar Matthean phrase 'The kingdom of heaven may be compared to' (22.2), but no hint is given of just how the story is thought to shed light on the kingdom, apart from the gnomic saying appended in verse 14, 'For many are called, but few are chosen.' This saying picks up the theme of the last part of the story only; it is a general, proverbial observation which comments on one aspect of the story but leaves much else uninterpreted. As Schottroff points out, the (later) Rabbinic parables give support to the notion that when in Judaism any human situation is linked with 'the kingdom of God', it is more often than not in wry awareness of the contrast between God's order and human order than of similarity between them (2006, pp. 41–5). In this story Jesus plays his characteristic role of the sharp but self-effacing observer–narrator who sets up a scene for his hearers to contemplate, then takes a back seat as they do so.

Plot

The central conflict of the plot, as of The Great Banquet, is the resistance to the king's dignity put up by some of his subjects. Its resolution is the king's restoration of his honour through the inviting of new guests, and the maintenance of that honour through holding the one improperly dressed to account and having him brutally punished. As always, the ending of the story shows where its weight lies, and, as so often, it takes the form of a character's direct speech. The king's command to the attendants to bind and punish the man focuses the hearers' minds on the harsh reality of absolute power and leaves a rotten taste in their mouths.

In the early part of the plot it is worth noting a difference from The Great Banquet analogous to the difference between Matthew's and Luke's versions of The Rebellious Tenants. In Luke, when the banquet is ready, there is just one sending of a slave (14.17), but the excuses by three people are recounted individually, in their own direct speech (14.18–19). In Luke's version of The Rebellious Tenants, the owner sends three individual slaves in succession (Luke 20.10–12). In Matthew, the king sends slaves on two occasions to those invited to the wedding feast (22.3–4), and the excuses on the second occasion are recounted generally: 'But they made light of it and went away, one to his farm, another to his business, while the rest seized his slaves, mistreated them, and killed them' (22.5–6). Similarly in Matthew's version of the tenants story, there are two sendings of various slaves, whose treatment with varying degrees of severity by the tenants is described in general terms (21.34–36). No great weight is to be given to these differences when it comes to understanding the plots, but that is the point: they are matters of the Evangelists' styles, representing different ways of advancing a narrative.

Another noteworthy feature of the plot in Matthew's story is the use of a fast-forward technique in 22.7. The detail of the king sending his troops to destroy the murderers and burn their city has usually been taken by modern commentators as an allegorical addition by Matthew, referring to the destruction of Jerusalem, and ridiculously interrupting the realism of the story, as if such a person would dispatch an army 'while the food was getting cold on the table'. But the refusal of the invitation (particularly because it is violent) is an act of rebellion, so the king's response is quite realistic, and it is a standard plot technique to finish off one part of a story before returning to events which happened earlier. So there is no need to see the king's vengeance taking place at precisely that moment. It completes the treatment of the rebels, before the storyteller returns to what, as we have already seen, is the main focus of the plot: the restoration of the king's honour, first by filling the empty places and then by ensuring the respect of their new occupants.

Reflection

As a tale steeped in the power dynamics of first-century Judea or Galilee, and possibly echoing real events with which hearers would have been familiar, The Wedding Feast focuses attention, like that of the tenants, on the logic and consequences of resisting authority. Here, too, while the king is briefly shamed in the story, he reasserts his authority ruthlessly.

Those who heard this story, including especially the Jewish leaders, would be reminded of the ruthlessness of their imperial masters, and the dangers of failing to conform to their wishes. Like The Great Banquet, this story describes an overturning of the social order. As 'both bad and good' enter the banqueting hall (v. 10), the respectable who thought they could get away with flexing their political muscles lie under threat of destruction (v. 7). But the danger for the new guests, too, is exposed (vv. 11–14).

Like the story of the tenants, this story does not give a direct warning. It hints at a social upheaval in which a crowd 'both bad and good' may benefit. But its sombre account of the workings of imperial power forms a laconic reminder from Jesus to all, of whatever social class, that it is not lightly to be confronted. If there is a text which helps us in more direct language to feel the realistic, historical force of this story, it may be Matthew 24.40–41, pointing to dramatic social upheaval: 'Then two will be in the field; one will be taken and one will be left. Two women will be grinding meal together; one will be taken and one will be left.'

The Ten Virgins (Matt. 25.1–12)

Setting

The wedding customs presupposed in The Ten Virgins entail marriageable girls aged about 12 accompanying the bridegroom, with his bride and their entourage, in a celebratory procession into the wedding banquet in his house. Bailey (2008, p. 271) offers the interesting information that many Greek, Latin and Syriac versions include the bride as well as the groom, presumably reflecting knowledge of the customs. He writes of a 'disorganized, exuberant parade' winding its way through the village (p. 272). This was a way of young women placing themselves 'on the marriage market, which was, as a rule, regulated by their fathers and potential husbands' (Schottroff, 2006, p. 29). Their task is to be ready to escort the bridegroom on this important night.

Events unfold in what one might call a lightly tragic manner, but always staying within the bounds of realism. The girls fall asleep when the bridegroom is delayed. When they are aroused by a cry that he is coming, they get up and prepare their lamps. At this point the 'foolish' who had not brought spare oil ask for some from the 'wise' who have done so. The 'wise', not unexpectedly, refuse, sending the 'foolish' off to the shops to get some. Apparently dealers might be open, though it was late in the evening. The bridegroom comes while the 'foolish' are away, the 'wise' accompany him into the banquet, and when the others eventually arrive they are excluded, despite pleading to be admitted.

The realism of the story is often thought to be threatened by the bridegroom's words in verse 12, 'Truly I tell you, I do not know you.' There is an echo here of the words of Jesus in Matthew 7.23, 'Then I will declare to them, "I never knew you".' The language of the story may well have been coloured by this saying and/or vice versa, though it is not as similar-sounding in the Greek as in the English (25.12: *ouk oida humas*; 7:23: *oudepote egnōn humas*). However, it may be later allegorizing which causes us to hear these words of the bridegroom in a more spiritual or transcendent sense than the natural one which, surely, they can easily bear. The bridegroom has not even seen the 'foolish' virgins. If the custom was that they offer their own services, and the 'wise' have said nothing to him, he has no reason to think that he was ever going to have more than five escorts. Of course he does not know them. And why should he admit to his banquet young women who, as far as he is concerned, have not fulfilled the customary duty at all? Exclusion from a 'banquet' has wider resonances in later Christian theology, but such resonances are not developed here.

The mindset into which the story taps is closely connected with the OT concept of wisdom as prudence (Schottroff, 2006, p. 30). Two verses cited by Schottroff form particularly interesting background. First, there is the depiction of the ideal wife in Proverbs 31.18: 'Her lamp does not go out at night.' Second, there is the comment in Sirach 22.4: 'A sensible [LXX *phronimē*, the same word as used in Jesus' story for 'wise'] daughter obtains a husband of her own, but one who acts shamefully is a grief to her father.' The story thus plays on the earthy 'wisdom' which recognized, from an often paternalistic perspective, what a woman's behaviour 'ought' to be like.

Character

The bridegroom is a stock character whose personality is not developed at all. His exclusion of the unknown girls at the end is neither compassionate nor (by the standards of Jesus' anti-heroes) particularly harsh. On the one hand, this final scene 'reveals the ugly face, the hard reality of a society that defines women in terms of their accommodation, subjection, and marriage' (Schottroff, 2006, p. 31). Exclusion from the banquet is not just a matter of missing a party; the girls are exposed as not playing by the rules of the game, and their chances of bringing honour to their families (especially fathers) by finding a good match take a knock. On the other hand, there is no fierce punishment like that exercised by the kings of 18.23–35 or 22.2–13, or the propertied man in 25.14–30.

In a patriarchal society, hearers would recognize that the behaviour of the 'foolish' virgins was indeed 'naïve' (Schottroff's translation, 2006, p. 29). Furthermore, they would probably see the 'prudence' of the 'wise' girls displayed in their refusal to give oil to the 'foolish' as well as in their initial preparations. Certainly the ending of the story seems (uncomfortably to modern hearers) to validate this choice not to share, giving the story the feel of a proverbial maxim: the clever (Schottroff's translation) are rewarded while the naïve are punished.

Schottroff rightly points to the evaluation of the 'clever' girls' behaviour that a thoughtful hearer familiar with Hebrew Scripture and Jesus' own teaching surely makes:

> There is no need even to bring the commandment of love of neighbour into play to show that, measured against the biblical tradition of the shaping of human relationships, the clever women are behaving in an unsolidary manner and are subjecting themselves to the socially accepted condition of competition.
>
> (Schottroff, 2006, p. 31)

But would Jesus' hearers have made that evaluation? Or would they, at least at first, have seen the story as validating the more prudential and self-serving aspects of their 'wisdom' tradition? Does Jesus as narrator give any guidance on this?

Point of view

At first sight, the answer to this question is uncompromising. This story is an unusual one among Jesus' full narratives in the clear labelling of the characters by the narrator: 'foolish' and 'wise'. This brings the story closer than most of the others to some of Jesus' shorter similitudes, especially Mathew 7.24–27, in which those who obey Jesus are compared to a wise man who built his house on a rock, and those who do not are compared to a foolish man who built his house on the sand. In characterizing the virgins in this way, the narrator directs a hearer's response to them from the start and appears to approve of the actions of the 'wise', as according with the wisdom tradition.

But what tone of voice does Jesus use? That is a key question that all attempts to imagine an original telling of his stories must ask, as performance criticism highlights (see Ward and Trobisch, 2013, pp. 56–60). What if, in the telling of the story, Jesus placed the oral equivalent of speech marks around the words 'wise' and 'foolish' wherever they occur? In that case, his perspective would sound rather different. The events of the story would be presented more neutrally, as expressing an expected chain of cause and effect, but without passing explicit moral judgements on anyone.

Plot

The numerical balance between the five 'wise' and five 'foolish' virgins is a familiar plot device, bringing out the starkness of a contrast. The question which a hearer immediately asks is 'Will the lamps of the "foolish" burn for as long as they need to without spare oil?' Tension increases as the bridegroom is delayed and all the virgins fall asleep. Here, the audience wonders whether all ten will miss their chance. Will their lamps still be alight when he arrives? Crisis then comes as the bridegroom's arrival is announced and they wake up. The 'wise' have the oil with which to relight their lamps, the 'foolish' do not, so attention refocuses on the latter. What will they do? When the 'foolish' ask for oil from the 'wise', what will the 'wise' respond? The answer 'no' comes as hard, yet predictable, and prompts the further question: what next? Tension is maintained as hearers wonder whether the 'foolish' will get back in time from the dealers. With an ugly thud, the climax comes. The 'wise' are ready to accompany the party into the banquet, but the 'foolish' arrive too late, and their request for admittance is refused.

Characteristically, the story ends with the bridegroom's direct speech: 'Truly I tell you, I do not know you' (v. 12). The end-stress of this moment leaves the emphasis of the story on the hard realities of Jesus' world. What, then, are the story's wider implications?

Reflection

There is something rather brutal about the implication of the story that the world works on an 'everyone for him/herself' basis – not dissimilar to the way the man without the wedding garment in 22.11–14 seems left out on a limb with no one to come to his aid. But I am much less sure than I was (S. I. Wright, 2009, p. 21) that we should hear in this a strong warning to keep one's head down and 'play the system'. Rather, the story seems, as Schottroff suggests, to focus with minimal narratorial comment on exhibiting the ruthlessness of the system itself, and in the very harshness that it portrays, to speak of the injustice that is the 'beginning of the birth pangs' (Matt. 24.8) and a harbinger of the nearness of God's kingdom (Schottroff, 2006, pp. 34–7). We should be cautious about taking the words 'wise' and 'foolish' at face value.

The Talents (Matt. 25.14–30)

Setting

Although The Talents is similar to one strand of The Pounds in Luke 19.11–27, the element concerning the nobleman's claim to the throne and those resisting it is missing. Also, as with the Lukan Great Banquet and Matthean Wedding Feast stories, there is remarkably little similarity in the Greek wording between the stories in the two Gospels. (This suggests, incidentally, the intriguing possibility that the 'Q' source supposedly used by Matthew and Luke contained no stories told by Jesus; but that is something we cannot pursue here.) We treat The Talents separately, therefore, although briefly, because much that can be said about its setting, character, point of view and plot has already been said with reference to The Pounds in Chapter 9.

The 'man' who goes on a journey in Matthew 25.14 is not claiming a throne. He is, however, extremely wealthy. A 'talent' was about 15 years' wages for a labourer, whereas a 'pound' was only about three months' wages. So the slaves in the Matthew story are given vastly more responsibility than those in Luke's. There may be a touch of the storyteller's colourful exaggeration here. Yet as with the 'ten thousand talents' owed by the first slave in the story of the unforgiving slave (Matt. 18.24), the amounts, though imprecise, quite realistically indicate the fabulous wealth enjoyed by a few in contrast to the many. In this tale, unlike The Pounds, the master reckons with the varied 'ability' (*dunamin*) of the slaves in deciding how much to entrust to each (v. 15). The association of wealth and power is also seen in this story, though not quite as overtly as in The Pounds. The two faithful slaves are rewarded for their faithfulness by being 'put in charge' of many things (vv. 21, 23) when their master returns.

Two potentially unrealistic touches are found in the story. When the owner says to the faithful slaves 'enter into the joy of your master' (vv. 21, 23), this sounds like a spiritualizing of the scene. But is it? The Prodigal Son has been seen in a very spiritual way, yet the celebration and signs of welcome laid on by the father for his returning son are thoroughly earthly, human, physical. The story can be used to express spiritual reality so powerfully precisely because the scene it presents is so strikingly this-worldly, touching the depths of human experience. 'The joy of your master' may sound to Christian ears ethereal, and 'joy' is indeed a quality of the eschaton in Jewish literature (Beyreuther and Finkenrath, in Brown, ed., 1975, vol. 2, p. 357).[3] But there is no reason not to imagine this as an expression of the newly confirmed favour in which the faithful slaves find themselves with their owner. They are given greater responsibility and power, and with that, no doubt, are able to taste more for themselves of the opulence of his household.

The second potentially unrealistic touch is the final punishment of the 'worthless slave': 'throw him into the outer darkness, where there will be weeping and gnashing of teeth' (v. 30). This is certainly terminology which Matthew likes (see also 8.12; 13.42, 50; 22.13), and it brings an apocalyptic colouring to the story. But there is nothing unrealistic about the master's harsh treatment of the third slave. Again, brutal earthly reality lies beneath the exotic language, though that language invests it with extra significance.

Character

Little needs to be said about character here other than what was said about the characters in The Pounds. A man of such wealth as this is assumed, from the start, to be a man of overweening power. There is no surprise in his rewarding of the first two slaves with greater responsibility, nor the ruthless removal of all responsibility from the third, together with his harsh punishment. The third slave's estimation of him as a 'harsh man', with which, indeed, he implicitly agrees himself (v. 26), will be the view of ordinary hearers of Jesus from the start, only confirmed by events as they unfold.

As in The Pounds, hearers would feel a degree of identification with the three slaves. Though there might also be some initial suspicion of those so closely associated with this wealthy aristocrat, hearers would know well that for many people there was little choice. The choices the slaves make, to trade or to bury, reflect a genuine dilemma, and it is likely that listeners would have seen and sympathized with the logic of both. While recognizing the plausibility of the master acting as he did, and the imprudence, as it turned out, of the third slave's actions, they would have been unlikely to have accepted the master's valuation of him as 'wicked and lazy', with its consequent harsh punishment. But they may also have seen that this slave acted disappointingly. The master had, after all, seen some ability in him, despite recognizing his limitations (v. 15), and had taken a risk with him, of which he had not proved himself worthy.

Point of view

The narrator characteristically gives barely any clues as to his own stance. Indeed, there is a nice balance between the third slave's evaluation of the master and the master's evaluation of the third slave which makes the story poised. The narrator himself evaluates neither, but invites hearers to observe the unfolding logic of events.

Plot

Without the element of claiming a throne, the plot of The Talents is simpler than that of The Pounds. The implied question set up by the opening is what success the slaves will have in fulfilling their commission. The entrusting of talents to the slaves is carried out slightly differently from that of pounds in Luke's story. Here the slaves are given three different amounts. The first two make a 100 per cent profit on their investments, much smaller than the profit made by the traders who were entrusted with the pounds. In this respect, therefore, the more exaggerated sound of the initial quantity of money in Matthew is balanced by a more sober reckoning of the slaves' achievement. But the difference at this point between the two stories is essentially a difference of narrative art. The contrast between the first two and the third slaves can be made equally by giving them the same amount initially and setting two vast profits against no profit at all (Luke), or by giving them different amounts 'according to their ability' and setting two good profits against no profit at all (Matthew).

Whereas Luke's story does not disclose how the slaves have done until they give their account to the nobleman, Matthew narrates their activity (25.16–18) as well as the account they give of it (25.19–30). This fills some of the space that Luke's story takes up with the throne-claimant element. More significantly, it increases the suspense, as the audience first find out what the slaves did, but then have to wait till they report it to find out how the master will react. The emphasis of the plot falls heavily on the decree against the third slave from the master's mouth in the closing verses. This outcome will have been heard as a near-inevitable consequence of the third slave's misjudgement of the prudent conclusion to draw from his assessment of his master's character. He has failed to latch on to the survival tactics necessary to the time.

Reflection

The lack of the throne-claimant strand in the story shifts the emphasis away from the danger of an open challenge to the authority of one of the élite to the more subtle but everyday danger of the demands of the political environment. The plutocrat's treatment of the third slave is as unreasonable as the host's treatment of the man without the wedding garment. But as in The Wedding Feast and The Ten Virgins, the outcome revolves around not fairness, still less compassion, but the brute realities of the time.

Like The Ten Virgins, The Talents should not, I think, be heard as urging the way of 'prudence' (*contra* an element of my approach in S. I. Wright, 2002, p. 147). Rather, it exposes the harsh truth of how the interactions between the powerful and their dependants in the present and imminent time of crisis and upheaval are likely to play out, without any obvious recommendation for action in their light.

Part 4

GATHERING THE ECHOES

11

Jesus the storyteller

The time has come to pose the questions of what exactly our hearing of the stories of Jesus in the preceding chapters may tell us about Jesus himself, how this relates to the rest of the Synoptic picture of his life and death, and how this way of hearing them advances scholarly debate and relates to wider theological concerns.

In brief, I believe that a serious focus on the stories of Jesus as stories has opened up many new insights and possibilities for understanding. More specifically, I believe that the combination of factors outlined in Chapter 3 and assumed as an explicit or implicit substructure in Chapters 4—10 – orality, memory, testimony and performance – together with the disciplines of reception history and, especially, narrative criticism – has enabled us to get a tighter grip on the dynamics of their original telling. While an awareness of the mechanisms of an oral culture and of the vagaries of memory allow a lower degree of certainty than modern scholarship has tended to claim about the thrust of an original performance, it also, along with a sense of the importance of testimony, subverts the now traditional sharp distinction between the Evangelists' performances and those of Jesus. This has meant that though Jesus' 'intention' has emerged more tentatively (and strangely) than those interested in the stories' theological import might wish, the boundaries between my hearings of the Evangelists in Chapters 4—6 and my hearing of Jesus in Chapters 7—10 are fuzzier than critical scholarship normally expects. To readers disappointed on either ground, I can only say that this is where my study has led me and that this seems an appropriate balance for the nature of my subject.

In what follows I will first gather together some threads from what we have heard in the stories in Chapters 7—10 that may enable us to piece together a picture of the 'implied teller'. I will then relate this picture to other elements of the Synoptic portrait of Jesus, taking for granted, as always, that that portrait has been filtered by various factors including the Evangelists' own concerns and theology, but using evidence that is generally held to be overwhelming. Finally, I will locate my hearing in the story of scholarship and point to its theological significance.

Jesus the implied teller

Chapters 7—10 have been an exploration of what insights may emerge when we attend seriously to the stories of Jesus *as stories*, rather than as 'parables' with all the irresolvable questions of definition which that raises. We have used some of the main categories of narrative criticism to imagine how Jesus' audiences would have received these stories, followed their threads, entered their emotions and responded to their characters and conclusions. In so doing we have tried to capture more closely than has usually been the case the moment of an original oral telling, recognizing of course that there will have been many such moments and that ultimately they are beyond our recall. The focus on possible 'hearings' underlines both the richness of the stories and the impossibility of recovering a single original 'meaning' or thrust. Yet a remarkable outline emerges of the 'implied narrator'. We will approach this through a summary of what has emerged from our study of the setting, character, point of view and plot of these stories.

Setting

I have been testing the hypothesis that Jesus' stories are essentially realistic, reflecting the real world in which Jesus lived – its social structures, its cultural customs, its ambiguities, its difficult choices, the logic of its political dynamics, the memories, scripts and mindsets which shaped his hearers' view of life. Through this exploration I have become more convinced than ever that this hypothesis takes us a very long way in accounting for the stories as we have them and dealing with the problems which they have regularly thrown up for interpreters, such as (sometimes) puzzling logic and the harsh edges of powerful characters. There are, indeed, some uses of language in the various Gospel records which hint at dimensions beyond realism. But none of these, I believe, should divert us from hearing them as designed to lead their hearers into a believable, known world and open up for them in intriguing ways the urgent questions it poses.

The perception of realism in the parables has been common at least from Jülicher onwards. The question, however, is what we consider the purpose of this realism to be, and that is primarily where my dissatisfaction with previous approaches (including, to some extent, my own) has lain. Realistic stories, however brief, are not translatable into other rhetorical forms without loss. They may be rich in suggestiveness, in metaphor, metonymy or other turns of speech; individual elements (such as the father of the lost son in Luke 11.15–32), or entire narrative sequences (such as that whole story), may point tellingly towards wider, deeper, realities on various levels (e.g. the character of God, the story of Israel, or the travails of humankind). But to overlook the story in the interests of such 'meanings' is to overlook that which prima facie the Evangelists have left us. Whereas much modern scholarship has found the Evangelists' fingerprints all over the stories Jesus told, I find it a most impressive fact that whatever 'spin' tradition, memory and theology may have put upon them in their Gospel contexts, their character as realistic stories has been preserved. This allows us to hear their strange rhetoric as the speech-acts of one who is (here) not concerned to persuade, or reveal, or promise, or warn, but rather invite keen observation and reflection.

Character

An essential element in all the stories is the way in which they invite reflection on characters. People are presented in them with minimal description, but are often recognizable as particular social types. Their thoughts, actions and responses are then opened for scrutiny by audiences who will, from their own perspectives, have a range of evaluations of and degrees of sympathy towards them.

Moreover, it is through the process of the hearers' identification with the characters that the specific situations depicted in the stories open up on to a wider world. It is not that the stories are saying 'the "spiritual" world is like the "ordinary" world'. Rather, through portraying a slave, a tenant, a father, a toll-collector, they invite listeners to see themselves, or someone they know well, within the narrative, and thus make its world their own. The stories appear to come from one who is both immersed in his world and concerned to relate to others within it.

Point of view

We have seen that clues to the narrator's point of view in Jesus' stories are often sparse. Events are narrated with minimal comment and direction on how hearers are to regard them. Herein lies one of the most important results of a narrative-critical enquiry. The stories of Jesus do not advance an argument (*contra* e.g. Jeremias, 1963 (1947), and aspects of my own chapter 'Parables and Persuasion', S. I. Wright, 2000b, pp. 182–226). They present a series of events for the hearers to enter into and ponder, and then draw conclusions.

Nevertheless, though Jesus may be a restrained commentator in his stories, they certainly disclose the point of view of a keen observer, whose interests are revealing. 'Themes' are a significant element of a story's rhetoric (Resseguie, 2005, pp. 46–8), and identifying them is a useful way of directing attention to the interests of the implied teller. Narrative themes are not discrete 'topics of discussion' but threads woven with each other in various combinations, with varying degrees of prominence in different stories. We can trace a variety of themes from Jesus' surroundings in which, his stories strongly suggest, he took a sharp interest.

Three stories focus on the natural process of growth, and obstacles to it (The Sower, The Wheat and the Weeds, and The Barren Fig Tree). Although realistic stories, they are rooted in the organic connection between growth in the human and natural worlds (or 'the natural and the spiritual order', as Dodd put it, 1936 (1935), pp. 21–2 – though I am uneasy about the dualistic connotations of Dodd's language here). Therefore they have immediate resonance beyond the purely agricultural environment with the human one.

The specific theme of obstacles recurs much more widely in the stories – as, perhaps, is to be expected, since plots regularly revolve around conflict. A king's slave is hard-hearted (The Unforgiving Slave), a vineyard-owner's rent-collection is thwarted (The Rebellious Tenants), a widow's case is ignored (The Widow and the Judge): these are only some of the most obvious instances of those tensions that we have observed in play in all the plots we have studied.

Violence is a frequent theme (The Unforgiving Slave, The Good Samaritan, The Pounds, The Rebellious Tenants, The Wedding Feast). So is wealth and its use (The Unforgiving Slave, The Good Samaritan, The Rich Fool, The Great Banquet, The Prodigal Son, The Shrewd Manager, The Rich Man and Lazarus, The Pounds, The Labourers in the Vineyard, The Wedding Feast, The Talents). As a subset of this, debt and its remission (or otherwise) is a specific focus in The Unforgiving Slave, The Prodigal Son, and The Shrewd Manager.

Contrasts regularly appear between the utter helplessness of some and the compassion, or otherwise, of others: The Unforgiving Slave, The Good Samaritan, The Great Banquet, The Prodigal Son, The Rich Man and Lazarus, The Widow and the Judge, The Labourers in the Vineyard, The Wedding Feast. Two interesting threads enrich and vary this theme. On the one hand, the motives and character of those who, on particular occasions, seem to act rightly and generously may be decidedly mixed or at least ambiguous (The Unforgiving Slave, The Great Banquet, The Shrewd Manager, The Widow and the Judge, The Wedding Feast). On the other hand, those in need of help sometimes show themselves feisty and decisive (The Prodigal Son, The Shrewd Manager, The Widow and the Judge).

The latter thread connects with a wider theme of wisdom and folly. The stories often pose implied questions about the prudent way to act in demanding situations (e.g. The Shrewd Manager). Sometimes characters are caught short in situations whose real demands for wise action they had not realized (The Rich Fool, The Rich Man and Lazarus, The Pharisee and the Toll-Collector, The Ten Virgins).

Nearly all the stories open up, from one angle or another, the theme of hierarchy, or other more subtle status-relationships, within Jesus' society. Only The Sower simply concerns one man and his soil. Even The Wheat and the Weeds and The Barren Fig Tree contain brief evocative dialogues between master and servants. The Rich Fool has just one character and God, but the implied presence of others is highlighted precisely in the man's self-absorption, and others will inherit all his possessions.

Finally, one of the most pervasive themes in the stories is the reversal of fortunes. This can have either a 'comic' or a 'tragic' twist. In, for example, The Sower, The Good Samaritan, The Prodigal Son and The Shrewd Manager, gloomy beginnings contrast with hopeful endings. In The Unforgiving Slave and The Rebellious Tenants, in contrast, hope and relief are quickly succeeded by disaster. In some stories, a stark contrast is drawn between the reward of some and the punishment of others (e.g. The Rich Man and Lazarus, The Pounds, The Talents). In The Labourers in the Vineyard there is a surprising equalization of fortunes. In many, characters are seen in a light unexpected by hearers: most strikingly, The Good Samaritan, The Rich Man and Lazarus, and The Pharisee and the Toll-Collector.

Identifying these themes helps us to see clearly the fields of Jesus' observation and attention. To characterize these as 'this-worldly' is correct, but not if that means we forget that, for Jesus and his hearers, the natural–supernatural distinction does not hold the ideological sway that it has held during much of modernity. God is, for them, as much a part of these scenes as their human players, even though, apart from one occasion (Luke 12.20), he remains an unseen and unheard presence.

This yields the impression of a storyteller who is not only celebrating his world as it is, in its diversity of people, its comedy, its hopeful potential, but also unremittingly honest about its darker side. In the ability to identify and envisage compassion, forgiveness and reconciliation Jesus seems to show the beat of his own heart. In the envisaging of harshness, cruelty and degradation he shows how close he is to the suffering of many of his contemporaries.

The themes on which the stories focus betray the intense fascinations of the storyteller, but taking 'point of view' seriously impels us to be cautious about using them as direct evidence of a particular standpoint or purpose – precisely because the evaluative point of view they disclose is so understated. If we refrain from the traditional figurative identifications that point beyond the stories themselves, it will seem forced to press them into service as encodings of a particular view of the kingdom of God, whether understood as imminent and apocalyptic, present or 'inaugurated'. In this sense, I believe Dale Allison is partly right: the ambiguity of Jesus' parables makes them unsuitable as primary evidence for Jesus' expectation concerning the kingdom (2010, pp. 116–18). However, their focus on current circumstances undoubtedly betrays Jesus' belief that the present was a time imbued with critical significance.

Our study also suggests that it is unnatural to hear Jesus' stories as directly self-referential. The one which has been most commonly seen thus, The Rebellious Tenants, makes good sense, as we have seen, in realistic terms. The phrase 'beloved Son' certainly re-echoes with the identity of Jesus for Mark and Luke. The story is steeped in the atmosphere of violence which is indeed soon to overwhelm Jesus. But that does not limit the situation, or its potential resonance, to the violence meted out to Jesus by certain Jewish leaders. There had been, could be and would be other victims and other perpetrators. Precisely the enquiry into 'point of view', then, uncovers a narrator who is self-effacing and sharply focused on the scenes of his surrounding world.

Plot

Our study of the stories' plots has shown how all can be read as a logical unity, and I have suggested that this is a far more adequate way of conceiving the

stories' cogency than to say that they make one (or more) 'points'. Some plots
are 'resolution' plots, portraying how a problem is solved (e.g. The Wheat and
the Weeds); others are 'revelation' plots, disclosing a surprising truth (e.g. The
Pharisee and the Toll-Collector). We have also seen a frequent use of direct
speech by a main character at or near the end, reinforcing the familiar narrative
law of end-stress. This highlights attention on the outcome of the various
tensions and conflicts which generate the plots. An effect of this is to underline
a wry sense of inevitability in the dénouement of events, combined sometimes
with genuine tragedy (The Rebellious Tenants, The Pounds, The Talents) or
carnivalesque-type comedy (The Great Banquet). The outcome of the plots
does not necessarily imply any recommendation by the narrator on a course of
action to be taken in the light of the story, but it does focus hearers' minds on
processes of cause and consequence which are familiar. Here we return to the
point made above that the stories cannot be forced to yield a particular
understanding of the kingdom of God. Certainly their plots are in no way
explicit about the timing of God's kingdom's consummation. But their taut
tension and sense of a sure though sometimes mysterious purpose conveys an
unmistakable mood of urgency. They are not mere discussion-starters or
thought-provokers. In this sense, they sit well with the reported view of Jesus
that the kingdom of God was present, spatially and temporally (Luke 17.20–
21).

Overall reflection

It would, of course, be possible to challenge this whole approach by saying
that I have brought the analytical categories of setting, character, point of view
and plot to the texts, rather than derived them therefrom; that in truth, these
are minor or irrelevant aspects of their rhetoric; that we should go back to
calling them 'parables' defined as similes or metaphors which serve to compare
or identify one thing with another. To this I would respond that I have only
used these analytical categories following an initial identification of these texts
as bearing the rhetorical form of story, and that it is the categories of simile,
metaphor or indeed 'parable' itself which are the real culprits obscuring their
true rhetoric.

   I believe that the narrative-critical exploration of the stories yields two
overall conclusions about their place in our construal of the historical Jesus.
On the one hand, the stories tell us less about Jesus' 'theology' or 'message' or
'thinking' than has usually been supposed (as evidenced in my account of
scholarship in Chapters 1 and 2). A story which is transparently the
communication of a 'view' of the storyteller ceases to be a story that has
interest and power, and we have seen that Jesus' stories are not transparent in
this way. They work their magic through the traditional threads of the
storyteller's art, uniquely chosen and woven in each case. To miss that
weaving is to miss not just a little, but the great majority of what they are and
say.

On the other hand, the stories actually tell us more about Jesus' 'praxis' than has usually been supposed. The fact that storytelling was such a characteristic mode of Jesus' speech is a significant *datum* of his way of operating. It means, for example, that the way we generalize about Jesus' words often needs to be qualified. Did Jesus 'proclaim' the kingdom of God? Yes, but the stories hardly count as 'proclamation'. Did he 'teach' the law of God, and a way of true wisdom? Yes, but the teaching style of Jesus as revealed in his stories surely challenges the regular scholarly assumption that reduces teaching to 'what' is taught while disregarding the 'how' (Melchert, 1998, pp. 216–17). Herzog's portrayal of Jesus as 'pedagogue of the oppressed' (1994) captures this sense of Jesus' teaching as an empowering event, inviting but not forcing the participation of the hearers (though it underplays the aspect of Jesus' storytelling as a public activity, with ordinary crowds or groups of suspicious authority figures, or both, and the disciples listening in). Charles Melchert shows that Jesus' approach was to 'evoke learning' in a 'non-coercive manner', like Israel's sages whose thinking is collected in the 'Wisdom Literature' (1998, pp. 240–69). Crossan has shrewdly argued that Jesus' particular understanding of God's kingdom as non-violent and entailing collaboration between God and humans is matched by his parabolic form of communication, which does not compel the hearer to adopt a particular viewpoint but requires their co-operation, in entering the parabolic world (2012, pp. 133–6). They are challenging, but not aggressive, 'delicately provocative and gently subversive' (p. 135); '*a collaborative* eschaton *requires a participatory pedagogy*' (p. 134, Crossan's italics).

Jesus' stories not only illuminate his praxis, they are also part of it. Like his other sayings, in their different ways, they are speech-acts, which 'do' something as much as they communicate anything; or rather, they communicate by the doing as much as by the saying (cf. N. T. Wright, 1996, p. 176, picking up the emphasis of the New Hermeneutic). Conversely, his acts are as much a part of his 'wise teaching' as his words (Melchert, 1998, pp. 269–71).

The stories compel us to look beyond familiar categories to describe the stance and persona of their teller. Some good suggestions have been made. We might say that Jesus' stories are the supreme examples of what Edward F. Beutner says about his parables generally: 'A parable is a little like a joke, but not an entirely innocent joke' (2007, p. 33). Or, in the words of veteran parable scholar Robert W. Funk: 'Jesus may be described as a comic savant. He was perhaps the first standup Jewish comic. A comic savant is a sage who embeds wisdom in humor; a humorist shuns practical advice. Comic wisdom refuses to be explicit' (2007, p. 90). To claim that Jesus was a 'joker' or 'comic savant' is not frivolous; it helps to force our attention on to the liveliness of Jesus' rhetoric. It is not, however, sufficient to capture the evidence, particularly the intense seriousness of focus and purpose revealed in both the teller's keen observation of his world and his tight plots.

N. T. Wright applies to the parables John P. Meier's comment that 'It is almost as though Jesus were intent on making a riddle of himself' (N. T.

Wright, 1996, p. 631, citing Meier, 1994, pp. 453–4).[1] This underlines the element of self-exposure in the stories, paradoxically arising from their very indirectness of form. Still more profound, maybe, is the label 'fool' or 'jester' (e.g. Frost, 2010; Campbell, 2008). The 'fool' in culture and literature is one who has the privilege – or takes the risk – of speaking truth to power, through a repertoire of verbal and enacted strategies, by turns comic, creative, satirical and eccentric (see Frost, 2010, pp. 1–11). Or, in Campbell's words:

> [T]he jester seeks to startle and dislocate people – especially those in power – so they might be released from their common-sense presuppositions and see and live in the world in new and creative ways ... The jester melts away those elemental assumptions that are supposedly 'written in stone.' That is, he or she subverts the myths, rationalities, and presuppositions that others take for granted, but that often are the ways of death not life.   (2008, p. 3)

These epithets capture the sense that, in his stories, despite (or because of) their extreme restraint in offering a 'point of view', Jesus was performing an act that was risky in itself and of a piece with the riskiness of everything else we can know of his praxis. 'If they really were to see and understand there might be a riot', writes N. T. Wright (1996, p. 179): yes, but even in their narrative indirectness there was risk enough. In a similar vein, Robert J. Miller argues that in the similitudes The Treasure in the Field and The Merchant in Search of Fine Pearls, the protagonists mirror Jesus' own attitude as a 'fool' who single-mindedly, dangerously and joyfully campaigned for the kingdom of God and called others to do so (2007, pp. 76–82).

Jesus' stance as narrator, self-effacing and detached, yet piercingly perceptive of the world around, is that of the 'fool' who challenges a whole system from its roots up. Or, to use terms from classical drama, Jesus – *pace* the implication of Reimarus! – is very far from being a braggart or *alazōn*, using inflated rhetoric, claiming to know far more than he does. The stories of Jesus, surely, are the words of a subtle but disturbing *eirōn*, who appears to know far less: and that is by no means in spite of his Jewishness, but surely an expression of it.[2] Also highly suggestive, and relevant to stories as actions, is David McCracken's portrayal of the scandal, stumbling block and offence caused by Jesus in the Gospels (1994).

Identifying the implications of the story-form as a speech-act enables us to get more glimpses of a rounded Jesus, who wasn't ruled by a diary divided up between 'teaching' and 'doing miracles', 'meals with sinners' or 'being kind'. This was a Jesus who seemed to be constantly finding new ways of saying things in an indirect, oblique, quizzical form, sometimes quite an extended one. The presence of all these puzzling and provoking stories, more or less undisturbed in their narrative form, in the earliest layers of Christian tradition is strong support for the characterization of Jesus as one who regularly refused to be too open about what he thought he was doing, who he thought he was, and what he was claiming.

Yet 'joker', 'comic savant' and 'fool' may all suggest a merely eccentric individual, rather than a person steeped in the Scriptures and traditions of his people. Particularly the first two epithets are too redolent of the Jesus Seminar's Jesus, defined according to his words alone, subversive of anything and everything, but not a figure in whom word and action, speech and suffering are closely integrated. Jesus' stories certainly attest to a profound concern with true (and sometimes paradoxical) wisdom, but this is not the wisdom of an isolated sage. It derives from the communal tradition of Israel where 'wisdom' is closely tied to Torah and the fear of YHWH. Jesus repristinates this wisdom, but does not turn his back on it in favour of some vaguely defined 'radicalism'. In particular, Jesus' storytelling surely supports the claim that he acted as one of Israel's prophets (e.g. N. T. Wright, 1996, pp. 147–474; Herzog, 2005, pp. 99–124; Horsley, 2012, pp. 67–157).

As we have seen, the rhetoric of story, though ambiguous, yet has direction and thrust, and this fits with the classic prophetic ethos and vivid style. The Rebellious Tenants clearly worked on the hearers the same kind of infuriation that the message of a prophet like Jeremiah stoked in the powers that be. If any one story played a part in the chain of events which led to Jesus' death, this was surely it. Jesus also displays the prophetic concern for penetrating to the really important elements of Torah (e.g. Mic. 6.6–8). He contrasts in narrative those concerned with details of the Torah with one who exhibits obedience to its undergirding thrust (The Good Samaritan). He displays in narrative a conventional contrast between 'prudence' and 'naïveté' without endorsing it (The Ten Virgins). Storytelling of Jesus' kind is an act of interpretation and also of questioning prevailing mores. Like the prophets, he focuses on different aspects of the society around him, particularly from the viewpoint of its downtrodden members, and invites fresh perspectives on it. As Herzog writes:

> Jesus the prophet interpreted what was happening to the people of Galilee who were being increasingly squeezed by colonial domination and internal exploit-ation. He taught them to read their distressing situation not as God's will but as a consequence of the violation of God's covenant.   (2005, p. 113)

There is no real precedent in the Hebrew prophets for storytelling of the style or scale of that of Jesus. In addition, Jesus did not have access to the centres of political power as some of the prophets did (Herzog, 2005, p. 114). But there is in figures such as Elijah, Amos, Jeremiah and Ezekiel ample precedent for the figure on the edge and yet in the midst, troubling Israel with perplexing words that are also acts and acts that are also words, not only identifying with the people but also speaking truth to power. He is indeed a 'social prophet', leading a movement of renewal 'from below'. But he finds himself frequently at odds with his own followers, a lonely figure who must patiently re-educate them with fresh, envisioning means such as story, if that movement is to have transforming effect. Stories such as The Great Banquet no doubt needled the Pharisaic élite, but would also have been mind-stretching for hearers of any and all classes, as Luke's representation of frequently mixed audiences suggests. It is this prophetic reimagining of Jesus' hearers' world that, in essence,

Crossan deals with in his highly suggestive study of the stories of Ruth, Jonah and Job as 'challenge parables' anticipating those of Jesus (2012, pp. 65–88).

It is precisely in the conjunction of the meaning of words in combination (as in a story) and the 'performance' in which those words are uttered that the force of a speech-act lies.[3] Thus none of the details of the stories we have sought to hear falls by the wayside impotent. In combination they are powerful: just as they were doubtless powerful to engage their original hearers, so they are powerful now to evoke some haunting, silhouetted lines of their original speaker.

The stories of Jesus in the context of his life

What specific links, then, can be made between the stories of Jesus and the other things he did, said and suffered?

Despite their indirectness, the tales of one who appears to be a clown or a fool can cut to the quick. It is not inappropriate to see the stories of Jesus as one element of his overall persona and action that led, ultimately, to his death, though this must not be misstated. Jesus did not die for the 'truth' of his parables, as Eduard Schweizer said (1971 (1968), p. 29, and see p. 30 above), as if they contained some new conceptual disclosure. But the 'act' of his stories must have been deeply provoking. In his stories, in other words, Jesus acted as in other respects he was perceived as acting: as one outside the normal systems and structures of Rabbinic argument and praxis, in the risky space of a self-claimed authority.

How do the stories relate to the other elements of Jesus' praxis that led, eventually, to his death? I begin with the rest of Jesus' reported sayings. There is no space for a full survey of links between these and the stories. It is important to note, however, that we should not try to turn all the other sayings of Jesus into narratives, with the peculiar characteristics of narrative – just as stories should not be turned by interpreters into beatitudes or similes or denunciations or proverbs. Certainly, a number of his similitudes contain or imply a brief snatch of narrative. But it is part of the glory of the deposit of material that has come down to us from Jesus through the memory and traditions of his followers that a whole range of rhetorical forms is preserved. Any overall appraisal of Jesus' words must take this exciting variety into account. Jesus uttered many kinds of saying, including announcements of God's kingdom, and the judgement and blessing it entailed, in much more direct form than his stories.

However, an argument might be mounted against my approach to the stories, which resists the identification of a character in a scene with God, on the grounds that in some of Jesus' shorter sayings some such identification is both natural and intentional. For example, is not God like the shepherd who goes searching for his one lost sheep (Luke 15.3–7)? And, if that is the case, what is the knock-on effect for hearing stories like The Prodigal Son?

I will make two responses to this argument. First, as I have just said, it is clear that Jesus used an abundant range of different speech-forms. There is no a priori reason why we should lump several together and assume that they all 'worked' the same way. This has been the mistake of many scholars who have said things like 'Jesus "could not" have used allegory'. I argue that these stories are realistic wholes drawn from the human world because that seems to me the natural way to take them. It does not mean that I want either to claim that all Jesus' speech-forms work in this way or to deny that he ever spoke of God under human figures.

Second, though, if we examine the shorter sayings that are nearest rhetorically to stories, those beginning 'Suppose ... ' or 'Which one of you ... ', we find, in fact, that the implied comparison between God and an individual character is as comically contrasting as it is comparative, and this creates a mood similar to the quirky detachment of the full-blown stories. In truth, if other elements of Jesus' teaching are taken seriously, God is very unlike a reluctant friend (Luke 11.5–9), an unclean shepherd (Luke 15.3–7), a woman who has lost a coin (Luke 15.8–10), a master who will not serve his servants (Luke 17.7–10), or one who cuts an unfaithful slave in pieces (Luke 12.42–48). The logic of these parables is grounded in the fundamental unity of 'how things work' in God's world: in the images they might suggest of God they show an ironic awareness of the impossibility of truly imaging him.

Turning to Jesus' wider career, the integration of his stories into its various events is seen in the way that their themes, identified above, are echoed in the memories of his interactions with people preserved in the Gospels. In N. T. Wright's words, indeed, 'The parables made sense only within the context of Jesus' whole career. They echoed, reflected, interpreted and indeed defended the main thrusts of Jesus' work and themselves set up other echoes in turn' (1996, p. 181). We might add that it is supremely the stories which exemplify this.

Thus Jesus' concern for people's everyday needs, to be supplied through the processes of germination and growth in the natural world, is documented in the multiplication of loaves and fishes (Mark 6.30–44), which provides an interesting parallel in 'miracle' to the story of The Sower (Eve, 2009, pp. 107–10). Jesus himself and his followers face the obstacles of opposition and conflict, and Jesus falls victim eventually to the wider political dynamics of repression and rebellion, being crucified as a would-be revolutionary – having the most brutal violence meted out to him though he had committed none himself. He is in the dock of a show trial (Herzog, 2005, pp. 215–27) and for him there is no favourable verdict like that eventually given to the widow in Luke 18.1–8.

Jesus not only told stories about indebtedness. He also announced a year of jubilee (Luke 4.16–21) and instructed his followers to pray that their debts would be forgiven as they had forgiven others (Matt. 6.12 / Luke 11.4). He not only told stories about wealth and poverty; he practised a lifestyle of poverty, relying on God alone and the support of those who identified with his cause, and encouraged his followers to do likewise, thus putting a sharp question mark against all reliance on riches (Luke 8.1–3; 9.58; 12.22–34; 18.18–25). The compassion he showed to actual people (e.g. Luke 7.13) mirrors the compassion portrayed in his stories. He interacted with all classes and types, from a blind beggar (Luke 18.35–43) to Herod the tetrarch and Pilate the Roman governor (Luke 23.1–12). His group of followers included fishermen, a toll-collector and a would-be revolutionary (Luke 6.12–16). He dined both with the disreputable (Luke 5.29–32) and Pharisees (Luke 7.36; 11.37). Large crowds listened to him with delight (Mark 12.37) even while he responded astutely to the most scholarly and able members of the Jewish hierarchy (Mark 11.27—12.37). He had close dealings with non-Jews as well as Jews (e.g. Mark 7.24–30; Luke 7.1–10; 17.11–18). His praxis demonstrated the equal regard for all which emerges both comically and tragically in the surprises, reversals and equalizations of his stories. In other words, the world of Jesus' imagination as it is revealed to us in his stories is a reflection of the world he inhabited and influenced himself. Though he hides himself behind the narratives, his life reflects back upon them, and they upon it.

The stories in Christian theology and wider scholarship

Finally, some reflections on how I see the kind of 'hearing' of Jesus I have advocated as contributing to scholarly debate and theological thinking. As we saw in Chapters 1 and 2, theological assumptions and categories have been woven into debate about Jesus' parables from the beginning until now. The history of parable scholarship is therefore also, in some degree, a history of theological reception (even among those who, especially from the late twentieth century, have tried to distance themselves from orthodox theological premises in reading the New Testament), and I will not attempt to unravel that cord here.

An early stage of reception of the stories into traditions of reflection about Jesus is seen in the Gospel of John, which strikingly contains none of the stories we have studied. Some familiar images from the Synoptics are transmuted into self-revelatory sayings by Jesus ('I am the bread of life', John 6.35; 'I am the good shepherd', John 10.11, 14; 'I am the true vine', John 15.1). As is well known, Jesus in John regularly 'speaks' through long discourses. The absence of the rhetorical form of Jesus' stories from John is one of the most obvious pieces of evidence that John is doing something different from the Synoptics. Rather than attempting to reflect the varied speech-forms Jesus actually employed, he has sought to present the truth of Jesus as it has come to him in a more inventive way, in which belief about Jesus is more closely fused with truth portrayed as coming from Jesus' mouth. This used to be seen mainly as a 'theological' move by John. But our study highlights that it is also a literary one. The reproduction of Jesus' storytelling has given way to a more explicit presentation of the storyteller in which he reveals truth about himself more openly and directly.[4]

The history of Christian interpretation of the stories can be seen as a development of this trend. Their angularity and refusal to fit into neat doctrinal or theological patterns was often ironed out through their use as teaching and preaching tools, though there remain beautiful examples of the allegorical 'method', particularly when it is used with self-consciously imaginative freedom (see the examples in S. I. Wright, 2000b, pp. 62–112). Jülicher, in stripping away allegory, continued to obscure their character as stories through reading them as similes expressing the highest form of human morality. In particular, his emphasis on their having just one 'point' reduced their rich realistic polyvalence to the ears of several generations of scholars. Making the connection between Jesus' stories and his proclamation of God's kingdom, with the various meanings that may have had in the Judaism of Jesus' day, has certainly helped to restore something of that realistic polyvalence, though it continues to be reduced whenever they are 'translated' into 'plain teaching' of any kind.

Some of the most accurate renderings of Jesus' stories and of Jesus as a storyteller, I have argued, come from recent scholarship which seeks to outline the contours of a Jesus who is fully immersed in his culture and society (Herzog, Schottroff, N. T. Wright), and sets his storytelling within that matrix. The Jesus Seminar has also done valuable service in highlighting the rhetoric of fiction (especially Hedrick), though its approach needs to be broadened by showing more fully how the stories fit with Jesus' other sayings, his actions, his way of life, the opposition he aroused, and ultimately with his death.

It is important, in conclusion, to say that neither my hearing of the stories nor that of these other recent scholars need imply that they lack theological significance. To say that Jesus was not 'teaching about God' in his stories does not mean that a theological vision does not lie behind them. Nor does it challenge any Christian convictions about the identity of Jesus himself. Those for whom stories such as The Prodigal Son or The Talents hold a cherished position in their understanding of God's love or his accounting will, I hope, be led to new and deeper insight through the 'hearings' I have traced in this book, rather than rejecting them altogether. Insofar as the Evangelists themselves have lent weight to such familiar positions (as Chapters 4—6 suggest they do to some extent, but not as much as often thought), those positions may form part of a canonical hearing which need not, however, exclude other hearings. Positively, I hope that the portrayal of Jesus as a person for whom storytelling was a significant element of his dealings with people of all kinds will clarify the human profile of the one who stands at the root of Christian theology and faith. If the old adage that Jesus proclaimed God's kingdom while the Church proclaimed Jesus is hopelessly polarized, the stories Jesus told open a window on a much more nuanced and historically satisfying picture of his human activity. They do not 'proclaim' God's kingdom, though Jesus did so in other times and ways. Nor do they give 'teaching' about his 'identity'. Rather, they reveal the standpoint of one who observed contemporary Jewish life in its richness, its potential and its urgent demands, and, with idiosyncratic, humorous, deep-sighted penetration, narrated some of its possibilities, then left his hearers and their successors to enter his narratives, if they would.

Notes

Introduction

1 A convenient list of occurrences of the word *parabolē* in the New Testament is found in Snodgrass, 2008, pp. 567–9. All but two (Heb. 9.9 and 11.19) are in the Synoptic Gospels.

2 These are labels given by Snodgrass (2008) in the list mentioned in n. 1, referring to Matt. 15.15; Mark 3.23, 7.17; Luke 4.23, 5.36, 6.39, 14.7.

3 For example, in Jülicher's classic work (1910 (1886, 1898, 1899)), out of ten references to Aristotle in the Index to vol. 1, where he sets out his theory, only one is to the *Poetics* (p. 4) rather than the *Rhetoric*.

4 Charles W. F. Smith had a chapter on 'The Jesus of the Parables' at the end of his book of that title (1975, pp. 193–219).

5 Bernard Brandon Scott (2007b, p. 96) comments briefly on the parables' comparative lack of appearance in Jesus-scholarship, citing E. P. Sanders, John P. Meier, J. Dominic Crossan and Marcus Borg. Crossan (2012) does, however, offer an intriguing hypothesis about how Jesus' parabolic fictions inspired the Gospel genre.

6 One thinks of narrative criticism, narrative ethics, narrative theology, narrative therapy, narrative homiletics and others. Businesses and politicians are said to set out their proposals as part of a 'narrative' that will be attractive and persuasive to employees, clients or potential supporters.

1 Eclipsing the stories of Jesus: from Reimarus to Jülicher

1 On this ancient reading see S. I. Wright, 2000b, pp. 69–71, 76–9.

2 Douglas Oakman has sought to revive Reimarus's conception of a thoroughly 'political' Jesus (2012: see pp. 3–22, 'Revisiting Reimarus').

3 As pointed out by Reimarus's editor Talbert in a footnote, the evidence for this alternative Jewish conception has been shown to be lacking.

4 Reimarus's comment that 'Of the kingdom of heaven, Jesus speaks to the people in parables, out of which they could gather what they pleased' (1970 (1768), p. 145) seems inconsistent with his main thrust, in that it implies that Jesus intended up to a point to veil his true meaning.

5 Modern examples of scholars' inclination to exclude elements of Jesus' stories on the basis of their supposed literary inconsistencies can be found in the works of Crossan and Scott on the parables. For example, Scott excludes the concluding verses (vv. 27–31) of the parable of The Rich Man and Lazarus (Luke 16.19–31) because the story, in his view, 'is about boundaries and connections' and has thus come to an end 'once Abraham pronounces the chasm' (Scott, 1989, p. 146) (discussed in S. I. Wright, 2000b, pp. 167–8).

6 This passage in Matt. 25.31–46 is often excluded from lists of 'parables' by scholars, because the comparison between the judgement and the separation between sheep and goats is not mentioned after v. 33. In any case, it is not a story.

2 Recovering the stories of Jesus: from Wrede to the present

1 Blomberg, 2012 (1990), pp. 37–8, shows how Wrede's view has not entirely disappeared, citing Elian Cuvillier, *Le concept de parabolē dans le Second Évangile*, Gabalda, Paris, 1993.

2 We may compare here the prophetic past tenses of Mary's *Magnificat* (Luke 1.46–55). Mary is, to be sure, recalling God's deeds in Israel's history, but at the same time speaking prophetically about what he is to do.

3 Schweitzer does not use John's Gospel as a primary source, but one wonders whether here he is also influenced by John 4.35–38, in which Jesus draws an explicit comparison and contrast between the harvest of grain – which is still four months off – and that of people – whose time has already come. Schweitzer, however, imagines the literal harvest as nearer than this, envisaging the Baptist's movement as having started in the spring (Schweitzer, 2000 (1913), p. 325).

4 At least two other book-length works of this time and afterwards have related the parables of Jesus closely to his eschatological proclamation: Ladd (1966) and Beasley-Murray (1986).

5 On this book and what it expresses of Bultmann's view of the relationship of Jesus and Judaism see the comments of Sanders (1985), pp. 26–8.

6 Similar examples are found in Bultmann, 1935 (1926), pp. 94–6 (The Talents and The Good Samaritan).

7 On the issue of the criteria of authenticity, see Theissen and Winter, 2002; Keith and Le Donne, eds, 2012.

8 For an elaboration of the view that Jesus' parables do work by 'metaphor', indeed often by allegory understood as a chain of metaphors, see Boucher, 1977. Etchells (1998) fascinatingly discusses the parables as working through a crossing of the metaphorical (i.e. as having a strange or other-worldly reference) and metonymic (i.e. as evoking an aspect of Jesus' everyday world).

9 For a classic statement of the way in which narrative works as metaphor, with particular reference to the parables, see Ricoeur, 1975, discussed briefly in Chapter 3 below.

10 Marshall (1973 (1963)) offered a brief critique of Dodd and other scholars who denied that Jesus could have spoken of his own return, commenting that the '*prima facie* interpretation of many of [the parables, such as The Talents / Pounds] in terms of the parousia of the Son of man after a certain undefined interval is not only the most natural interpretation of them individually, but is also in keeping with the teaching of Jesus as a whole' (p. 45). 'Prima facie' is an over-bold concept to employ for interpreting any of Jesus' sayings, not least his stories.

11 On the precursors and nature of Bultmann's stance see Thiselton, 1980, pp. 212–23.

12 Storie also mentions Bailey's failure to distinguish between the 'public account' of a social custom and the reality of how it was experienced; his tendency to assume a positive relationship between dominant parable characters and God; his overlooking of violence in the parables; and his underestimation of the effect of power disparities on the poor, especially women.

13 There was indeed an anti-Jewish thread in some twentieth-century studies of Jesus, though it would be unfair to accuse a scholar such as Jeremias of deliberately fostering this. On this thread see Casey, 2010, pp. 4–9. One of the scholars Casey

cites as pro-Nazi and anti-Jewish is Paul Fiebig, who had produced important early works on the parables in reaction to Jülicher (1904, 1912).

14 Amos Wilder had previously written of the 'war of myths' in connection with Jesus' parables (1982).

15 Cf. my own argument that elements of the 'voice' of Jesus are preserved by the Evangelists and, indeed, by the various subsequent traditions of interpreting the parables, from the Fathers to the present (2000b).

16 N. T. Wright's reading of the parables is critiqued by Snodgrass, 1999; his reading of The Prodigal Son is expanded in great detail by Bailey, 2003.

17 See also the comments on N. T. Wright's limited application of his reconstructed Jesus to social ethics in Perrin, 2011.

18 For a summary of responses to Herzog's 1994 work, including Hedrick's own critique, see Hedrick, 2004, pp. 75–6.

3 Jesus' stories: tools for a fresh hearing

1 Cf. the reader-response model of how narrative works advanced by Wolfgang Iser, 1974, 1978, and the extremely helpful account in Thiselton, 1985, of the necessity of sensitivity to 'reader-response' or 'hearer-response' when dealing with Jesus' parables.

2 In S. I. Wright, 2000b, I explored the potential for describing this kind of evocation more accurately as the trope of 'metonymy' (pp. 30–61) or 'synecdoche' (pp. 193–226) rather than metaphor. In literary criticism, realistic writing may be described as 'metonymic' because a focus on specific segments of reality powerfully evokes the whole, as, for instance, Ernest Hemingway's precisely drawn *For Whom the Bell Tolls* brings to life the entire mood and scope of the Spanish civil war. See the work of David Lodge (1977), drawn on by Ruth Etchells (1998) in her work on the parables; see further S. I. Wright, 2000b, pp. 186–7 and notes.

3 I realize that in the following I fall foul of two of what Paul Foster (2012) claims are the three 'dead-ends' in Jesus research: orality and memory studies (the third is the use of the Fourth Gospel).

4 I am grateful to Francis Watson for a discussion which reminded me to make this point.

5 On the Gospels as memory and testimony see also Borg, 2011, pp. 43–4.

6 I am grateful to Larry Hurtado for his comments on this.

7 A brief section on the parables as narrative, touching on character and plot, is found in Donahue, 1988, pp. 20–5.

8 See the critique of structuralist theory as applied to the interpretation of texts in Ricoeur, 1976. The structuralist work of the SBL Parables seminar in the early 1970s is discussed by Perrin, 1976, pp. 168–81. French structuralist work was also carried out on Gospel texts, including some of Jesus' stories (see The Entrevernes Group, 1978 (1977)).

9 Here again I find myself close in approach to Green, 1997 (p. 12). He writes that by Luke's 'social setting' he means 'more than the world available to us through the narrative as a closed system, but less than the world often represented to us by historical-critical enquiry'. My focus in Part 3 will be Jesus' social setting, not Luke's, but the same applies: attention to the stories requires attention to their social world, but understanding them does not depend on a full reconstruction of that world in every detail.

10 I find it hard to imagine the bloodthirsty tales of David or the Maccabees not being gripping bedtime fare for Jewish boys in Jesus' time (told and retold from memory, not usually read!), or Jewish girls not being enthralled by the stories of Ruth, Esther or Judith.

11 An example may be The Rich Man and Lazarus (Luke 16.19–31). See Bauckham, 1991.

4 Hearing the stories through Mark

1 Two very helpful accounts of the difficult verses Mark 4.10–12 are found in Thiselton, 1985, pp. 111–13, and Snodgrass, 2008, pp. 157–64. For a brief, clear analysis of the difference between these verses and their parallels in Matthew and Luke see Hedrick, 2004, pp. 30–5, though I do not agree that Mark's rendering of this scene gives us no clues at all about Jesus' approach or intention. Myers, contrary to Hedrick, argues for the unhelpfulness of divorcing such sayings from their literary context for a socio-literary reading (2008 (1988), pp. 169–70).

5 Hearing the stories through Matthew

1 Carter offers a fuller account of the story within Matthew's narrative (2001, pp. 370–5) which deals with the paradoxes of the king's character, seen as unlike the God Matthew has presented (e.g. 5.43–48), yet in the end compared to God. Throughout his commentary he highlights how Matthew presents God's reign as both like and unlike human empire.

2 Cf. Carter, 2001, p. 398: 'The parable challenges audiences of disciples to embrace this alternative egalitarian lifestyle and to view social structures and interactions from that perspective which is fundamental to God's empire.'

3 'Q' is the label given to material common to Matthew and Luke.

6 Hearing the stories through Luke

1 Green comments that 'As with many of the Lukan parables, this one draws its significance in part from its realism and in part from its transparent points of contact with the larger narrative' (1997, p. 674). He reflects that while, on the one hand, Luke seems to use this story to point to 'the coming of judgement on those who refuse the nature of God's rule', on the other hand, the analogy between the nobleman and Jesus is 'parodic or ironic' (p. 675).

7 Hearing the stories in Galilee

1 See p. 47. Shortly before writing this section I had a conversation with Dave Leeman about story which helped me clarify this point.

2 I am grateful to Azar Ajaj for this insight, and to the wonderful Nazareth Village, an attempt based on an excavated first-century vineyard to reproduce accurately the farming landscape and practices of Jesus' time on the edge of modern Nazareth.

8 Hearing the stories on the way: 1

1 On the significance of characters and their designations or names in the stories traditionally labelled 'example stories', see Tucker, 1998, pp. 248–64.

2 The frequent use of participles in Greek makes this a more tightly constructed sequence in the original: five of these verbs are in participle form.

3 'Nobody would remember the Good Samaritan if he had only good intentions. He had money as well' (Speech to the General Assembly of the Church of Scotland, 1980).

4 For example, John Calvin, who rejected the Fathers' allegorical treatment but retained its most objectionable element, seeing in the story Jesus' description of the 'cruel neglect of love' on the part of 'the Jews and priests in particular' (1972 (1553), II, p. 38, discussed in S. I. Wright, 2000b, p. 78).

5 Scott, 1989, p. 112, suggests that many would have had a more positive view of the younger son, as one who fulfilled the familiar cultural script of the younger brother who comes out on top, like Jacob. On associations between Jacob and the prodigal see Bailey, 2003. But Scott deliberately abstracts the story from its Lukan context. For Pharisaic hearers there would be nothing to sympathize with in the younger son's behaviour.

9 Hearing the stories on the way: 2

1 I have recently benefited from Tim Ford's doctoral work-in-progress on the stories of Luke 16 and from discussions with him.

2 There is another hint of the liberation theme in this verse. The people of Israel lived in 'tents' during the feast of Booths, a joyful celebration of their exodus from Egypt.

3 For other readings along these lines see Kitchen, 2002, and Keesmaat and Walsh, 2011.

4 On this story see also Vearncombe, 2010.

10 Hearing the stories in Jerusalem

1 On the differences between Isa. 5.1–2 and Mark 12.1 see Herzog, 1994, pp. 101–2.

2 I am grateful to Elizabeth Raine for pointing out to me the close link between the end of Matt. 23 and the end of Matt. 21.

3 References given here include Isa. 66.10, 14; Joel 2.21, 23; Zech. 10.7; Tobit 13.25; 1QH 13.6; 1QM 4.14; 13.12–13; 14.4.

11 Jesus the storyteller

1 Crossan reserves the term 'riddle' for Mark's understanding of the parables (2012, pp. 13–27), in contradistinction from Jesus' own praxis which he characterizes as 'challenge' (pp. 45–112).

2 For this classical distinction see the discussion of irony in Resseguie, 2005, pp. 67–75. For discussion of Reimarus see Chapter 1 above, pp. 9–12.

3 Technically this is known as the 'illocutionary' force of an utterance: i.e. not simply what the words mean in the abstract but what they do in a context.

4 Crossan argues (2012) that the Synoptic Gospels, too, in their record of supposedly 'factual' material are creating 'parables' for particular audiences. This is a suggestive line of thought but remains to be fully investigated and tested.

Bibliography

Allison, Dale C. (2010), *Constructing Jesus: Memory, Imagination and History*. SPCK, London.

Bailey, Kenneth E. (1976), *Poet and Peasant*. Eerdmans, Grand Rapids.

Bailey, Kenneth E. (1980), *Through Peasant Eyes*. Eerdmans, Grand Rapids.

Bailey, Kenneth E. (2003), *Jacob & the Prodigal: How Jesus Retold Israel's Story*. IVP, Downers Grove, Ill.

Bailey, Kenneth E. (2008), *Jesus Through Middle Eastern Eyes: Cultural Studies in the Gospels*. SPCK, London.

Baird, J. Arthur (1969), *Audience Criticism and the Historical Jesus*. Westminster Press, Philadelphia.

Bauckham, Richard (1991), 'The Rich Man and Lazarus: The Parables and the Parallels', *New Testament Studies* 37, pp. 225–46.

Bauckham, Richard (2006), *Jesus and the Eyewitnesses: The Gospels as Eyewitness Testimony*. Eerdmans, Grand Rapids.

Beasley-Murray, G. R. (1986), *Jesus and the Kingdom of God*. Eerdmans, Grand Rapids; Paternoster Press, Carlisle.

Beutner, Edward F. (2007), 'A Mercy Unextended: Matthew 18.23–34', pp. 33–9, in Edward F. Beutner (ed.), *Listening to the Parables of Jesus*, Jesus Seminar Guides. Polebridge Press, Santa Rosa, Calif.

Bindemann, Walther (1995), 'Ungerechte als Vorbilder? Gottesreich und Gottesrecht in den Gleichnissen vom "ungerechten Verwalter" und "ungerechten Richter"', *Theologische Literaturzeitung* 11, pp. 956–70.

Black, Matthew (1946), *An Aramaic Approach to the Gospels and Acts*. Clarendon Press, Oxford.

Blomberg, Craig L. (1983), 'Midrash, Chiasmus, and the Outline of Luke's Central Section', pp. 217–61, in R. T. France and D. Wenham (eds), *Studies in Midrash and Historiography*, Gospel Perspectives 3. JSOT Press, Sheffield.

Blomberg, Craig L. (2012 (1990)), *Interpreting the Parables*, 2nd edn. IVP Academic, Downers Grove, Ill.; Apollos, Nottingham.

Borg, Marcus J. (2011), *Jesus: Uncovering the Life, Teachings, and Relevance of a Religious Revolutionary*. SPCK, London.

Boucher, Madeleine (1977), *The Mysterious Parable: A Literary Study*, Catholic Biblical Quarterly Monograph Series 6. Catholic Biblical Association of America, Washington, DC.

Breech, James (1983), *The Silence of Jesus: The Authentic Voice of the Historical Man*. Fortress Press, Philadelphia.

Brown, Colin (ed.) (1975), *New International Dictionary of New Testament Theology*, 3 vols. Paternoster Press, Exeter.

Brueggemann, Walter (2004), *An Introduction to the Old Testament: The Canon and Christian Imagination*. Westminster John Knox Press, Louisville, Ky.

Bultmann, Rudolf (1935 (1926)), *Jesus and the Word*, trans. Louise Pettibone Smith and Erminie Huntress. Ivor Nicholson & Watson, London.

Bultmann, Rudolf (1963 (1921)), *History of the Synoptic Tradition*, trans. J. Marsh. Blackwell, Oxford.

Calvin, John (1972 (1553)), *A Harmony of the Gospels Matthew, Mark and Luke*, 3 vols, trans. T. H. L. Parker and A. W. Morrison. Saint Andrew Press, Edinburgh.

Campbell, Charles L. (2008), 'Principalities, Powers and Fools: Does Preaching Make an Ethical Difference?', *Homiletic* 33.2, n.p., <http://www.homiletic.net/index. php/homiletic/article/view/3289/1522>, accessed 19 December 2013.

Carter, Warren (2001), *Matthew and the Margins: A Sociopolitical and Religious Reading*. Orbis Books, Maryknoll, NY.

Casey, Maurice (2002), *An Aramaic Approach to Q: Sources for the Gospels of Matthew and Luke*, Society for New Testament Studies Monograph Series 122. Cambridge University Press, Cambridge.

Casey, Maurice (2010), *Jesus of Nazareth: An Independent Historian's Account of His Life and Teaching*. T&T Clark, London.

Conzelmann, Hans (1960 (1953, 1957)), *The Theology of St Luke*, 2nd edn, trans. Geoffrey Buswell. Faber & Faber, London.

Crossan, John Dominic (1973), *In Parables: The Challenge of the Historical Jesus*. Harper & Row, San Francisco.

Crossan, John Dominic (1980), *Cliffs of Fall: Paradox and Polyvalence in the Parables of Jesus*. Seabury Press, New York.

Crossan, John Dominic (1991), *The Historical Jesus: The Life of a Mediterranean Jewish Peasant*. HarperCollins, San Francisco.

Crossan, John Dominic (2012), *The Power of Parable: How Fiction by Jesus Became Fiction about Jesus*. SPCK, London.

Dewey, Joanna (1994), 'The Gospel of Mark as an Oral-Aural Event: Implications for Interpretation', pp. 145–63, in Edgar V. McKnight and Elizabeth Struthers Malbon (eds), *The New Literary Criticism and the New Testament*. Sheffield Academic Press, Sheffield.

Dodd, C. H. (1936 (1935)), *The Parables of the Kingdom*, rev. edn. Nisbet & Co., London.

Donahue, John R. (1988), *The Gospel in Parable: Metaphor, Narrative and Theology in the Synoptic Gospels*. Fortress Press, Philadelphia.

Dowling, Elizabeth V. (2007), *Taking away the Pound: Women, Theology and the Parable of the Pounds*. Continuum, London.

Drury, John (1985), *The Parables in the Gospels: History and Allegory*. SPCK, London.

Dunn, James D. G. (2003), *Christianity in the Making, Vol. 1: Jesus Remembered*. Eerdmans, Grand Rapids.

Dunn, James D. G. (2005), *A New Perspective on Jesus: What the Quest for the Historical Jesus Missed*. SPCK, London.

Dunn, James D. G. (2011), *Jesus, Paul, and the Gospels*. Eerdmans, Grand Rapids.

Etchells, Ruth (1998), *A Reading of the Parables of Jesus*. Darton, Longman & Todd, London.

Eve, Eric (2009), *The Healer from Nazareth: Jesus' Miracles in Historical Context*. SPCK, London.

Fiebig, Paul (1904), *Altjüdische Gleichnisse und die Gleichnisse Jesu*. J. C. B. Mohr (Paul Siebeck), Tübingen.

Fiebig, Paul (1912), *Die Gleichnisreden Jesu im Lichte der Rabbinischen Gleichnisse des Neutestamentlichen Zeitalters*. J. C. B. Mohr (Paul Siebeck), Tübingen.

Ford, Richard Q. (1997), *The Parables of Jesus: Recovering the Art of Listening*. Fortress Press, Minneapolis.

Foster, Paul (2012), 'Memory, Orality, and the Fourth Gospel: Three Dead-Ends in Historical Jesus Research', *Journal for the Study of the Historical Jesus* 10.3, pp. 191–227.

Frei, Hans (1974), *The Eclipse of Biblical Narrative: A Study in Eighteenth and Nineteenth Century Hermeneutics*. Yale University Press, New Haven and London.

Freyne, Sean (2004), *Jesus the Jewish Galilean: A New Reading of the Jesus-Story*. T&T Clark International, London and New York.

Frost, Michael (2010), *Jesus the Fool: The Mission of the Unconventional Christ*. Baker, Grand Rapids.

Fuchs, Ernst (1964), *Studies of the Historical Jesus*, trans. Andrew Scobie, Studies in Biblical Theology 42. SCM Press, London.

Funk, Robert W. (1982), *Parables and Presence: Forms of the New Testament Tradition*. Fortress Press, Philadelphia.

Funk, Robert W. (2007), 'Jesus of Nazareth: A Glimpse', pp. 89–93, in Edward F. Beutner (ed.), *Listening to the Parables of Jesus*, Jesus Seminar Guides. Polebridge Press, Santa Rosa, Cal.

Funk, Robert W., Hoover, Roy W., and The Jesus Seminar (1997), *The Five Gospels: What Did Jesus Really Say?* HarperCollins, San Francisco.

Goodman, Martin (ed.) (2012 (2001)), *The Apocrypha*, The Oxford Bible Commentary. Oxford University Press, Oxford.

Green, Joel B. (1997), *The Gospel of Luke*, The New International Commentary on the New Testament. Eerdmans, Grand Rapids.

Havelock, Eric (1984), 'Oral Composition in the Oedipus Tyrannus of Sophocles', *New Literary History* 16, pp. 175–97.

Hedrick, Charles W. (1994), *Parables as Poetic Fictions: The Creative Voice of Jesus*. Hendrickson, Peabody, Mass.

Hedrick, Charles W. (2004), *Many Things in Parables: Jesus and His Modern Critics*. Westminster John Knox Press, Louisville, Ky.

Heidegger, Martin (1971), 'The Origin of the Work of Art', pp. 32–7, *Poetry, Language and Thought*. Harper & Row, New York.

Hengel, Martin (1968), 'Das Gleichnis von den Weingärtnern Mc, 12.1–12 im Lichte der Zenonpapyri und der rabbinischen Gleichnisse', *Zeitschrift für Neutestamentliche Wissenschaft* 59, pp. 12–21.

Herzog II, William R. (1994), *Parables as Subversive Speech: Jesus as Pedagogue of the Oppressed*. Westminster John Knox Press, Louisville, Ky.

Herzog II, William R. (2005), *Prophet and Teacher: An Introduction to the Historical Jesus*. Westminster John Knox Press, Louisville, Ky.

Horsley, Richard A. (2008), *Jesus in Context: Power, People and Performance*. Fortress Press, Minneapolis.

Horsley, Richard A. (2012), *The Prophet Jesus and the Renewal of Israel: Moving beyond a Diversionary Debate*. Eerdmans, Grand Rapids.

Hultgren, Arland J. (2000), *The Parables of Jesus: A Commentary*, The Bible in Its World. Eerdmans, Grand Rapids.

Iser, Wolfgang (1974), *The Implied Reader*. Johns Hopkins University Press, Baltimore, Md.

Iser, Wolfgang (1978), *The Act of Reading*. Johns Hopkins University Press, Baltimore, Md.

Jeremias, Joachim (1963 (1947)), *The Parables of Jesus*, rev. edn, trans. S. H. Hooke. SCM Press, London.

Jeremias, Joachim (1971), *New Testament Theology, Vol. 1: The Proclamation of Jesus*. SCM Press, London.

Johnson, Luke Timothy (1977), *The Literary Function of Possessions in Luke–Acts*, Society of Biblical Literature Dissertation Series 39. Scholars Press, Missoula.

Jones, Geraint Vaughan (1964), *The Art and Truth of the Parables: A Study in Their Literary Form and Modern Interpretation*. SPCK, London.

Josephus, Flavius (1959), *The Jewish War*, trans. and ed. G. A. Williamson. Penguin, Harmondsworth.

Jülicher, Adolf (1910 (1886, 1898, 1899)). *Die Gleichnisreden Jesu*, 2 vols, 2nd edn. J. C. B. Mohr (Paul Siebeck), Tübingen.

Jüngel, Eberhard (1962), *Paulus und Jesus: Eine Untersuchung zur Präzisierung der Frage nach dem Ursprung der Christologie*. J. C. B. Mohr (Paul Siebeck), Tübingen.

Käsemann, Ernst (1964 (1960)), *Essays on New Testament Themes*, trans. W. J. Montague, Studies in Biblical Theology 41. SCM Press, London.

Keesmaat, Sylvia C., and Brian J. Walsh (2011), '"Outside of a Small Circle of Friends": Jesus and the Justice of God', pp. 66–91, in Nicholas Perrin and Richard B. Hays (eds), *Jesus, Paul and the People of God: A Theological Dialogue with N. T. Wright*. SPCK, London.

Keith, Chris, and Le Donne, Anthony (eds) (2012), *Jesus, Criteria, and the Demise of Authenticity*. T&T Clark, London.

Kingsbury, J. D. (1969), *The Parables of Jesus in Matthew 13: A Study in Redaction-Criticism*. SPCK, London.

Kitchen, Merrill A. (2002), 'Re-reading the Parable of the Pounds: A Social and Narrative Analysis of Luke 19:11-28', pp. 227–46, in David Neville (ed.), *Prophecy and Passion: Essays in Honour of Athol Gill*. Australian Theological Forum, Hindmarsh, SA.

Kloppenborg, John (2006), *The Tenants in the Vineyard: Ideology, Economics, and Agrarian Conflict in Jewish Palestine*, Wissenschaftliche Untersuchungen zum Neuen Testament 195. J. C. B. Mohr (Paul Siebeck), Tübingen.

Ladd, George Eldon (1966), *Jesus and the Kingdom: The Eschatology of Biblical Realism*. SPCK, London.

Le Donne, Anthony (2011), *Historical Jesus: What Can We Know and How Can We Know It?* Eerdmans, Grand Rapids.

Linnemann, Eta (1966 (1961)), *Parables of Jesus: Introduction and Exposition*, 3rd edn, trans. John Sturdy. SPCK, London.

Lodge, David (1977), *The Models of Modern Writing*. Arnold, Leeds.

Longenecker, Richard N. (ed.) (2000), *The Challenge of Jesus' Parables*, McMaster New Testament Studies. Eerdmans, Grand Rapids.

McArthur, Harvey K., and Johnston, Robert M. (1990), *They Also Taught in Parables: Rabbinic Parables from the First Centuries of the Christian Era*. Academie, Grand Rapids.

McCracken, David (1994), *The Scandal of the Gospels: Jesus, Story and Offence*. Oxford University Press, New York and Oxford.

McFague, Sally (1975), *Speaking in Parables: A Metaphorical Theology.* Fortress Press, Philadelphia; SCM Press, London.

Marguerat, Daniel, and Bourquin, Yvan (1999), *How to Read Bible Stories,* trans. John Bowden. SCM Press, London.

Marshall, I. Howard (1973 (1963)), *Eschatology and the Parables,* The Tyndale Lecture 1963. Theological Students' Fellowship, London.

Meier, John P. (1994), *A Marginal Jew: Rethinking the Historical Jesus, Vol. 2: Mentor, Message and Miracles.* Doubleday, New York.

Melchert, Charles F. (1998), *Wise Teaching: Biblical Wisdom and Educational Ministry.* Trinity Press International, Harrisburg, Penn.

Meyer, Ben F. (1979), *The Aims of Jesus.* SCM Press, London.

Milavec, Aaron (1989), 'A Fresh Analysis of the Parable of the Wicked Husbandmen in the Light of Jewish–Catholic Dialogue', pp. 81–117, in Clemens Thoma and Michael Wyschogrod (eds), *Parable and Story in Judaism and Christianity.* Paulist Press, Mahwah, NY.

Miller, Robert J. (2007), 'The Pearl, The Treasure, The Fool and The Cross', pp. 65–82, in Edward F. Beutner (ed.), *Listening to the Parables of Jesus,* Jesus Seminar Guides. Polebridge Press, Santa Rosa, Calif.

Moore, Stephen D. (1989), *Literary Criticism and the Gospels: The Theoretical Challenge.* Yale University Press, New Haven and London.

Moxnes, Halvor, Blanton, Ward, and Crossley, James G. (eds) (2009), *Jesus beyond Nationalism: Constructing the Historical Jesus in a Period of Cultural Complexity.* Equinox, London.

Myers, Ched (2008 (1988)), *Binding the Strong Man: A Political Reading of Mark's Story of Jesus.* Orbis Books, Maryknoll, NY.

Oakman, Douglas E. (2012), *The Political Aims of Jesus.* Fortress Press, Minneapolis.

Parker, Andrew (1996), *Painfully Clear: The Parables of Jesus.* Sheffield Academic Press, Sheffield.

Perrin, Nicholas (2011), 'Jesus' Eschatology and Kingdom Ethics: Ever the Twain Shall Meet', pp. 92–112, in Nicholas Perrin and Richard B. Hays (eds), *Jesus, Paul and the People of God: A Theological Dialogue with N. T. Wright.* SPCK, London.

Perrin, Norman (1976), *Jesus and the Language of the Kingdom: Symbol and Metaphor in New Testament Interpretation.* SCM Press, London.

Powell, Mark Allan (1993), *What Is Narrative Criticism? A New Approach to the Bible.* SPCK, London.

Reimarus, Hermann Samuel (1970 (1768)), *Fragments,* ed. Charles H. Talbert, trans. Ralph S. Fraser. Fortress Press, Philadelphia.

Renan, Ernest (1935 (1863)), *The Life of Jesus,* trans. A. D. Howell Smith. Watts & Co., London, <www.infidels.org/library/historical/ernest-renan>.

Resseguie, James L. (2005), *Narrative Criticism and the New Testament.* Baker Academic, Grand Rapids.

Ricoeur, Paul (1975), 'Biblical Hermeneutics', *Semeia* 4, pp. 29–145.

Ricoeur, Paul (1976), *Interpretation Theory: Discourse and the Surplus of Meaning.* Texas University Press, Fort Worth, Tex.

Sanders, E. P. (1985), *Jesus and Judaism.* SCM Press, London.

Schleiermacher, Friedrich D. E. (1997 (1864)), *The Life of Jesus,* ed. Jack C. Verheyden, trans. S. Maclean Gilmour. Sigler Press, Mifflintown, Penn.

Schottroff, Luise (2006), *The Parables of Jesus*, trans. Linda M. Maloney. Fortress Press, Minneapolis.

Schweitzer, Albert (2000 (1913)), *The Quest of the Historical Jesus*, 1st complete edn, trans. W. Montgomery, J. R. Coates, Susan Cupitt and John Bowden. SCM Press, London.

Schweizer, Eduard (1971 (1968)), *Jesus*, trans. David E. Green. SCM Press, London.

Scott, Bernard Brandon (1989), *Hear Then the Parable: A Commentary on the Parables of Jesus*. Fortress Press, Minneapolis.

Scott, Bernard Brandon (2007a), 'On the Road Again: The Leased Vineyard', pp. 21–31, in Edward F. Beutner (ed.), *Listening to the Parables of Jesus*, Jesus Seminar Guides. Polebridge Press, Santa Rosa, Calif.

Scott, Bernard Brandon (2007b), 'The Reappearance of Parables', pp. 95–119, in Edward F. Beutner (ed.), *Listening to the Parables of Jesus*, Jesus Seminar Guides. Polebridge Press, Santa Rosa, Calif.

Sellew, Philip (1992), 'Interior Monologue as a Narrative Device in the Parables of Luke', *Journal of Biblical Literature* 111.2, pp. 239–53.

Shillington, V. George (1997), 'Engaging with the Parables', pp. 1–20, in V. George Shillington (ed.), *Jesus and His Parables: Interpreting the Parables of Jesus Today*. T&T Clark, Edinburgh.

Smith, Charles W. F. (1975), *The Jesus of the Parables*. United Church Press, Philadelphia.

Snodgrass, Klyne R. (1983), *The Parable of the Wicked Tenants*, Wissenschaftliche Untersuchungen zum Neuen Testament 27. J. C. B. Mohr (Paul Siebeck), Tübingen.

Snodgrass, Klyne R. (1999), 'Reading and Overreading the Parables in *Jesus and the Victory of God*', pp. 61–76, in Carey Newman (ed.), *Jesus and the Restoration of Israel: A Critical Assessment of N. T. Wright's Jesus and the Victory of God*. IVP, Downers Grove, Ill.; Paternoster Press, Carlisle.

Snodgrass, Klyne R. (2008), *Stories with Intent: A Comprehensive Guide to the Parables of Jesus*. Eerdmans, Grand Rapids.

Snodgrass, Klyne R. (2013), 'Preaching *Jesus'* Parables', pp. 45–58, in Ian Paul and David Wenham (eds), *'We Proclaim the Word of Life': Preaching the New Testament Today*. IVP, Nottingham.

Stegemann, Ekkehard W., and Stegemann, Wolfgang (1999 (1995)), *The Jesus Movement: A Social History of the First Century*, trans. O. C. Dean Jr. T&T Clark, Edinburgh.

Stern, Frank (2006), *A Rabbi Looks at Jesus' Parables*. Rowman & Littlefield, Lanham, Md.

Storie, Deborah (2009), 'Review of Bailey, Kenneth E., *Jesus through Middle Eastern Eyes: Cultural Studies in the Gospels*', *Pacifica* 22, pp. 96–109.

Strauss, David F. (1994 (1840)), *The Life of Jesus Critically Examined*, 4th edn, ed. Peter C. Hodgson, trans. George Eliot. Sigler Press, Ramsey, NJ.

Tannehill, Robert C. (1986), *The Narrative Unity of Luke–Acts: A Literary Interpretation*, Vol. 1: *The Gospel according to Luke*. Fortress Press, Minneapolis.

Tannehill, Robert C. (1990), *The Narrative Unity of Luke–Acts: A Literary Interpretation*, Vol. 2: *The Acts of the Apostles*. Fortress Press, Minneapolis.

The Entrevernes Group (1978 (1977)), *Signs and Parables: Semiotics and Gospel Texts,* trans. Gary Phillips, Pittsburgh Theological Monograph Series 23. Pickwick Press, Pittsburgh, Penn.

Theissen, Gerd, and Merz, Annette (1998 (1996)), *The Historical Jesus: A Comprehensive Guide,* trans. John Bowden. SCM Press, London.

Theissen, Gerd, and Winter, Dagmar (2002), *The Quest for the Plausible Jesus: The Question of Criteria.* Westminster John Knox Press, Louisville, Ky.

Thiselton, Anthony C. (1980), *The Two Horizons: New Testament Hermeneutics and Philosophical Description with Special Reference to Heidegger, Bultmann, Gadamer and Wittgenstein.* Paternoster Press, Exeter.

Thiselton, Anthony C. (1985), 'Reader-Response Hermeneutics, Action Models, and the Parables of Jesus', pp. 79–113, in Roger Lundin, Anthony C. Thiselton and Clarence Walhout, *The Responsibility of Hermeneutics.* Eerdmans, Grand Rapids; Paternoster Press, Exeter.

Tolbert, Mary Ann (1979), *Perspectives on the Parables: An Approach to Multiple Interpretation.* Fortress Press, Philadelphia.

Tucker, Jeffrey T. (1998), *Example Stories: Perspectives on Four Parables in the Gospel of Luke,* JSNT Supplement Series 162. Sheffield Academic Press, Sheffield.

Vearncombe, Erin K. (2010), 'Redistribution and Reciprocity: A Socio-Economic Interpretation of the Parable of the Labourers in the Vineyard (Matthew 20.1–15)', *Journal for the Study of the Historical Jesus* 8.3, pp. 199–236.

Via, Dan Otto (1967), *The Parables: Their Literary and Existential Dimension.* Fortress Press, Philadelphia.

Ward, Richard F., and Trobisch, David J. (2013), *Bringing the Word to Life: Engaging the New Testament through Performing It.* Eerdmans, Grand Rapids.

Weiss, Johannes (1971 (1892)), *Jesus' Proclamation of the Kingdom of God,* trans. R. Hyde and D. Holland. SCM Press, London.

Wilder, Amos N. (1982), *Jesus' Parables and the War of Myths.* SPCK, London.

Wilder, Amos N. (1991), *The Bible and the Literary Critic.* Fortress Press, Minneapolis.

Wolter, Michael (2009), 'Jesus as a Teller of Parables: On Jesus' Self-Interpretation in His Parables', pp. 123–39, in James H. Charlesworth and Petr Pokorný (eds), *Jesus Research: An International Perspective.* Eerdmans, Grand Rapids.

Wrede, William (1971 (1901)), *The Messianic Secret,* trans. J. C. G. Greig. J. Clarke, London.

Wright, N. T. (1996), *Jesus and the Victory of God,* Christian Origins and the Question of God 2. SPCK, London.

Wright, Stephen I. (2000a), 'Parables on Poverty and Riches', pp. 217–39, in Richard N. Longenecker (ed.), *The Challenge of Jesus' Parables.* Eerdmans, Grand Rapids.

Wright, Stephen I. (2000b), *The Voice of Jesus: Studies in the Interpretation of Six Gospel Parables.* Paternoster Press, Carlisle; Wipf & Stock, Eugene, Or., (2007).

Wright, Stephen I. (2002), *Tales Jesus Told: An Introduction to the Narrative Parables of Jesus.* Paternoster Press, Milton Keynes.

Wright, Stephen I. (2009), 'Debtors, Laborers and Virgins: The Voice of Jesus and the Voice of Matthew in Three Parables', pp. 13–23, in B. J. Oropeza, C. K. Robertson and Douglas C. Mohrmann (eds), *Jesus and Paul: Global Perspectives in Honor of J. D. G. Dunn for His 70th Birthday,* Library of New Testament Studies 414. T&T Clark, London.

Young, Brad H. (1998), *The Parables: Jewish Tradition and Christian Interpretation*. Paulist Press, Mahwah, NJ.

Zimmermann, Ruben (ed.) (2007), *Kompendium der Gleichnisse Jesu*. Gütersloher Verlagshaus, Gütersloh.

Zimmermann, Ruben (2009), 'How to Understand the Parables of Jesus: A Paradigm Shift in Parable Exegesis', *Acta Theologica* 29.1, pp. 157–82.

Index of stories and parables

For convenience, the stories and parables are often referred to in the main text by means of a conventional title, rather than repeating their biblical reference frequently. This index enables readers to trace them by name rather than biblical reference. A substantial discussion is indicated in bold.

Index of ancient and biblical texts

Index of modern authors

Index of names and subjects